Development Dilemmas

NGO Challenges and Ambiguities

Edited by

ALAN WHAITES

World Vision

Many of the resources mentioned in this book are available on various websites. To locate them, enter the name of the book or article, the author, or the organisation in a good search engine.

Printed in the United States of America.

10 09 08 07 06 05 04 03 02 01   5 4 3 2 1

Published by World Vision International, 800 W. Chestnut Avenue, Monrovia, California 91016-3198, U.S.A.

Library of Congress Cataloging-in-Publication Data

Development dilemmas : NGO challenges and ambiguities / edited by Alan Whaites.
       p. cm.
Includes bibliographical references.
   ISBN 1-887983-38-4
  1. Economic assistance—Developing countries. 2. Non-governmental organizations—Developing countries. 3. Poverty—Developing countries. I. Whaites. Alan.
   HC60 .D4748 2001
   338.91—dc21

                             2001008615

Permissions:
Major portions of chapter 6 are taken from Bruce Bradshaw, *Change Across Cultures*, published by Baker Academic, a division of Baker Book House Company, © 2002. Used with permisison of the publisher.

Editor in Chief: Edna Valdez. Senior editor: Rebecca Russell. Copyediting and typesetting: Joan Weber Laflamme/jml ediset. Cover concept and design: Crooks Design Inc. Photo: Corbis Images.

♻ ∞ This book is printed on acid-free recycled paper.

Development
Dilemmas

Contents

103250

Contributors

Bruce Bradshaw is Assistant Professor of Economic Development at Bethel College in Newton, Kansas. He previously served as the director of Transformational Development Research at World Vision International. He is the author of *Change Across Cultures: A Narrative Approach to Social Transformation* (Baker Books) and *Bridging the Gap: Evangelism, Development and Shalom* (MARC).

Don Brandt has served for 16 years as Senior Researcher, World Vision International, engaged in a variety of socio-economic-political issues, including early warning/disaster mitigation, microenterprise development, and research related to strategic decision-making. The focus of his current position involves policy and advocacy. He is the author of several books and articles.

David A. Chandler worked in Southeast Asia for 10 years as an expatriate manager for World Vision International. Posted in the Philippines, Cambodia, Thailand and Myanmar, he served in a number of capacities, including advisor to the Country Director in the Philippines and Cambodia, regional liaison for USAID-funded projects, and manager of the Myanmar Project. In 1994 he moved to Yangon, Myanmar, as Country Director. He opened the permanent World Vision office there. He has a B.A. and M.Ed. from Duke University, and an M.B.A. from Yale University.

Kelly Russell Currah is Senior Consulting Adviser at World Vision International and an Associate at the New Economics Foundation in London. As part of his responsibilities regarding World Vision's policy on transnational corporations, he has participated in a number of international development initiatives among NGOs, governments and businesses such as the Global Movement for

Children. He has also done research and written on business-NGO engagement for academic journals and the mainstream press.

Warren Nyamugasira received a bachelor's degree in economics from Makerere University (Uganda), and obtained a master's degree in economics and a social studies degree from the University of Wales (University College of Swansea), UK, specialising in development policy and planning. Nyamugasira has worked for Scripture Union of Uganda, World Vision in Uganda and Rwanda, Uganda Debt Network and is currently the National Coordinator of the Uganda National NGO Forum, a platform for all NGOs working in the field of policy advocacy and lobbying in Uganda. He also founded the Advocacy Centre for Strategic Social Change, an NGO working to promote alternatives to current development paradigms.

Abikök C. Riak is based in Manila with the World Vision Asia Region Disaster Management Office. Providing support in relief and development contexts, she works with the different national offices in the region to build capacity in programming in conflict areas. This includes co-ordinating the mainstreaming of peace-building initiatives in the Philippines, Myanmar, Sri Lanka and Indonesia. Before moving to the Asia region, she worked with World Vision in Sudan, where she managed the Local Capacities for Peace (Do No Harm) implementation project.

Kathy Vandergrift, Senior Policy Analyst for World Vision Canada, also chairs an NGO Working Group on Children and Armed Conflict in Canada and co-chaired the Children and Armed Conflict Caucus for the UN Special Session on Children. She co-ordinated production of the NGO Action Plan for the First International Conference on War-affected Children, entitled "Peace Is Every Child's Right."

Alan Whaites has worked in relief, development and advocacy for more than 10 years, including time spent living and working in Pakistan, Laos and Thailand. After post-graduate studies in the politics of Africa and Asia at London's School of Oriental and African Studies, he became Policy and Research Manager for

World Vision UK before moving to the World Vision Partnership Office as Director for International Policy and Advocacy. A regular contributor to development journals and conferences, he is based in his home country, the United Kingdom.

Introduction

NGOs:
Facing Dilemmas and Answering Critics

ALAN WHAITES

Development, and perhaps more particularly the world of NGOs, is in a transitional phase. The heady days of civil society in the 1990s have given way to sharper external critiques and also to a new series of challenges for which development workers must become prepared. The catch phrases of the last decade, from *new world order* to *globalisation,* point to the increasing fragmentation in development policy, partly a result of the diverging fortunes of developing states themselves. These contextual changes and emerging challenges pose questions relevant to all who are interested in international development.

Those questions lie behind the issues addressed in this volume, issues that spark both hope and despair – a combination not unusual in the world of development. Entrenched problems of states suffering long-term conflict – including the use of child soldiers, proliferation of small arms, and manipulation of aid – feature in a number of chapters. Elsewhere authors look at orthodox solutions to development problems offered by the Washington consensus. Empirical evidence of recent decades, for example, does show considerable room for hope that poverty can be overcome – but not without changes to the neo-liberal formulas put forward by the Organization for Economic Co-operation and Development (OECD) donors and the International Monetary Fund (IMF).

The range of issues covered in this volume reflects the breadth of dilemmas that face development workers. Aid professionals have become acutely conscious that even the most local of problems is shaped by its wider context and is likely to have hidden political connotations. Yet as development practitioners become more attuned to the complexities that surround them, they are also increasingly questioned by audiences in both North and South. Initial debates about NGO practice in relief situations, for example, have been followed by questions regarding the campaigning work of activist NGOs.

The contributors to *Development Dilemmas* unashamedly take positions that may seem contentious and subjective. Some commentators have questioned the legitimacy of such NGO analysis and the basis on which development practitioners might question the actions of "legitimate" actors such as governments. For the authors involved that basis is often the experience and intimate knowledge of real issues that only proximity to the everyday dilemmas of development can bring. In a chapter on human rights and operational work in constrained contexts, David Chandler writes as someone who struggled to build up a development programme in a difficult environment while keeping a constant eye on the question of humanitarian ethics. When discussing the problem of balancing core organisational principles with the compunction to offer relief in the midst of conflict, Abikök Riak speaks from the perspective of a staff person caught in a tragic environment in which none of the available choices is easy.

The authors of *Development Dilemmas* map out only a fraction of the micro- and macro-problems that face NGOs, yet the honesty of the perspectives offered suggests that development practitioners do bring something unique to the shifting sands of the development debate. Even so, it would not be right to offer a collection of essays on dilemmas facing development without looking at the critique of civil society that has emerged in recent years. The days are now gone when NGOs could speak and assume that they had a right to be heard; increasingly, the role of NGOs is as much a part of the discussion as the perspectives they raise.

Introducing *Development Dilemmas* therefore means looking seriously at the external critique. This volume is, after all, largely about challenging assumptions and arguing a cause.[1] True, the critique of civil society that has emerged in recent years has been partly a stung response from some of those who have fiercely advocated the benefits of globalisation and liberalisation.[2] Yet despite this genesis some of the points raised do pose serious questions for NGOs to consider.

IN DEFENCE OF CIVIL SOCIETY'S VOICE

Chief amongst the questions raised by the critique are the issues of legitimacy and accountability. With the democratisation of much of the developing world and pioneering attempts to consult directly with the poor, is it still appropriate for civil society to be treated as a legitimate voice on the issues? And, as NGOs comment on the challenges of development, who holds NGOs accountable for the views they express? None of the arguments put forward in *Development Dilemmas* presumes a divine right to speak. Yet the authors are realistic enough to know that if all commentators on development had to meet the stern criteria proposed by civil society's harshest critics, there would be total silence.

NGOs, like all institutions, are flawed, but critics should recognise that the flaws affect a wide range of other organisations, including the institutional targets of NGO advocacy. A tremendous hypocrisy results, however, from posing questions of legitimacy and accountability to NGOs without comparative analysis of bodies such as the World Bank and IMF. *The Economist,* for example, in its article during the International Monetary Fund World Bank Group Annual Meeting in Prague, held September 19-28, 2000, failed to mention that all of Africa has only two executive directors at the World Bank – hardly an example of adequate representation.

The poor of the developing world remain remarkably disenfranchised from the international, inter-governmental institutions that daily shape their lives – an archaic situation that the New Economics Foundation report "It's Democracy, Stupid" has done much to make clear.[3] *The Economist* also failed to mention that the Bretton Woods institutions themselves sometimes find NGOs a useful element in their relations with the OECD states, whose agendas, after all, are often domestic rather than international. Bank and Fund staff regularly leak to NGOs the documents that help NGOs point to problems.

Reasonable people want access to more than one point of view and are willing to accept that their critics might have valid points. In the 1980s and early 1990s the World Bank latched on to civil society – particularly NGOs – as a means to implement social safety nets for Structural Adjustment programmes without going through the out-of-favour state. Western donors saw in civil society a way to strengthen democratic forces. Perhaps ironically, support from Western institutions was complemented by forces of globalisation that allowed new civil society movements to organise over the Internet.

Operational NGOs, working alongside communities in poor countries, were instrumental in constructively helping the World Bank and IMF to grasp the impact of key Structural Adjustment policies on important areas of human capital formation. NGOs were the first to experience the impact of user charges on schools and health centres, largely because they had to move very quickly to pick up some of the slack. NGOs also pointed to the failure of OECD states to liberalise markets in the rich North (the Bank estimates that this costs the poor US$150 billion per year). Put simply, the NGO critique helped policy-makers (perhaps reluctantly) to better understand the ultimate consequences of their policies.

THOSE WHO PICK UP THE PIECES . . .

It is the very failure of international policy that created the context for the growth and prominence of NGOs. Civil society faced a double imperative: first, to offset some of the social damage caused by bad policy (such as Structural Adjustment programmes – induced cuts in social spending); and second, to force international government action in situations where NGOs were clearly inadequate to address the scale of the problems involved (such as Ethiopia in 1985 or Rwanda in 1994). In effect the failure of policy and often the vacuum caused by its absence pushed NGOs into the foreground and bestowed on them an obligation to speak.

The legitimacy of the NGO voice, however, cannot be limited to times of extreme crisis. Western development policy, after all, has been inadequate not sporadically but constantly. Indeed, the shallowness of that policy is made clear by the repeated tendency of international policy-makers to fall back on three standard responses to post–Cold War problems in the developing world. (The choice of response often depends more on location than on the scale of the human suffering. Note the response to a European conflict such as Kosovo and reaction to the appalling tragedy of Angola).

The three responses can be summarised as:

1. *Punitive Economic Action* – Punitive economic action taken against rogue states (including trade sanctions, withheld aid and conditionality) has become the defining element of North-South relations. New and much vaunted signs of Northern concern (including the global AIDS fund) are derailed and devalued by the insistence of OECD states on determining priorities for expenditure. Sanctions, meanwhile, have become a knee-jerk staple of Western policy. Trade and other sanctions are a blunt instrument, more effective against civilians than states. Yet sanctions are applied in response to everything from human rights abuses to poor labour practices or the failure to liberalise domestic markets (despite the OECD's own closed door to poor counties' agricultural goods). Sanctions have a poor record of achieving political objectives.[4]

2. *Humanitarian Crisis Management* – Failures in Western Official Development Assistance (ODA) policy and donor unwillingness to invest in political impact assessments when developing conditionality packages (most notably for Structural Adjustment programmes) have played their own role in state erosion in the South. The economic and political influences that lead to third-world conflicts are not entirely external, but invariably they are also not completely domestic. Yet the response of OECD states has been not to look at long-term strategies for conflict reduction but instead to developing a short-term relief and response mentality. In this regard Somalia continues to cast a long shadow over Western thinking with a preference for long-range or proxy humanitarian interventions.

3. *Agreements Without Implementation* – If the moral force of international law is gradually being eroded, then the OECD need look no further than its own abysmal record for implementation in finding a cause. The long hours of haggling over UN summit declarations, new codes and international conventions are ironic, given the consistency with which major players proceed to ignore the commitments involved. The outcry over the decision of the United States to abandon its Kyoto goals in 2001 was an unusual public airing of the wider problem of non-compliance. Indeed the failure to implement conventions is sometimes made inevitable by the lack of ratification by key states. Reform of the monitoring systems for such agreements is long overdue.

Each of these three responses has, over recent years, replaced real policy-making by the UN Security Council and OECD states.

None of these policies has the potential to promote constructive development, they are instead fire-fighting tools that reflect a crisis-focused approach to development. What happens when Western policy goes wrong? When the tools of international policy are themselves the cause of humanitarian damage? Who calls the gatekeepers of "global good governance" to account when they seek to starve a state into submission? The policy interventions of developed states propel NGOs as observers with a rationale of assisting the poor to speak vocally of the problems that result. Lacking legitimacy? Perhaps. Not sufficiently accountable? Possibly. But even so, for NGOs silence can hardly be an option.

Recently the World Bank and IMF have frankly admitted, in background documents for Poverty Reduction Strategy Papers (PRSPs), that real progress towards goals will not occur without increased aid and liberalisation of Northern markets. The failure of OECD states to respond to these dynamics is symptomatic of a failure of global values – willing acceptance that gross inequality, wasted opportunity and conflict are simply the way things are. NGO practitioners are inevitably caught up in the consequences; indeed, it might even be argued that past silence makes NGOs partly to blame for this malaise. Failure to build a constituency for aid and development in the North has allowed governments the room to pursue a policy of neglect.

Building such a constituency will mean uniting with churches, unions, political parties and all those with a commitment to the poor. It's an old truism, but an important reality nevertheless, that a genuinely broad-based movement is needed to persuade rich countries to abandon ultimately self-destructive economic policies. It is difficult to conceive of such a movement without organised civil society – particularly development NGOs in a seminal role. Defence of civil society as a legitimate voice on issues affecting the poor does not mean no room to improve. Questions of legitimacy and accountability demand frankness and honesty in order to build on advances already made.

PUTTING HOUSES IN ORDER

All this does not mean that NGOs do not have questions to answer. The critique of civil society should raise issues amongst practitioners concerning the role of NGOs in the development debate. In the past it has often been the friendlier criticism of academia that has helped NGOs to be responsive to weaknesses and issues of concern. Now the criticisms of those who challenge the NGO right to speak should also lead to creative thinking within civil society concerning the underlying problems involved. Such thinking might also help us to ask whether NGOs have used their voices as wisely as they could have done, or whether greater access to those with power has actually dulled civil society's own ability to critique.

Why, for example, have NGOs come so far so fast? For civil society to maintain a legitimate role in global policy debate, NGOs need to be wary of the reasons for the warm welcome received at the tables of those with power. Why do international institutions of the world (IMF, World Bank, World Trade Organization [WTO]) court a movement that is largely unaccountable, usually sharp-tongued and sometimes self-indulgent? The answer is that the new orthodoxy of civil society inclusion is as convenient and useful for the global institutions as it is for the NGOs with whom they want to work.

The World Bank, WTO and IMF have been under increasing pressure to make themselves accountable to the people most directly affected by their activities, particularly the world's poor. In lieu of consulting directly with these constituencies, NGOs[5] have become a useful substitute for listening to the communities and families at the grass roots of development. This labour-saving scenario is fuelled by the tendency of NGOs to identify their own interests with those of the people whom they claim to represent.

NGOs must be the first to say that consulting with civil society experts does not absolve institutions from the need to listen directly to the poor. Indeed, the World Bank has shown what can be done. At the end of the 1990s it commissioned the respected academic Robert Chambers to work with a team in surveying the views of the poor in 60 countries.[6] The results were widely considered ground-breaking, and certainly surprised many in the Bank with the insights produced. This "voices of the poor" approach needs to be replicated as an on-going, continuous part of decision-making frameworks within the Bank.

If global institutions need to listen to those whose lives are changed by institutional policies, then NGOs should take care to differentiate their own interests from those whom they claim to represent. These painstaking and perhaps painful processes might entail the greatest blasphemy – recognition that poverty cannot be ended through small-scale, grass-roots development alone. In reality, NGOs are organisations just like the World Bank and IMF and, as such, are inevitably drawn to a worldview that underlines their own relevance to issues they hope to address.

BY-PASSING GOVERNMENTS

Civil society as a convenient partner for dialogue is complemented by another central reason for the warm welcome extended to NGOs, a reason centring on the role of NGOs in relation to often-eroded third-world states. NGOs first came to prominence in the days of Structural Adjustment, when the World Bank found NGOs useful for what became known as "gap filling." Adjustment forced developing states to cut expenditure on health and education, leading to howls of protest in the North. NGOs rapidly became a non-state way of delivering services to the poor, especially among institutions committed to shrinking the role of the state.[7]

The problem today is that the state, in most developing countries, suffered significant erosion of capacity as a result of these policies, leaving the World Bank and IMF with a frustrating development problem.[8] Erosion of the third-world states through adjustment policies led increasingly to a "brain drain," or flight of the most talented civil servants from government service, and to increasing of corruption as the states' capacity to police themselves waned. Today the Bank and Fund often seem to despair of the state as a partner for long-term development change. The latest trend, therefore, is the call to work with forces of social capital: those traditional societal structures (tribal chiefs, the church) that offer continued potential to circumvent the state – inevitably a process where issues of scale require partnering with NGOs.

Although flattering, this attention to NGOs by institutions such as the Bank and Fund masks a real lack of action to address the diminishing sustainability of third-world states.[9] The Bank and Fund have opted for changes of language rather than policy. Their response – the new Poverty Reduction Strategies – is billed as an attempt to offer programme ownership back to the states concerned. The rider, however, is that those states must collaborate closely with the Bretton Woods institutions, and their economic policies will still effectively be decided from 19th Street in Washington, D.C.

Failing infrastructure of governments in the Third World is as much a problem for civil society as for financial and political power wielders. Aside from the moral issues of denying the poor the right to accountable and responsive government, some very practical issues are also involved. The state ultimately is the key co-ordinator for successful delivery of development services, ensuring that school curricula meet common standards, that goods can be shipped to markets and that contracts are honoured.[10] There is, therefore, no inconsistency in NGOs recognising that an accountable and responsible state is essential to hold the ring amongst competing interest groups.[11]

SPEAKING TO THE POINT

The fact that NGOs sometimes confuse their voice with that of the poor or help global institutions to by-pass the state does not mean that civil society has nothing to contribute. Finding real solutions requires recognising each of the actors who should be party to the process.

As an NGO worker I was stunned by the inconsistency of protestors at the infamous battle for Seattle, particularly their treatment of representatives of the third-world states that many claimed to be protesting to protect. (To be fair, the treatment of some demonstrators was worse, but this justifies nothing). Even so, and although I remain an advocate for positive/constructive engagement with global institutions on issues of justice, I would still argue for the right of the nonviolent activist groups to protest. Institutions such as the World Bank and IMF are acutely aware of the differences between activist and professional wings of civil society. Influential NGO advocacy groups suggest the institutions are following a

> tried and true strategy of "divide and rule." The goal is simple: to split civil society into "good" and "bad," "civil" and "uncivil." The "good" are those who accept the overall direction of globalisation . . . and behave nicely when they are invited to meet with the rich and powerful. The "bad" are those who don't.[12]

My experience in advocacy among global institutions persuades me that they can and do learn and change – there can be no question that the World Bank, for example, came a long way in the 1990s. Even so, there is still room for criticism of the Bank and even more to decry the work of the IMF, which has only recently accepted poverty alleviation as a goal of its activities. The Bank, for its part, can still behave like an alcoholic on the slide, relapsing into funding projects that conflict with its own stated ecological and social concerns.

NGOs, therefore, must commit to stand against attempts by global institutions to divide and rule. The cause of the poor is too important to allow access to those with power to come at the expense of substantive contributions and critique. Among the spectrum of tools available to those who advocate for poverty reduction, those who favour constructive dialogue must remember the vital role of those who gathered around the G8 in Birmingham, England, in 1998 in bringing debt-relief forward.

Defending the right of all groups to be heard does not necessarily mean that we can agree on the issues. Indeed, it is helpful to recognise that the role of some of the activist groups can be destructive. Many of those who gathered at Seattle and Prague were opposed to development itself. Romanticised views of poverty and belief that the poor should be denied consumer goods available to the rich can be hallmarks of anti-globalisation groups, themselves a product of globalising forces. (Anarchists in Seattle were carefully organised through the Internet and had travelled from around the world.)

The need for civil society to accept its own diversity and recognise that division is inevitable was spelled out clearly in the People's Millennium Forum in May 2000 – an event that pointed to the sheer impracticality of addressing civil society as a uniform phenomenon. The People's Millennium Forum was a typically brave and worthy initiative on the part of the United Nations bringing together NGOs at the UN's own New York headquarters, providing an opportunity to unite behind a common platform of recommendations. Yet this was a meeting that most of the world's largest Private Voluntary Organisations (PVOs) opted to avoid. Those who did attend soon became mired in the basic incongruity of 1200 organisations all trying to press for 1200 issues to be included in the same short declaration of action.

The broad brush of civil society is simply *too* broad to produce anything coherent en-masse and, amongst the squabbling, the voices of real grass-roots movements from poor countries often become lost. Indeed, the small-issue focus of NGOs that made de Tocqueville see them as such a constructive part of democratic society can also make it difficult for each to see the wider picture involved. NGOs tend to view the world by "scaling up" their own areas of expertise, usually leading to lack of appreciation of the macro-environment in which their own and everybody else's issues are faced.

ACCOUNTABILITY

The freedom of civil society to define the parameters of its role, and to say virtually anything on any issue, has led to a cacophony of NGO pronouncements on the state of the world. Some of these have greatly added to the debate and provided catalysts for political change and reform. Others, divorced from pragmatic reality, are less helpful. Rich country NGOs can mix a romanticised view of poverty ("simplicity" of third-world life) with disregard for empirical evidence, producing fanciful plans to address everything from global warming to inequities of world trade. Ultimately this is the luxury of a movement some of whose members remain more accountable for their fund-raising and expenditure than for their pronouncements – and who will never need to risk implementing the very recommendations they make.

The special contribution of civil society has also often been the art of critique or the negative campaign rather than promotion of a real vision for change. Landmines, debt, slavery . . . civil society, particularly in the rich world, usually knows more clearly what it wishes to abolish than to build. The Spanish political scientist Manuel Castells suggests that civil society builds havens, not heavens.[13]

In essence, civil society has a great deal to do with the need to find identity in an atomised world. And the search for identity means choosing a self-defining cause. For most, that cause will relate to a clear and visible objective, almost always achieved by removing a definable part of the policy status quo. The world would, of course, be a better place given the removal of bad policies, laws and injustices. The poor, however, also gain by articulation of a call for positive change, a call that at present is more likely to come from distant, less well-resourced voices of their own grass-roots social and political movements. Perhaps it is in finding a positive vision for change that faith-based organisations should have a marked edge, and indeed Bruce Bradshaw argues that such groups do have a unique role.

Even so, the issues that NGOs in the rich world choose to pursue and those they choose to ignore are enmeshed in that crucial issue of accountability. Even member NGOs, archetypal providers of new identity for the suburbs and young professionals of the rich world, enjoy a public audience relatively ill-informed about highly technical areas of work. NGO boards do play a crucial role, but some are chosen more for the name-recognition of their members with the public than the wisdom they bring to bear.

The accountability gap has led even the strongest advocates for civil society to call for serious change. Alan Fowler, in a document prepared for the United Nations, touches on a number of areas in which NGOs need reform:

> It is incorrect to assume that forces that create poverty, exclusion and injustice exist only in governments, public policies and market institutions. They lie within civil society as well. In other words, civil society encompasses contending power relations and group interests that can both advance and impede poverty reduction, equity, inclusion, justice and other social development objectives.[14]

Michael Edwards, a theorist central to the modern civil society movement and now director of the Civil Society and Governance Programme at the Ford Foundation, has also suggested a series of reforms. His proposals include limiting aid that can be directed through rich country NGOs and introducing new codes of conduct for civil society organisations, effectively creating a certification for those deemed accountable.[15] Changes proposed by Edwards, or Alan Fowler, would bring some increased accountability and legitimacy, but without tackling the fundamental problems of state erosion and direct articulation by the poor.

Even the oldest organisational bodies that have stood between society and the state, such as the church, have had to adapt structurally to maintain their sense of connection to the people they seek to embrace. The church, which its adherents would say has a mandate to transform society, has itself been transformed by changing understandings of legitimacy and accountability, but without necessarily undermining its original mission and beliefs. In the same way modern civil society can maintain the vibrancy of its beliefs and principles while striving for more accountable structures.

Ultimately, civil society at its best contributes valuable insights to the policy arena. In many countries civil society has been responsible for securing from the political system major social changes (ranging from abolition of slavery to creation of adequate social safety nets). The crucial factor to note, however, is that for such change to be possible an effective political system and state must also be in place, structures that provide potential for citizens to secure democratic change. A step towards this is for NGOs to accept that theirs is not the only legitimate voice. Indeed, the new orthodoxy of civil society inclusion must be widened to enable greater openness to the direct voice of the poor and the encouragement of the political process itself.

NGOs might also look at how they can help to create a better environment for the more neglected world of political society. "Political society" consists of the usually overlooked institutions of the organised political fray, including political parties themselves – the bodies that in government must try to build the heavens their manifestos optimistically proclaim. Through political society, comprehensive frameworks for social transformation are developed, and through elections they are put to the popular test. Investment in the growth of civil societies in poor countries by the governments and institutions of the rich world should not be at the expense of this equally important field.

Civil society should complement the development of institutions that can better unify and channel the social and political aspirations of poor-country citizens through democratic processes. To a degree, that will mean giving greater space to the development and evolution of grass-roots political movements that seek to articulate local issues (including radical groups such as the landless peasants movement of Brazil).

The greatest challenge is for rich-country NGOs to take a step of humility by recognising the limitations they face, as many of the chapters that follow clearly do. Rather than simply promoting their own roles as political commentators on issues affecting the poor (based on professional expertise), they must also address the political poverty of those they want to represent. Political disempowerment and voicelessness are themselves part of the process of marginalisation familiar to most of the developing-world poor. Tackling political poverty is therefore as much a task of poverty eradication as any other. Alan Fowler finished his comment on the potential pitfalls of civil society by stating that "civil society is essentially political in its meaning. The civic arena contains roots of power differences that are used to perpetuate poverty and exclusion."[16]

Civil society has a real and legitimate role in the education of political society on issues in which it has expertise. *Development Dilemmas* is one example of how NGOs can attempt to play this role. In many societies, civil society also plays an invaluable part by stimulating policy debate through the contribution of substantive ideas. While true that in many countries of the world political society is weak, repressed or riddled by the corruption that eats away at many attributes of the state, civil society is neither inherently more accountable nor necessarily more honest. NGOs are part of the solution, not the answer to the ills of the world. As has always been the case, the poor will need to find political leaders of stature and integrity who can take up the challenges (many articulated by civil society) of inequality and marginalisation, if change is to occur.

NOTES

[1] *The Economist* (23–29 September 2000).

[2] See, for example, *The Economist* (29 January–4 February 2000).

[3] "It's Democracy, Stupid," New Economics Foundation, London (2000).

[4] See "Still Stacking Up the Bodies: The Failure of Humanitarian Windows," Briefing by World Vision UK (1998).

[5] This includes both rich-country-based NGOs and also those many poor-country NGOs that are staffed by the articulate, educated and urban middle class with whom the institutions are able to engage easily.

[6] The study has led to a three-volume series of publications (*Can Anyone Hear Us?, Crying Out for Change, From Many Lands*). See especially Deepa Narayan et al., *Crying Out for Change* (Washington, D.C.: The World Bank, 2000).

[7] Alan Whaites, "Let's Get Civil Society Straight: NGOs and Political Theory," *Development in Practice* 6/3 (1996).

[8] See Sam Jones, *Stolen Sovereignty: Globalisation and the Disempowerment of Africa* (Milton Keynes: World Vision UK, 1998).

[9] Jean-Francois Bayart et al., *The Criminalisation of the State in Africa* (Bloomington, Ind.: Indiana University Press, 1999); see also Patrick Chabal and Jean-Pascal Daloz, *Africa Works: Disorder as Political Instrument* (Bloomington, Ind.: Indiana University Press; Oxford: James Currey, 1999).

[10] See Bayart et al., *The Criminalisation of the State in Africa*; Chabal and Daloz, *Africa Works*. Also see Christopher Clapham, *Africa and the International System* (Cambridge: Cambridge University Press, 1996), Section III, particularly chap. 9.

[11] Whaites, "Let's Get Civil Society Straight: NGOs, the State, and Political Theory," in *Development, NGOs, and Civil Society*, ed. Deborah Eade (Oxford: Oxfam Publishing, 2000).

[12] Nicola Bullard, "It's Time for 'Uncivil' Society to Act," paper presented at the Mantinese Congress "Nuove regole per il nuovo millennio," Florence, Italy, 18-20 March 2000 (published by "Focus on the Global South" at website www.focusweb.org).

[13] Manuel Castells, *The Power of Identity*, vol. 2 of *The Information Age: Economy, Society and Culture* (Oxford: Blackwell, 1998), 64.

[14] Alan Fowler, *Civil Society, NGDOs and Social Development: Changing the Rules of the Game*, UNRISD Occasional Paper G1 (January 2000).

[15] Michael Edwards, *Democratising Global Governance: Rights and Responsibilities of NGOs*, The Foreign Policy Centre, London (June 2000).

[16] Fowler, *Civil Society, NGDOs and Social Development*, 7.

1.

Genuine North-South Partnerships

Putting Shared Values Before Money

WARREN NYAMUGASIRA

*Northern and international NGOs and their Southern coun-
terparts and civil society proclaim themselves true partners in
development. However, the Northern bias still shows itself in
the South. Is there anything that the sector can do to redress
the imbalance? The author argues that there is, if NGOs step
back from money-only mediated processes of what seems defective development.*

The North-South relationship, as defined in the stated goals, objectives and mission statements of most Northern and Southern NGOs,
is supposed to be one of equal partnership, founded on shared values and goals, and on principles of mutual respect, self-reliant,
people-centred development (Smillie 1995). People are supposed
to determine what they want to do and how they want to do it.
Where external assistance in the form of money and ideas becomes
necessary, it is meant to supplement indigenous knowledge and local
resources, with a view to graduation, as direct assistance becomes
unnecessary. Yet from the perspective of those from the South working among many NGOs, there is a glaring gap between rhetoric and
reality. The relations are unequal and socially constructed. They revolve around money from the rich North to the poor South and one-
way communication where the South does the bidding of the North.

The so-called Southern partners are often just subcontractors who must still refer back to the North for every major decision. Southern indigenous knowledge, even from the NGO staffs themselves, let alone from the poor, is devalued, and there is insincerity in giving recognition and praise. Why is this the case and is there anything that can be done to redress the situation? This chapter argues that the South must re-claim its right to strategize, to organise and lead, to invest as it sees fit and without strings attached, to theorize and to speak if true development is to be realised.

This Southern perspective draws mainly from the experience of NGO staff in a few African countries with which the author is familiar. The essay examines the historical context in which "partnership" was born and argues that with the dawn of globalisation and liberalisation, the need for hiding behind the "partnership veil" seems to have become unnecessary, although the verbiage remains. The essay discusses the impact of the Northern behaviour on the South, with special reference to the staffs of international NGOs, before going on to make recommendations of what should be done urgently to redress the glaringly unacceptable imbalance.

NORTH-SOUTH PARTNERSHIP

When Northern NGOs began their operations in the South, "development" was something conceived, managed and paid for by "outsiders" from the North (Smillie 1995, 181). It was a one-way flow of money and ideas. Over time, however, and with the emergence of a strong challenge from the South, the relationship between Northern and Southern players has begun to be portrayed as that of partnership. Partnership in effect evolved with the push for political independence and the emergence of strong Southern NGOs and civil society that started to demand recognition from the dominant North. As a result, Northern NGOs, sensing a threat to "development" that was quickly becoming a growth industry, came up with the rhetoric about partnership with Southern counterparts out of fear that they would otherwise be denied a role in the South. Partnership therefore became a survival strategy developed in the face of increasing Southern pressure and autonomy. Born out of conflict, by and large, it became a strategy designed out of necessity as a kind of hiding place, a disguise, while in reality very little changed in the way development was conceived and paid for and in the way major decisions were made.

One of the key developments in this evolution of partnership was the "nationalisation" of paid staff among international NGOs (Smillie 1995) as more and more nationals of Southern countries were hired into top managerial and technical positions. What never changed was the role these national staff played in the decision-making processes. In many respects today's "development" still is something controlled, if not conceived, by those outsiders who pay for it. It is immaterial that they may not be physically present at the site in the South. In fact, with the advent of liberalisation and globalisation of the 1980s and 1990s, Northern partners have found that they no longer need to disguise the way they deal with their Southern counterparts. The "veil" can be and has been lifted. By coincidence or design, there is no more need for a hiding place. Partnership is once again openly a one-way street, characterised by power imbalance and dominated by money. It is like a buffet lunch, where donors and Northern NGOs through whom funds are channelled take what they like from what the South presents for support and leave the rest (Smillie 1995, 185). The way staffs of NGOs from the South perceive the development dilemma of unequal partnerships is that while NGO rhetoric emphasises the role of Southern NGOs and Southern partners (whom Northern NGOs fund) as being critical to successful development, in reality the Southern partners are often just sub-contractors who must still refer back to the North for every major decision. The staffs themselves, along with the other partners, have no independent voice in the so-called partnership.

NGO staffs with their civil society counterparts who have been at the forefront of third-world development through operational programmes and policy influencing are concerned that despite all their commendable efforts, poverty has defiantly increased. They are aware that the phenomenon of increasing poverty can be attributed to many factors, such as the wrong or inappropriate development models employed by governments and international financial institutions. It is also influenced by unbalanced terms of trade and imperfect operations of market systems, bad governance (such as corrupt political leadership) and so on and so forth. But it should be acknowledged, even by NGOs, that the North-South unequal relations have played an important role in undermining the NGO/civil society development efforts and effectiveness, or worse, directly contributed to the increase in levels and intensity of poverty.

A POOR IMITATION OF THE VOICE OF THE POOR

In "NGOs and Advocacy: Poor Imitations of Authentic Southern Voices," this author challenged the widespread perception that Southern NGOs best represent the authentic voices of the Southern poor (Nyamugasira 1997). I argued that, despite the commendable work they do, both Northern and Southern NGOs still offer a poor imitation of the voice of the poor. The present essay uncovers a key factor contributing to this state of affairs. It examines more closely the unequal relationship that exists between Southern development workers and their Northern partners, on the one hand, and the people they strive to serve, on the other. In this, staffs of Northern and international NGOs are in the same boat as – and sometimes worse off than – their counterparts working with Southern or in-digenous NGOs. Many are dedicated to serving their people the best way they know how. They go to geographically and socially remote places to try to reach the poorest so as to bring to them services they so badly need. And this is sometimes acknowledged. For example, in Uganda senior government officials often state publicly that agencies like World Vision, ActionAid and Oxfam reach the poor whom the government cannot. For that reason the government allocates resources from the poverty eradication fund to supplement activities of such NGOs. These are not isolated or exceptional cases. Therefore staffs of international NGOs are baffled and frustrated that they are not making the kind of lasting impact they work so hard to attain. There is even an irony: As NGOs have proliferated and increased the number of nationals on their staffs, now estimated to be 19 in every 20, the authentic voice (of the poor and that of Southern staffs) has become less distinct when important decisions are made. "How can this be?" national staffs ask themselves. One possible explanation is behavioural imitation.

Southern-based NGO staffs have tended, perhaps without intend-ing to and in most cases without realising it, to treat their members and those they strive to serve the very way they are treated by their Northern counterparts and supporters. The North systematically devalues the contribution of Southern partners, including that of their Southern staff. In turn, NGO staffs not only fail to articulate the voice of the poor, their roots, but also have underrated or placed limited value on that very voice when they make those decisions their Northern sponsors allow them to make. Worse still, these staffs silence and suppress the independent voice of the people, expecting them to comply with instructions, to do as they are told. The thinking is clear: If we can comply, so can you.

Southerns (1996) notes that when NGOs partner with the poor in the South, the people "have no independent voice or authority over the NGOs in their midst," irrespective of whether they are Northern, international, or Southern. Vink (1993) contends that it is naive to assume that because nationals in the South work in their own country, among their own people, they communicate as equals with their target groups. Most important, poor people also report that NGO staffs are not only rude and forceful, but they are also poor listeners (Narayan 2000). Many Southern-based NGO staffs actually feel that there is psychological distance between them and their people, alienation so great and widespread that it is a cause of much frustration and disillusionment among them.

The honest NGO staffs in the South know and accept that not only are they poor listeners, they also do not communicate well with their roots. But instead of doing something to reverse the situation, they argue and "fight" among themselves as to who is the more authentic representative of the people. On and off there have been intense conflicts among staffs of Southern and Northern NGOs for recognition as the *bona fide* representatives of the voice of the poor. This can only be a symptom of an identity crisis. They do not know who they are. They do not know whom they represent. Southern NGOs see staff of Northern NGOs as agents of "outsiders" whose agenda they are hired to push. When they work in isolated places, they are accused of being there for ulterior motives and perhaps illicit deals or for some other motive other than altruism. (Actually, when pushed, the issue becomes that of pay. Staffs of Southern NGOs are very jealous of what they perceive to be the large salaries of the staff of international NGOs. They surmise that if their clout were reduced, perhaps, somehow, they would get a bigger piece of the "pie." Meanwhile the North sits and watches passively and occasionally adds fuel to the fire by showing preference for one group over another.) The truth is that both staffs are at best only proxies of the voice of the poor. On their part, the poor see all NGO staffs and consultants as self-appointed beneficiaries of their plight, making a living as professionals out of dealing with their poverty and humanitarian crises. They see NGOs as threatened with extinction if they (the poor) no longer needed or accepted their financial assistance.

THE COSTS OF SELF-PERPETUATION

On their part, many national staff of NGOs have been wondering whether the very NGOs they work for do not in effect exist by continually projecting to the Northern media and donors an image of the South as victimised, helpless, weak and incapable of coping without Northern intervention. They are weary of the often portrayed idea that "these children will die or terribly suffer irreparable damage unless you give money," which implies that the children's own social support mechanisms and culture are deficient and incapable of providing rescue or care. NGO staffs from the South are increasingly uncomfortable with the marketing messages and approaches of their Northern counterparts. They believe that an unintended impact of such marketing is that consumers of such messages, including donors, are not likely to respect "Southern voices" if all they hear about them are unending pleas for money.

Clearly, a lot of what goes on in the name of development is money driven. Money has taken centre stage and a life of its own. Raising money, large amounts of it, has become an end in itself. Fund-raisers have done market research and established "the most effective" fund-raising approaches, messages, pictures and dollar handles. Coupled with the aspiration of Northern NGOs to become the biggest fund-raising agencies, to capture the biggest market share, and to gain the most influence over their publics, raising lots of money has become an obsession, a trap. But there is another side to it. In that the South asks for and expects to receive more and more money from the North each year, the South has become an accomplice. So, we have ended up with a situation where Northern NGOs measure success largely by the amount of money they raise each year and the South by the amount they receive. A "healthy

trend" is considered to be one where the North projects to raise
and the South projects to receive an ever-increasing amount – irrespective of what the poor want to do and what resources they already have. Development has turned into the process of shifting
money, of one-way giving and one-way receiving, a kind of give-
and-give and take-and-take situation. It has become almost incon-
ceivable to think of development partnerships that are not money
based.

THE COSTS OF NORTHERN LANGUAGES AND OUTLOOKS

Yet genuine partnerships for development are dependent on non-
monetary factors (the so-called soft aspects) such as effective communication: listening, learning and always reaching out to make
connections with and to affirm others. If viewed in the right perspective, money matters and is a useful element in promoting development, but genuine partnerships must involve talking, looking, touching and even intuition, applying the "sixth sense." Giving
others a voice, security and equality of rights, not just money, should
be the basic essentials of a fulfilling life without which it is non-
sense to talk of real partnership for development (Edwards 1999,
232).

While there is no shortage of words among NGO staff, both
North and South, and between them and their partners, there is
little effective communication. One of the hindrances to effective
communication, besides the deafening noise generated by money,
is the fact that there is no common medium of communication. On
the one hand, it is the South that has to learn the North's mother
tongue, which it has never mastered enough to have the necessary
confidence of an equal partner at a round table. On the other hand,
and to compound the problem, the language is often coded and
expressed in jargon that makes no sense to those outside a specific
context. Words do not always mean what they say on their face
value. There is no need looking up the word in a dictionary. To
make matters worse, most forms of expression from the South
have been rendered useless or inapplicable. We don't write much
to express ourselves; rather, we tell a story, which in most cases is
impossible to translate and only makes sense in a mother tongue.
We dance and give gifts when we are happy. We cry when we are

sad. It is Kenneth Kaunda, the former Zambian head of state that employed crying in public as a form of expression when he was saddened by an appalling human state of affairs. He became known as the weeping president. In doing what he did he was being a true African. Nelson Mandela, Yoweri Museveni, and many other African leaders dance with the people when they and their people are jubilant. In meetings in the North, we want to dance or cry but we fear we will be ridiculed. So we become tongue-tied, frustrated, and often go away often without saying a word, whereas there is so much we would wish to communicate. When we do express ourselves, our stories and parables make little sense to those to whom we are trying to talk.

In most NGOs the standard language for reporting and all other communications is English or perhaps French. They are known as the international languages of business. You can't get anywhere in NGO business without them. In the days of Mwalimu Julius Nyerere's Tanzania, we used to meet with colleagues from there and see them painfully struggle to communicate in English. They would appear mediocre or even incompetent. But when they had the chance to express themselves in Swahili, which is second nature to every Tanzanian, they suddenly became alive, animated and sounded very competent indeed, even sophisticated.

In the 1980s I attended an academic course in the United Kingdom. I was already a university graduate, having done all my education in English. The course I was attending would only award a diploma or a certificate. I registered for the diploma, sure that I would sail through with distinction. My tutors were less sure, and they found a way to tell me so: "No African has up till now successfully passed this course at the diploma level. Only one lady from Rwanda managed to pass it at certificate level. She would have made the diploma had she not come from a Franco-phone background." I was advised to "pursue the course at certificate level." Although my confidence level was significantly diminished, I insisted on pursuing the course at the diploma level and passed it successfully, but not with distinction. Later, when I returned to the same country to pursue a master's degree in economics, I refused to have my confidence undermined. I passed with commendation – an equivalent of a distinction.

Working in Rwanda, a predominantly Franco-phone country, in a senior position for World Vision for four years, I found myself at the receiving end of the incompetence charges when my staff wrote reports in faltering English, the standard for all our donor reporting. Yet when these people expressed themselves in French, or better still in Kinyarwanda, their mother tongue, they were truly impressive. But unless one put himself or herself in the shoes of those struggling to express themselves in a second or even third language, one cannot know how demoralising the remarks about incompetence (based only on the inadequacy of a foreign language facility) are. When repeated often enough, as is the tendency, the people concerned develop a complex. They come to believe that indeed they are incompetent. Roland Bunch (World Vision 1999), quoting Schumacher (1973), argues that "people who are convinced that they are ignorant or incompetent will, in fact, become incompetent." They then lose their poise and all enthusiasm, the driving force behind partnership. And as Bunch (1995) again points out, "Enthusiasm is known by many other names: determination, drive, commitment, motivation, inspiration . . . a willingness to make sacrifices in order to reach a goal . . . to step out into the unknown, to experiment and to work together towards a common end." When all that is quashed, life loses meaning. Enthusiasm quashed is a life denied. In the business of development, those who do such things to their supposed partners deserve to die As de Senillosa (1999, 101) aptly puts it:

> Non Governmental Development NGOs (NGDOs) that are committed to defending the interests of those worst affected by the present economic and political system and to working alongside them in this must denounce mechanisms and processes of oppression and exclusion. They may also have to oppose NGDOs that are motivated by interests which ultimately impede the eradication of poverty and the full participation of men and women in the process of emancipation, and the efforts to create a society which arises from their own perceptions and priorities.

There should be a difference between requirements by academic institutions and standards of development partners. In the latter, competency in a Northern mother tongue should not be allowed to overshadow the other qualities and competencies that Southern partners bring to the partnership for their own (Southern) development.

One should not need a foreign language to serve his or her own people well. Really. What is needed are community degrees (discussed in Nyamugasira 1998), entrenchment in the life and culture of the people, and an inspiration and determination to improve them.

This author has observed that when someone from the North expresses himself or herself in Swahili, Kinyarwanda, Luganda, or Kichewa, the languages of Africa, however falteringly, the people they are talking to are impressed. Some time ago I was talking to someone from the West who had lived and worked as a researcher in Rwanda for quite some time. She admitted to me that learning and using a few words of Kinyarwanda became such an effective entry point into the lives of the people she was researching amongst. This raises a serious question: Why is there so much tolerance for incompetent language facilities of Northerners in the South, when such tolerance for Southerners is totally lacking in the North? Surely this goes beyond the mere lack of courtesy. It is a development question, and the answer is that it is because of the unequal partnerships. The South knows where its bread is buttered, and so its people can afford to be tolerant. The reverse is not the case.

SOUTHERN ORIGINS, NORTHERN ENDORSEMENTS

There are discernible trends in the North-South relationship and behaviour. For example, it is universally accepted that development agendas should not grow from the minds of thinkers in the North, however brilliant these may be. Rather, they should grow out of practical development action and reflection experience in the South. In reality, however, a development idea can only be valid and supported if it resonates in and is "endorsed" by the North. Development indicators are made there, and if according to those indicators a project or person is pronounced by a consultant from the North to be successful, it is universally accepted to be so. This is the practice of the international institutions, corporations and agencies. This is the practice of development NGOs and donors. It could be a case of inherited cultural baggage.

To mirror this, Southern-based NGO staffs know that the ability to analyse life situations, structures of society and development processes is not their preserve or that of intellectuals and other development professionals (Muchina 1995). They know the poor have the potential to do this, and they treasure the "opportunity to work with our own people" (Smillie 1995). They even know that without effective participation and ownership by those being supported, there is no chance of sustainability for whatever initiatives they have tried to introduce. Yet they go ahead and behave contrary to what they know to be the truth, imposing their views of development and their priorities on the people. There is no effective consultation, and the little that takes place is for window dressing, a kind of tokenism.

THE ILLUSION OF CONSULTATION

Window dressing is something the South has suspected the North of being guilty of for a long time. Recently this was admitted to me by a senior staff member of a leading international financial institution when he told me that his "conversion" took place only three years ago. He also said this was the case with an even more senior staff friend of his at the same institution. They had been organising meetings, like the one we were attending when he told me this, supposedly to hear from the South with no intention of hearing what the South had to say. They would then return to the North to go ahead with their ideas as if the consultations had never taken place. Likewise, Southern-based NGO staffs know the right thing to do but fail to do it. They are from the community, but they are not of the community. They, perhaps without knowing it, behave like their benefactors. They have become conditioned to believe uncritically that real success is that which is pronounced from the North rather than what poor people say.

There are two issues here. The first is the devaluation of indigenous knowledge. The second is the use and abuse of recognition and praise. Because the North is perceived by the South not to value ideas except its own, the NGO staffs in the South do not, deep within themselves, believe the poor have ideas at all. After all, we go North to get knowledge. We read their books as set texts in all courses in the South, books whose authors may never have set foot on the African continent but whose prescriptions we take wholesale as the answer to Africa's problems, from economics to science. Because this has gone on for many decades, it has become dogma. Forms of recognition and praise have been used to prop this fallacy. Ms. Kaluwile, executive secretary of the National Association of Small and Medium Enterprises of Malawi, points out that Southern development thinkers and practitioners are weary of praise when it comes from the North, believing it to be a tool to co-opt good ideas and eventually return them as "intellectual property" of the North. Or they are suspicious that praise comes before a fall (private conversation).

Southern-based staffs who want to consult their communities for indigenous ideas quickly find that there is no time for them to do so. They live a life of constant apprehension about money, reports and keeping the donor happy. Money has killed all creative thinking from the South. As many NGO staff know, "more time is spent in accounting to Northern partners than in actually applying one's mind, judgement and energies to the work at hand" (Smillie 1995, 186). Money, or rather the love of it, as the Bible rightly says (1 Tim. 6:10) is the root of all kinds of evil. People in the South who have and want to apply their minds to real issues of development and change soon realise that working for a Northern or international NGO, or even starting one's own, is not a way to achieve this. Those who develop a good idea and have the language facility to document and speak for it spend the rest of their life globetrotting to workshops, seminars and conferences until their idea loses its cutting edge and appeal. This is how initiatives for strategic social change are stillborn or die in infancy, long before they ever come to fruition.

SOUTHERN NGO SURVIVAL STRATEGIES

If "partnership" is a survival strategy of Northern and international agencies, Southern counterparts too have their survival strategies. One is, If you can't beat them, join them. Most NGO staff members have accepted the terms of the partnership. Instead of "divorce" or "separation," they have opted to stay. They know that they help to implement ideas which are not their own. If the ideas happen to work, and some do, then well and good. If the ideas do not work, they accept that they are accomplices to something they were not sure would deliver in the first place. They are part of a show. They know that money and "voice" are power.

They know that they have neither. But they know that exhibiting certain behaviour towards the community gives them apparent power before their fellow staff and community members. The question that begs an answer is, Must the show go on?

Another survival strategy is silence. As Smillie comments, "Supplicants, of course, can't be overly picky, and many Southern NGOs have chosen to bear the problem in silence, attempting to make the best deal possible under the circumstances" (Smillie 1995, 185). Like their colleagues, staffs of international NGOs also adopt the same rule: Silence is golden. When in doubt, they say little or nothing at all. Not that they have nothing to say; they are only playing it safe. When they speak, they know that they must say only politically correct things, things that their Northern counterparts want to hear. As a staff member once said, "Often staff who hold differing views are perceived to be a threat." Dissent is not well tolerated. Unfortunately, dissenting voices are often the brightest, the best and the most creative.

Although Smillie says that recently there has been a growing chorus of complaint and criticism, this is from a few people from the civil society rather than international NGO staff. Basically, the silence of the Southern voices is deafening. This silence must be listened to attentively. The South says the most when it says nothing at all. The South takes seriously the sayings of a wise owl: The older I become, the more I see. The more I see, the less I say. The less I say, the wiser I become. By not fully disclosing what one is thinking, one can leave others to guess. Full disclosure is taken by some to be tantamount to committing intellectual suicide.

Silence can be also a sign of protest. In studies done on children of genocide in Rwanda, it was discovered that during therapy, when children were asked to draw, they tended to draw people with no mouths. The children were saying that when they speak, no one listens, so why bother. Ugandan artist Alex Bukulu, in his stage play "Thirty Years of Bananas," had full-size portraits of past presidents, some of whom had no ears. He did this to signify how little they listened during their presidency. It is time to draw people with large mouths and small or no ears, talking to people with no or small mouths and various sizes of ears to signify the disparity between those who have and use a voice and those who don't and use silence. In the meantime, the North speaks freely – a vocal minority, deciding what good development is, monopolising ideas, and successfully obtaining millions of dollars to be spent on unproductive projects. But do they know the Southern readings of their words?

Silence can be wisdom. It can also be protest. But silence, like verbosity, can and often does indicate a complex. Silence often betokens an inferiority complex, just as verbosity is a sign of superiority, of dominance, of power. Inferiority is humanity's worst killer. It kills both the mind and the soul. The weak do not speak for fear of saying the wrong things and being laughed at or misunderstood or penalised. "Superior" people are always talking, even when they have nothing to say. As a matter of fact, there is too much of nothing. Since all speech, oral or written, has to be in a language foreign to the Southerner, in a mother tongue to the Northerner, it may be entered into only with care and caution and at one's own risk. The silence of the majority needs to be carefully studied if its implications are to be fully understood. It may hold the key to redefining the whole concept of partnership. We ignore silence at our own peril. Speech should be a right for all humans. The Southern tongue needs to be liberated.

SOUTH-TO-SOUTH SILENCE

Southern staffs are products of their political environment in which South-to-South dialogue is underdeveloped. In fact, all South-to-South linkages are either very weak or non-existent. So is South-to-South NGO dialogue and networking. Dialogue that is not conceived and supported by the North carries very little weight. It is this single fact that makes the voice of the South absent in international forums, even when the South is the subject of the discussion.

There are explanations for this. One is the political influence the North has had on the South, the politics of divide and rule, often referred to as neo-colonialism. With such politics, incentives were provided to vocal influential personalities to weaken South-to-South collaboration. Where incentives failed, force and sabotage were resorted to. This had the effect of discouraging alternative viewpoints, let alone dissent. It destroyed independent thought.

The second explanation is financial. All development activities have always depended on the North for their bankrolls. It follows that Northern interests must always come first. The North will not financially support anything that can challenge Northern supremacy. As Abdul Mohamed (1999) contends, financial dependence on the North leads to intellectual dependence. No way round this problem has been sought.

The third reason relates to organisational ability in the South. Abdul Mohamed notes the scarcity of opportunities for African policy-makers, practitioners, and theoreticians to come together to analyse the African experience. The capacity of the South to organise, both in the political and NGO spheres, is frightfully underdeveloped. This capacity was destroyed during the long period of colonialism and neo-colonialism that now has been revived through liberalisation and globalisation. In particular, there is lack of access to communication technology; this hampers the efforts of getting people in the South to talk to one another. For example, according to a recent UNDP report, the poor countries of the South have 1 per cent of the global Internet users (PNUD 1999).

Oral methods of exchanging ideas are severely limited in their reach. When representatives from the South go to meetings and consultations in the North, they go with individual voices. They cannot speak collectively. They may be meeting for the very first time and the organisers do not allow them time to talk amongst themselves before the meetings start. When they speak, they compete with, contradict and repeat one another. They may not talk again until the next meeting. In contrast, the North seems well organised, eloquent and logical. People seem to know each other and to have a similar position on the key points and issues that matter. They seem to speak with one voice and are of one mind.

The fourth reason may be intellectual laziness. Organising an effective network takes a lot of hard work, as anyone who has tried has found. Keeping it running and making an effective input into the global dialogue requires dedication and a constant flow of ideas. It requires investment in research and analysis of relevant issues, things in short supply in the South.

The fifth reason may be poverty. Potential leaders are preoccupied by the struggle for survival and lack the time to think strategically. The poor will probably not read this book. Poverty, that killer "virus" that passes from mother to child, from generation to generation, destroys the capacity for long-term strategizing. People have to try to survive on a day-to-day basis. Investments are made on the basis of their short-term returns. The value in a strong voice is not apparent. This is unfortunate, because the value of effective advocacy is incalculable.

The potential that lies in the South to influence global directions is enormous. Without the South many aid agencies would cease to exist. In addition, the South has values of extended family, of interdependence, and of community which the global marketplace so badly lacks. As Field Wicker-Miurin has said (*Newsweek* 1999, 52), "As the world gets more and more complicated and anonymous, we can preserve our humanity by taking care of others as well as ourselves." Africa can give to the world relational as well as spiritual values.

The South with its population mass can and should exert more influence on decisions that affect the well-being of the global family. Conversely, the South has the most to lose when decisions continue to be taken in disregard of it. NGOs, which are ardent proponents of equity and equality, must set an example of how the voice of the South can better be heard. This must begin at home, within the NGOs themselves.

IS SINCERE RECIPROCITY ATTAINABLE?

In the present arrangement, in which money occupies a central place in what we call North-South partnership, equality is unattainable. Durable solutions are those that put money in its right perspective and then go beyond it. NGOs that believe in the language of partnership must find ways to make alliances that can have a life outside the financial relationship (Smillie 1995, 194). In conceptualising development, genuine partnership should be securely rooted in ideas and principles and shared values. Let money chase these, not the other way round. Is this a feasible proposition? Affirmative. For example, "Southern human rights organisations tend to get along a lot better with their Northern counterparts than development NGOs, because functionally, they share more intellectual common ground. Money . . . [is] not the basis for their relationship. In fact money may not enter into the equation at all" (Smillie 1995, 194).

Development NGOs can go even further and agree to a partnership based on sincere reciprocity. What cannot be reciprocated must be relegated to a secondary place in the relationship. What breaks up or nullifies partnerships is money-centred conditions and attendant sanctions. The commonest tool used, of course, is withholding money in order to force compliance. But money is only one part of this, important though it is. As long as the South has no sanctions of its own to apply to the North, either as a diplomatic "tit for tat," or simply to bring the North in line, there cannot be a meaningful North-South partnership. As long as the North does not experience the equivalent of a withholding of funding for lack of compliance with regard to an aspect of a development, it will never know how humiliating unequal partnerships are.

Some NGOs have devised peer reviews in which all stakeholders participate in a comprehensive review of the work of one of its offices, whether in the North or in the South. In what he refers to as "reverse evaluations," Smillie (1995, 194) quotes the Dutch NGO Novib as once having invited some of its partners to evaluate it.

Another possible approach is the microcredit, microenterprise model, now very popular among a number of international NGOs. The South has long been appealing for permission to go into commercial investments so that, over time, it can generate enough resources to run its activities with little or no direct financial injection from the North. This is already being done by some Asian NGOs. They see this as the only way to break away from dependency. And it has merits. It helps to create independent, self-sustaining mindsets. The microcredit, microenterprise model now being championed by many development agencies makes graduation into a self-governing entity that fully funds itself from interest proceeds charged to its clients a real possibility. If this were linked to the Area Development Programming (ADP) approach, also being championed by agencies such as World Vision and ActionAid, the cycle would be complete. The idea behind the ADP, relevant to this point, is that communities graduate into independent legal entities that can be fully responsible for the way they run their businesses.

Concerning language and cultural issues, the partners must engage in what can be called serious reduction criticism to try to identify substance from wrappings, from noise on either side. At the moment the trend seems to be to imitate global corporations (Smillie 1995). NGOs can lead the way in removing the language factor and cultural interference from the North-South partnership. Doing a reality check with the South periodically should do more to help match declaration with practice, rhetoric with reality. Ignacio de Senillosa (1998) suggests a cultural blending of North and South. But for this to be effective, the South must be willing to respond constructively and to reciprocate with its own reality check. North and South must regain hope that good can prevail over evil, that trust can become the central tenet of a genuine partnership.

The North and the South must work together to create interactive and mutually supportive networks. As a matter of urgency, the South must talk to itself and to its people more intensively than it services its relationship with the North. Attempts to draw distinctions among origins of agencies, an energy-consuming and emotion-consuming futile exercise, must be discouraged. This energy should be converted instead into a positive search for solutions for sustainable development in the South. More space should be created to allow the South to spend quality time and apply its critical faculties to this life-and-death matter. Conditions must be created that are conducive to African creativity. The South must re-claim its right to strategize its own development, to organise and lead it, and to speak for it in the language that best expresses what needs to be heard. Perhaps NGOs should step back from using money to dominate and drive the process of what seems defective development and try instead to get closer to Southern ideals, traditions and heartbeat for inspiring alternatives.

WORKS CITED

Bukulu, A. 1993. "Thirty Years of Bananas." The script of a stage play performed at the Kampala Cultural Centre.

Bunch, R. 1995. "Two Ears of Corn: A Guide to People-Centered Agricultural Improvement." Oklahoma: World Neighbors.

de Senillosa, I. 1998. "A New Age of Social Movements: A Fifth Generation of Non-governmental Development Organisations in the Making?" *Development in Practice* 8/1. This article also appears in *Development and Social Action*. A Development in Practice Reader. Oxfam, 1999.

Edwards, M. 1999. *Future Positive International Co-operation in the Twenty-first Century.* London: Earthscan.

Muchina, O. 1995. "Qualitative Indicators of Transformational Development." *Together* (October-December), 3–5.

Mohamed, A. 1999. "Conflict and Humanitarianism in Africa: New Challenges." Unpublished notes.

Narayan, D. 2000. "Voices of the Poor: Can Anyone Hear Us?" World Bank.

Newsweek. September 13, 1999.

Nyamugasira, W. 1997. "NGOs and Advocacy: Poor Imitations of Authentic Southern Voices." World Vision UK Discussion Papers, Number 4.

———. 1998. "NGOs and Advocacy: How Well Are the Poor Represented?" *Development in Practice* 8/3. This article also appears in *Development and Social Action*. A Development in Practice Reader. Oxfam, 1999.

PNUD. 1999. *Rapport Mondial Sur Le Developpement Humain 1999*. Paris, Bruxelles: De Boeck Universite.

Schumacher, E. F. 1973. *Small Is Beautiful: Economics as if People Mattered*. New York: Harper & Row.

Smillie, I. 1995. *The Alms Bazaar Altruism Under Fire – Non-Profit Organizations and International Development*. London: Intermediate Technology Publications

Southerns, R. 1996. "Advocacy: A Call for Renewed NGO Commitment." Unpublished paper.

Vink, N. 1993. "Communication Between Unequals: Development Workers and the Poor." *Bulletins of the Royal Tropical Institute: Culture and Communication* Number 329.

World Vision. 1998. "Qualitative Needs Assessment of Child-headed Households in Rwanda." Internal report.

World Vision. 1999. "Rwanda Emergency Agriculture Program." Evaluation report.

2.

Poverty, Prejudice and Development

Can NGOs Learn to Love Economic Growth?

ALAN WHAITES

The 1980s did much to spark the interest of development NGOs in the intricacies of macro-economics, particularly after the shock of the debt crisis. Yet it was without question the late 1990s which saw the flowering of their interest. The steady rise of global NGO coalitions, facilitated by email and Internet organising, has helped to foster new linkages both North-South and cross-sectorally (with environmental groups and others). By the end of the 1990s these coalitions were able to mobilise considerable lobbying resources and also large-scale street power in order to bring pressure to bear for debt relief, the scrapping of the Multilateral Agreement on Investment (MAI) and the postponement of a new round of trade talks.[1]

Long gone are the days when NGOs entered the corridors of treasury ministries with little more than a moral appeal for debt forgiveness, or when NGOs demonised the World Bank as the root of all evil. Today NGOs, with economists in tow, are interested in the details of policy, albeit with a focus that still revolves around the worlds of debt, adjustment, trans-national corporations (TNCs) and trade. The increasing economic sophistication of international NGOs has played a large part in their ability to influence the policy-making process. This combination of expertise and street power wedded to the emphasis in the 1990s on civil society enabled NGOs to gain access to the very institutions that they had long criticised.

Access and economic literacy are certainly critical if NGOs want to advocate seriously for macro-policies that directly benefit the poor. The tension for NGOs, however, is whether to use these new-found assets primarily to prevent policies that are bad or to promote those that bring maximum gain for the poor. This may seem like an unnecessary choice, until past practice is reviewed. With perhaps the honourable exception of Oxfam's 1999 *Education Now* campaign, the central economic advocacy of development NGOs has tended towards negative calls for redress rather than pointing towards new policy steps (scrapping of the MAI, cancelling debt, postponing trade talks).

The negativity of NGO economic advocacy has, to an extent, been a reflection of trends within the wider development community. Popular authors such as David C Korten, Susan George and Phil O'Keefe[2] have provided ample ammunition for a narrowly pessimistic view. A review of NGO briefings distributed at the now infamous World Trade Organization (WTO) meeting in Seattle in November 1999 provided a guide to the general approach being followed at the end of that decade. With few exceptions, the piles of documents pointed to proposed policies viewed as wrong, rather than offering a fundamentally different view of development.[3]

Does a negative bent to economic advocacy matter, if bad policies are consistently brought into the light? Yes, it does. Development, including human development, is a product of intentional policy, a process that means getting right the approach to an array of issues: from education to industry, from transport infrastructure to rural finance. The propensity towards the negative on the part of NGOs has let much go by; in the past it has reflected a failure to seize on good policy practice and then argue its cause to donors and Southern governments alike.

Some might hold that NGOs are simply weak at articulating successes in global poverty alleviation, preferring instead images of poverty, famine and disease. A less cynical view (taken here) is that the natural pressure to always scale up from micro-experience sometimes leads to a partial view of the issues at stake. If NGOs were to broaden their view and take in the range of empirical evidence available so far, then the ammunition for advocacy is vast. The progress of poverty reduction over the last few decades may not always agree with the myths that NGOs have tried to create – but just as clearly it contradicts the simplistic neo-liberalism with which many NGOs have tried to debate.

LETTING GO

Development is an intensely ideological business – as the poor have often found to their cost. This chapter is about broadening our perspectives to the point that our ideology is constructively shaped by the realities of development as it has taken place, a process that means being open to learning from any path that might bring closer a world of equity, accountability and empowerment. But, accepting the lessons of experience will mean letting go to some of the prejudices of the past. Ideology should, after all, be informed by empirical evidence rather than blinding us to the experience of the real world. Perhaps this is especially true for those protagonists of the Washington Consensus who have long argued for a path to development that has never successfully been implemented at all.

It is time to admit that no developed state has reached its current position of wealth by following the policies long advocated by the World Bank and the International Monetary Fund (IMF). This essay highlights the fact that recent experience (for example, the recent experience of states in Southeast Asia) runs contrary to the state shrinking and market opening conditionality forced on less fortunate souls. Similar arguments could also be made for those longer developed countries who began to open their markets after their wealth was achieved. Even the development aims of the neoliberal ideologues might be thrown into doubt, for their focus on gross national product (GNP) growth alone is not sufficient to bring about social development. We must be conscious of examples of growth so poorly distributed that it leaves a relatively rich country with 10 million people living on less than $1 a day (Brazil).

If neo-liberals need to let go their attachment to a recipe for development that has no claim to success, then equally NGOs need to look more closely at the role that GNP growth can play in improving the lives of the poor. The problem is that GNP growth too often has been portrayed as the ultimate goal rather than as a useful tool. GNP growth in itself does not equate to holistic development. Instead, it is people and communities who give development its meaning: reducing poverty, extending life, creating chances for fulfilment. Development, not just human development, is achieved when people gain power to change – to pursue their own goals, not only to aspire but also to achieve.

Increasing GNP does not bring development, but it can help bring a more holistic form of development closer. The problem for NGOs is that some of the apparent instruments of success in the past – industrialisation, capital flows and the promotion of growth – jar with the basic-needs philosophy that underpins most modern aid agencies. It is here that NGOs have much to let go. NGOs will need to speak not just about development failure but also about success.

NGOs, for example, have spent much of the last two decades focussed on the impact of debt in Africa and Latin America, while at the same time parts of Asia were enjoying economic growth at a breathtaking pace. It was the silence of their critics that allowed Western politicians erroneously to vaunt these as examples of free-market-driven success. These countries were, after all, largely ignored by development campaigners, who waited instead until the Asian recessions of the late 1990s to add their voice. The fact that development NGOs, many of whom were still operational in Thailand, Indonesia and Malaysia (and had been in Taiwan, Korea and Singapore), so willingly bought into the free-market rhetoric ensured that several advocacy opportunities were forgone.[4]

This essay argues that NGOs must review the lessons of the past, particularly of progress in human development, in order to advocate for policies that work. This will mean looking anew at traditional areas of concern (industrialisation, urbanisation) and learning to think of basic needs and rural work as elements of the picture, not the canvas as a whole. Most important, NGOs must stand ready to turn on its head their view of the micro-macro link, embracing the reality that usually it is the macro-micro that really matters more. Good macro-policy can bring straighter and faster roads from poverty, provided the vehicles are right. This chapter points to elements that must be considered as integral to such a commitment, particularly the key to much of the debate, the combination of state policy and income distribution as both corollaries and engines of human development and growth.

GROWTH AND HUMAN DEVELOPMENT

It is tempting to devote substantive space to an explanation of how progressive advocates for human development can come to embrace the idea of market-led economic growth, but this ground is already well-trodden by Bill Warren, Nigel Harris and others.[5] More important is the need to stress that it is a particular type of market-led growth that has proven to be effective in improving human development conditions. The discussion below examines some of the factors that helped create a socially beneficial path to growth for Southeast Asia. But first, it is useful to restate the degree to which human development in some states has taken place.

Stephen Haggard has shown that in the days before the Human Development Index (HDI) existed, the newly industrialising states (NICs) were already making strong progress when measured by the Physical Quality of Life Index (PQLI).[6] The advent of the HDI illustrated the dramatic progress made by Southeast Asian states on a range of social indicators. Comparative studies are often most illustrative, and Rhys Jenkins has compared the progress of Southeast Asian states with their Latin American counterparts, highlighting the greater progress they have made.[7]

Certainly achievement of high human development status by South Korea, Hong Kong and Singapore suggests that their development experience is worth closer review (of which it has received a great deal).[8] Perhaps more remarkable still is the experience of states which began the development process with less encouraging social indicators and significantly greater problems of scale. The overall experience of Indonesia and also China shows the poverty-reducing potential of economic growth. In both states rural poverty fell from over 30 per cent in 1978 to 14.3 per cent and 11.5 per cent respectively by 1990.[9]

The success in human development of some Asian states has been crudely characterised as evidence that market-driven economic growth is inherently poverty alleviating. In reality, lessons from the NICs are more complex and, for NGOs, considerably more interesting. Islam and Chowdhury have done much to dispel the myth that the labour intensive nature of export orientation alone is sufficient to foster social development.[10] True, increased employment does hold the potential of enabling the poor to purchase key social development needs such as education and healthcare, but more critical in NICs is the role of the state. Even in the most laissez-faire of the NICs, considerable state intervention has taken place to promote education, healthcare and in several cases low-cost public housing.

Policy was the counterweight to the reality that growth does not necessarily create the access and opportunity for social development. At an IMF sponsored conference in June 1998, Sen reminded the audience that even possession of incomes on the part of the poor does not create adequate conditions. Some guarantee must exist that the necessary services are available, and to the standard and degree of consistency necessary for the promotion of growth. Decent healthcare and education cannot be left to the chance of the market.[11]

This role of the state as a provider of poverty-reducing measures has reinforced the often noted tendency of NICs to exhibit relatively good patterns of income distribution (I make the assumption that more equal distribution is at least morally good). Although the income distribution picture has changed as these economies have matured, the initial role of distribution has usually been seen as an important factor both in achieving progress in human development and in accelerated economic growth. Indeed, the success of government economic policy in Southeast Asia has been linked to their promotion of good income distribution either directly or through provision of services and benefits.

States may pursue a range of policies intended to accelerate rates of economic growth, such as export orientation, fiscal balance, monetary stability and the encouragement of a high savings rate. Even so, this key lesson from Asia remains: growth must be seen as the generator of resources for social development interventions by the state. Private provision alone will not be sufficient. Indeed, relying on private provision only weakens the overall accountability and long-term efficiency of the state.[12] State-led social interventions also entail improving the distribution of resources between rich and poor, a corollary which governments should embrace not simply for the sake of social cohesion, but also to accelerate economic growth.

GROWTH AND THE POOR: EQUITY WORKS

In the past, economic growth was, for development activists, a fairly straightforward target for criticism, the charge being laid that a focus on economic growth produces only Dickensian exploitation, environmental degradation and a host of social problems. Much of this criticism was associated with market pressures to drive down costs through measures ranging from child labour to the repression of civil and political rights. Without challenging the argument that all of these problems can be a facet of a focus on growth, it is still worth noting that there are few examples of countries that have produced rapid improvements in human development indicators without rapid economic growth (Sri Lanka being the most famous exception).

Growth can produce appalling social conditions. The real point, however, is that this is not inevitable, there are even strong reasons why economic policy-makers should actively seek more equal growth. True, in the past, proponents of an emphasis on growth would have argued that high levels of inequality in developing countries were no bad thing. Concentrating wealth in the hands of a few would provide more resources for investment in new businesses, which could in turn generate greater employment and therefore income for the poor. In reality, without access to international markets or strong local demand, both of which make investment worthwhile, much of this money can simply disappear into high-earning foreign bank accounts or other investments overseas.[13] Wealth concentrated in the hands of a few also usually means disproportionate expenditure on luxury and imported goods.

While still arguing that growth leads to improved human development, the World Bank has made a leap towards recognising the importance of income equality. Better distribution of wealth creates higher and more stable demand for goods and services. In South Korea and Taiwan, for example, relative income equality within a framework of supportive economic policy allowed local industries to grow by producing goods for a healthy local market.[14]

Recent World Bank publications highlight positive factors resulting from equity, such as increased domestic savings rates and human capital formation.[15] Each of these is an important contributory factor to growth in its own right. Domestic savings can help to keep inflation in check whilst also providing potential loan capital for investment. In *The Lessons of East Asia: An Overview of Country Experience*, the World Bank made the point that achieving a "relative equality of income" was critical in the first generation of the newly industrialised economies of East Asia.

This factor was more of a change brought about by policy than an inheritance. Most other low and middle-income countries were not able to achieve similar equality of income or assets. Large land reform schemes in both Korea and Taiwan, China, did away with the landholding classes and made wage income the main source of advancement. Public housing investments in Singapore and Hong Kong were early priorities of governments bent on maintaining a national consensus on development policies.[16]

Studies such as those by Bruno, Ravallion and Squire and work by Griffin and Ickowitz reinforce the view that achieving higher growth is helped by improving equity and helping the poor to gain productive assets (for example, education).[17] Empirical studies even point to a negative relationship between initial inequality and subsequent economic growth.[18] It is perhaps ironic that these studies, based on data from developing economies over several decades, have originated with an institution often caricatured as irredeemably neo-liberal, namely, the World Bank. Griffith and Ickowitz go further still in their endorsement of equity as an appropriate policy goal, suggesting that growth and equity are mutually reinforcing.[19]

The key to achieving greater equity and, with it, better economic growth lies in the pursuit of deliberate policies addressing both issues together.[20] One approach to creating greater equality that has been found to work involves redistribution of land.[21] Other steps that have proven to be important involve equipping the poor as workers and entrepreneurs. Kanbur and Squire, looking at policies that have worked, write: "Another feature underlying the success of these countries was their emphasis on human development. They invested heavily in the education and health of their populations as a contributing factor to growth but also as a benefit in its own right."[22]

Interestingly, the late 1990s economic crisis in Asia affected the eight states studied in *The East Asian Miracle* in something of an inverse relationship to the degree of equality. A comparison of some of the states involved has been provided by Kamal Malhotra.[23] Equally, Amiya Kumar Bagchi has pointed to the economic disequilibrium and distortions that can arise in relatively unequal economies.[24] To assist in the study of these harmful income inequalities, economists have developed the Gini index, a measure of the extent to which the distribution of income deviates from a perfectly equal level (with zero representing perfect equality). In its 1989–99 review of world development, the World Bank found that all those states with a Gini score in excess of 50 were within the developing world.[25]

EXPLOITATION: ECONOMIC POISON

An initial reaction from many in development who witnessed the economic growth of NICs was to point to the perceived economic exploitation which such success was seen to involve. Reliance on low wages was certainly a key element in making early export orientation work, but rapid rises in productivity made economic growth compatible with rising real wages in Southeast Asian states.[26] Indeed, those states that have continued to rely on comparative advantage in labour costs as their primary economic asset have faired worse than their neighbours. In the case of Thailand, which has performed less well amongst NICs in income distribution, the failure to improve secondary and tertiary education levels has been a drag on growth, increasing vulnerability to new and cheaper exporting states.

Overall, the evidence suggests that exploitation is a poor mechanism for trying to achieve high levels of growth. In states such as Brazil, exploitation through income inequality helps to keep shallow the spread of consumer demand. The worst forms of exploitation, such as child labour, also bring few economic benefits while undermining human capital formation for the future. The labour standards study of the Organization for Economic Co-operation and Development (OECD) examined whether low labour standards had positive or negative impacts on the competitiveness of developing countries. Low standards included child labour, forced labour, lack of freedom of association, and restricted rights to organise and bargain collectively. According to the OECD:

> The study found no evidence that low-standards countries had a better global export performance than other countries; there

was not a correlation at the aggregate level between real wage growth and observance of freedom of association rights; there was some positive association between sustained trade reforms and improvements in core standards; finally FDI data suggest core labour standards are not important in most OECD investor decisions. The general conclusion therefore is that a) adoption of core standards would not hurt developing countries' economic performance or competitive position (indeed, higher standards might be helpful in the longer term); and b) the failure to observe such standards does not appear to constitute an important competitive advantage.[27]

Exploitation may not aid the growth prospects of developing countries, but problems such as child labour have been associated with the rise of low-cost, low-tech manufacturing sectors in developing urban environments. The example of the garment industry in Bangladesh and the disastrous impact of naive attempts by US legislators to solve the problem offer salutary reminders of the potential for producers to ignore the country's overall long-term interests.[28] It remains an open question whether problems such as child labour are a product of macro-economic policies or simply a sign of underlying poverty and need for income. Even so, it is a mistake to write such issues off as a "stage of growth" or a problem best solved by economic progress.

If growth is to do more good than harm and, in the process, achieve sustainability, then the externalities involved must be addressed. The need for effective state action and an adequate legal framework that can help redress abuses and ensure human capital formation is vital. The International Labour Organization (ILO) has developed labour standards offering safeguards for workers without enabling back-door protectionism on the part of states in the North. The seven conventions involved are, unfortunately, rarely implemented in full and lack accompanying positive international incentives that might aid their cause.[29] The presence of a weak state is often an obstacle to effective regulation for countries with endemic corruption or fragile political contexts. Inevitably the state must take centre stage in addressing wider externalities associated with growth.

FRIEND OR FOE:
URBANISATION AND INDUSTRIAL DEVELOPMENT

Potential threats to economic sustainability which governments of developing states face stretch beyond labour conditions to include environmental damage concomitant with industrialisation and social problems fuelled by explosive urban growth. NGOs have moved into cities in the last 30 years to provide clean water, education and healthcare. Efforts to organise and mobilise large slums have also generated some of the most innovative and successful new methodologies used by Northern and Southern NGOs. Despite advances made by development practitioners in meeting the needs of slum dwellers, many large NGOs seem to have remained mentally fixed in the village. A focus on the community as the core of development has led too often to the separation of the *basti*, slum, *barrio,* or township from the wider macro-urban issues involved.

Initially the analysis of NGOs in relation to macro-economic policy and urbanisation was not helped by the misconception that new urban dwellers were simply pursuing a mythical dream of modern consumer life. In reality the draw of the city is harshly practical. Urban poverty, although often appalling, can still be substantially more secure than conditions in the rural home. Jorge Hardoy and David Satterthwaite state:

> People's movements to or from cities are logical responses to the pattern of economic opportunities across the nation. Most decisions to move to the city are based on careful, logical and rational judgements; many result from information from people in the cities about job opportunities there.[30]

Governments might decry the fact that a city is growing rapidly, but they rarely ask why – or consider the extent to which their own policies are among the causes. Nor do they look at why people are leaving their original homes. In many cases migrants are small farmers forced off their land or agricultural labourers whose livelihood has disappeared because of soil erosion, low crop prices, or increasing concentration of land ownership.[31]

The solution offered by Hardoy and Satterthwaite is that governments must capture some of the proceeds of growing urban economies (often noticeable even where national GNP is stagnant) in order to invest in urban infrastructure and quality of life.[32] Such action, although desirable, is rarely easy with the urban economy dominated by the informal sector, and tax collection or leverage over private resources weak. Where states have sought to invest in their exploding conurbations they have also been criticised for their urban bias and denial of resources to the still more numerous rural poor.[33]

For development NGOs, dilemmas faced by Southern states in relation to urban policy, particularly during periods of structural adjustment and the pressure to focus on commodity exports, have gone largely unremarked (although environmental NGOs have been more vocal). The reality that cities are with us for the long term and offer a potential path away from commodity dependence demands a fuller NGO macro-policy response.

Pressure over issues such as the MAI, a new trade round, or TNCs must also recognise that for the cities of the South, such foreign investment, particularly in labour-intensive sectors, is actually a considerable prize. The states involved also need the large infrastructural multi-lateral loans NGOs so frequently despise (including for that traditional bogey, power generation). Perhaps most acutely, NGOs might look more seriously at one of the most demanding issues of all: bringing the informal sector (with which they often work) more fully into the formal sphere.

The unease felt by development organisations for the city is partly a reflection of their greater displeasure with the small-scale manufacturing or full-scale industrialisation on which cities feed. NGO advocates may berate the curse of commodity dependence and call for trade access for processed goods, but this usually falls well short of embracing the industrial path to growth. It is certainly the case that conditions for industrialisation in Southeast Asia have been very different from those prevalent in most of Africa, not least for the newest of the NICs, who absorbed vast amounts of investment from their richer neighbours. Nevertheless the urban-industrial sector remains a critical factor for human development across the developing world.

The continued growth of urban environments and the need of new entrants to the cities for employment suggests that NGOs should increasingly advocate for policies to facilitate manufacturing-sector growth, by both local government and international donors/trading partners. Such an approach will require a more nuanced position on issues of environmental sustainability. In the past the advocacy work of some groups, particularly in the environmental sector, has implicitly called for the Third World's poor to be permanently denied opportunity for the kind of consumer products taken for granted in the North. Environmental sustainability does not necessarily mean denying the right of the poor to aspire to ownership of consumer goods. Romantic ideas of the perfect un-commercialised life held by some amongst the middle class of the rich North are not, after all, seen in the same light in the slums of Rangoon, Calcutta, Nairobi or Sao Paolo.

Sustainable development will only be achieved if Northern states make substantial reductions in their own contribution to global pollution – a step that some, particularly the United States, have been determined not to take. As Peter Uimonen has pointed out, international structures, such as the WTO trade rules system, must include flexibility to allow adequate cross-border environmental agreements or national policy.[34] Countries of the OECD will responsibility for the ease with which new NICs can access the resources and technical capability needed for environmental sustainable manufacturing. Finally, a considerable burden will continue to rest on developing countries' regulatory structures, which are currently poorly placed to meet the challenge. Nick Robins and Alex Trisoglio state:

> Unlike previous industrial revolutions, the restructuring needed to achieve sustainable development will require conscious and deliberate changes in corporate goals, business practice and regulatory frameworks. . . . Governments need to provide an empowering framework and, within this, stimulate, cajole and sometimes force a long-term shift in industrial behaviour. This will involve the application of a range of policy tools at different levels from the global to the local.[35]

Proposals have been made on steps that could be taken by the NICs of Southeast Asia to address their serious environmental problems. Such proposals have recognised that in the short term, a focus on domestic issues is perhaps more practical than concentration on the need for global change.[36] The feasibility of domestic action in the developing world is, however, dependent upon the capability of the state, which has become a cross-cutting theme in discussions of achieving pro-poor growth.

INGREDIENTS FOR POVERTY-REDUCING GROWTH

Ironically, while structural adjustment programmes imposed on Africa during the 1980s were gradually eating away at the capability of the state, much attention was also focussing on the part played by governments in the success of the NICs. Although by the mid-1990s the World Bank was willing to recognise that the state did have a part to play, this was still a grudgingly defined and peripheral part at best.[37] Neo-liberals sought to point to extenuating circumstances for Asian states, including the relative autonomy of government from society. This view of Asia as free from clientelistic and patrimonial forces betrayed a weak grasp of underlying cultural factors, rudely exposed by later business/state problems in South Korea, Japan, Indonesia and Thailand.

The reality remains that the state played a crucial role through intentional policy in the success of the NICs, despite problems of corruption, occasional political crisis, periods of fiscal deficit and tendencies towards industrial planning. Actions by the state (and, in some cases, old colonial powers) created the beneficial income distribution mentioned above. The state invested in education and health. It was the state that pursued growth-promoting policies (low inflation, monetary stability, and the promotion of domestic savings) and encouraged export-based industries to grow. Today, it is also the state which holds the potential to implement those policies necessary to address continuing policy crises most developing states must face, particularly in relation to labour issues, the environment and urban growth.

Erosion of the state in many parts of the developing world, largely facilitated by the process of structural adjustment, therefore stands as one of the greatest development disasters of recent years. Effects of loan conditionality, particularly on states in Africa, have created a genre of development literature of its own. Sam Jones has described the process through which conditionality gradually weakened the resources and capabilities of the state.[38] Jean Francois

Bayart and others have suggested that these policies helped to criminalise the African state.[39] Elsewhere writers, particularly from Weberian schools, have pointed to the impact of the overall Western approach to Africa in debilitating the state.[40]

Certainly privatisation, user charges, civil society gap-filling and the ending of many subsidies only served to weaken autonomy.[41] But the demands made upon such states also created shifts in internal power and often brought political crises that served only to fuel elite competition for resources and the clientelistic grip. In implementing a stream of policies that undermined the African state, the World Bank and IMF perhaps did more to prevent pro-poor growth and prolong poverty than in any other of their many misguided approaches.

Northern thinkers may be able to write off erosion of the state as a natural by-product of globalisation, arguing that technology and capital flows make national borders increasingly obsolete. In reality, the OECD state has yet to disappear, but it is certainly becoming complex. States of the North are both more local (as part of a devolution trend) and more global (as multi-lateral bodies take on limited regulatory powers). The state, however, remains the broker and negotiator of the shifting power involved. Globalisation has changed the nature of the states concerned but hardly diminished their role. For developing states in Africa, the weakness of this lynch-pin level of the state distorts globalisation itself. Unable to broker between competing local units, it falls to ensuing conflict. Lacking technical capacity and expertise (and often dependent on goodwill) the African state is also no more than a weak global player.

Successfully promoting pro-poor growth will entail considerable investment in the capacity of the state, now made more difficult by the corruption conditionality has fuelled. In its work on principles for social policy, the World Bank has at least acknowledged that policy frameworks remain critical to success. Such a framework must include a commitment to investment as economic growth is achieved. Issues of income distribution and education play a primary role in sowing seeds for continuing economic growth. Over the long term, housing and infrastructure for a bearable urban environment must be put in place. Prolonged periods of growth also enable the development of those safety-net programmes that prevent the advent of recession causing a renewed crisis of poverty.[42]

FINANCE FOR DEVELOPMENT: THE ROLE OF AID

Aid has been getting an increasingly bad press in recent years, not least from those who work in the field. Perhaps the most damning studies have been those suggesting that official assistance does little to foster economic growth. Articles such as those by Peter Boone[43] and also by Craig Burnside and David Dollar have seemed to lend weight to the notion that aid is ineffective. As is often the case, discussion of the studies has tended to caricature their results. Burnside and Dollar suggest that much hinges on the performance of the government of the developing country. They also highlight the tendency for bilateral aid to follow donor interests rather than any serious desire to affirm and resource effective states.[44]

The inconsistency of donors identified by Burnside and Dollar underlines the conflicting pressures being exerted on the average developing state, creating a no-win situation in the end. States under pressure from multi-laterals may cut their capacity to govern in order to deliver the fiscal balance that is demanded without being rewarded with increased aid. Elsewhere weak states will be affirmed despite their corruption, clientelism and policy failure.[45] Inevitably this begs the question as to whether the problem is aid or the manner in which it is delivered. For aid to be effective, it must help to build the capacity of the developing state. Indeed, good policy secured through harsh conditionality will not produce the sustainability and good judgement modelled by successful examples of growth.

Instead, aid needs to help the state, but not just as a package of resources to fuel government largesse. Rather, it must be targeted and structured to help the state itself to create the conditions for growth, including regulatory frameworks, human-capital formation and expertise within the structures of government. Just as critically, aid must allow the stronger state the room it needs for its economy to grow. The interventionism of Southeast Asian states would soon fall foul of the conditionality prescribed by today's major donors and lenders. Yet as assimilationist theorists suggest, risk-taking has been integral to the achievement of Asian success.[46] Risk-taking by the state cannot be legislated for by the economists of the World Bank or the IMF and yet will be essential if states are to enjoy pro-poor growth.

If aid in the future is to make a difference for the poor, a final attribute will be needed – a level of consistency in its delivery that has previously been lacking. Oliver Morrissey and Robert Lensink have argued that it is the uncertainty of aid inflows that is most damaging to growth. This position leads them to question the role of conditionality in producing conducive environments for economic success. The key for Morrissey and Lensink is the role of aid in creating conditions that attract investment, which then fuels growth.[47]

The lesson seems to be that aid structures are seriously in need of reform. The need for consistency and room to manoeuvre has led to some interesting proposals, such as the idea of global-level and country-level development funds put forward by Michael Edwards. Edwards recognises the need for a system based on demand that includes consolidated funding and a long-term compact among all those involved. The former would underline the new image of aid as investment, not charity (reinforced by new sources of funding); the latter would focus on agreed goals, not top-down conditionality.[48]

In essence, such sweeping reform is desperately needed, even though using local boards may not be the best implementing approach. The lack of accountability of business and civil society (compared to the potential accountability of the state) mitigates against their involvement in an Edwards-style board. As research on Africa has shown, both groups are easily manipulated for clientelistic gain, a factor that might easily derail localised boards. Accountability for such funds, and also their chances of achieving success, instead depends squarely on the state, a reality that presses the issue of democratisation, and with it local community contact with and access to government, firmly to the fore.[49]

GLOBALISATION AND TRADE

The concept of globalisation has served as a smokescreen for many things, not least the erosion of the state that has been discussed above. Globalisation has also acted as convenient cover for the failure of OECD states to invest, either through Official Development Assistance (ODA) or Foreign Direct Investment (FDI) in the South. In 2000 the British government's Department for International Development produced a white paper (policy document) on globalisation that is typical of the prescription being offered to the poor. The document glides over the substantive infrastructure gap that limits ability to leverage globalising forces in the South, focussing instead on more limited issues, such as the digital divide. It also avoids mentioning that the technological change and trade/financial liberalisation at the heart of the forces we term globalisation are market driven in the North but often conditionality pushed in the South.[50]

For rich elites in developing states changes in technology, communications and trade have a very real impact, shown at its superficial level by the sprouting of television satellite receivers in many third-world cities. The impact of conditionality-driven trade and financial liberalisation has, however, been fundamentally more important to the long-term interests of the poor. Brett Parris has highlighted the inability of poorly resourced Southern states to take advantage of the trade rules to which they have been pressured to ascribe. Parris shows, in particular, the complexity involved in making a system such as the WTO respond to inequalities in trade relations between richer and poorer states. The net result is that poor states are forced to open their markets to their more powerful donors and creditors while Northern markets remain closed.[51] Some estimates suggest that this failure of the North to embrace its own liberalising message currently costs the South a staggering US$150 billion a year.

Trade is a critical issue for the future of poverty alleviation in the South, and the export-orientation route to growth will continue to be problematical for states hampered by Northern protectionism. The "everything but arms" language that has been used in relation to the European Union (EU) must for development advocates become a global goal. Yet trade, although necessary, will not be a sufficient route to economic progress and human development. Without the finance for development that is essential in order to leverage trading opportunities (ODA, FDI and so forth) and without the rebuilding of state capacity, trade alone will struggle to drive change.

POVERTY AND POWER

Achieving pro-poor growth therefore requires a combination of actions by both internal and external actors. The availability of greater finance for development and the liberalisation of Northern markets are both steps that require policy change by the governments of the OECD. Yet there are also key policy requirements for state structures in the South. Not least of these is the need for a new approach to accountability, itself an advocacy issue for NGOs.

Government accountability to citizens and the securing of human rights should be explicit policy objectives of every development NGO. Notwithstanding the fact that, while Western-style democracy represents one form of popular accountability, the post–Cold War assumption that it should be a norm has often weakened truly creative debate. The ability of citizens to exercise choice in the running of their country's affairs can take many forms. The form is therefore less important than the degree of real power exercised by people themselves.

Even so, accountability is a doubled-edge sword. Dependence on the support of disparate social groups has led to corruption and stagnation in both developing and developed states.[52] At worst, accountability can become the exploitation by elites of their supposed masters, often through manipulation of ethnic divides for temporary electoral gain. Such dangers are real, but the failure of accountability is not inevitable, nor have democratic states shown a greater tendency towards collapse or economic malaise (it can be argued that evidence points to the opposite).[53]

The role of accountability in securing pro-poor economic growth has been discussed by economists, political scientists and even the World Bank.[54] The key, however, is to give the instruments of governments sufficient incentive to seek the best interests of the poor. Mick Moore and James Putzel have shown that such incentives can be provided as much by ideology as by Western-style electoral systems. They also show that elsewhere it is political rather than civil society that holds out the greatest hope for the poor.[55]

The encouraging of political society (for example, political parties) is traditionally not seen as related to the NGO role (although some donors have been active in this area). Yet its development remains crucial to the aspirations of the poor.[56] Although NGOs, especially when based abroad, should have no place in trying to shape or guide the political activities of those they claim to serve, they can play an empowering part of sorts. NGOs can claim some legitimacy in three key areas of local political change: the first is to be faithful to the ideas of participation that many NGOs choose to espouse. This concept is essential if political society is to be robust. The second is to enable communities to become aware of concepts of human rights that have been globally accepted as core. And third, NGOs must not constrain the organisational development of those parts of civil society that will mutate into radical pressure groups or into political parties seeking to secure the interests of the poor.

The growth of political society must include a place for the poor if this growth is to be both sustainable and prone to the eradication of poverty. The building of political society and the strengthening of the institutions of the state are essential ingredients of accountable growth. The building of an effective state, in addition to facilitating pro-poor growth, also ultimately provides a vehicle of which the poor can gain control in order to secure further social action. In any case, political society and economic growth tend to make processes of democratisation more certain and sustainable and enable the poor to utilise the potential democracy offers. They are also mutually reinforcing over the longer term.[57]

CONCLUSION

In the last 40 years much has been achieved in the fight against poverty, not just in Southeast Asia but across the developing world. Improved immunisation, literacy, infant-mortality and life-expectancy rates benefit billions of people in both North and South. In the process, the tide of development theory has ebbed and flowed, occasionally to practical effect, as countries flirted with planning, import substitution and, more lately, capital account liberalisation.

At times those working at the grass roots of development, particularly NGOs, have articulated a simplified version of fashionable theoretical views, echoing the assumptions of dependency theorists, neo-Marxists, and basic-needs approaches to the issues. Many NGOs seemed content to pick and choose those views seeming to accord with a grass-roots agenda, although dabbling in the theory did little to foster an empirically based development paradigm of their own. Lack of a clear macro-worldview, combined with an eclectic approach to analysis, allowed the NGO movement to escape the head-on intellectual challenge of an emerging and unpopular neo-liberal orthodoxy, at the cost of any comprehensive answer to the liberalisation agenda.

Caught in the headlights of globalisation and a TINA worldview (There Is No Alternative), much of the NGO world has been prone to remain rooted in the solutions of their local worldview. Without the pressure of implementing large programmes or advising states directly on policy, aid agencies have lacked incentives to articulate a model of development beyond vague talk of "scaling up" the micro approach.[58] At times this has led NGOs to seem to suggest that everything from education, clean water or microenterprise might solve the developing world's ills. In effect, most civil society based development organisations have tried, and sadly succeeded, to sidestep questions of industrialisation, employment, fiscal balance and rotting infrastructure. A few serious forays into the macro arena have tended towards a focus on single areas of crisis, in which NGOs can critique a dimension of economic policy without needing to offer a comprehensive alternative model (debt being the outstanding case in point).

This chapter has argued that NGOs, perhaps particularly large international development NGOs, must break out of this tendency to view the world piecemeal – which often involves offering simultaneous contradictory views. Development activists need to work towards more consistent long-term goals embracing adoption of clear models of development. As the shifting sands of relief work have led to growing consensus on the principle of humanitarianism, so globalisation must force a willingness to coalesce around clear principles of poverty eradication. Clarity on the need to end poverty should propel NGOs to accept that development cannot be achieved at the grass roots alone. NGOs cannot avoid addressing the macro view. As NGOs embrace a willingness to challenge orthodoxies, as well as piecemeal elements of global economic policies, they must also learn to broaden perspective beyond failures of policy and learn to study success.

All advocates for development need to recognise that growth is a vital tool in the process of poverty eradication, but there is much analysis and advocacy to be done in ensuring that growth is truly

pro-poor in its effects. Pro-poor growth can be aided by the strengthening of political society able to press effectively the cause of accountability for the poor. Advocacy on growth, however, is not just
a question of calling for state provision, democracy, or aid. Central
to the advocacy of NGOs should also be a call for those policies
that will actually create growth, whether ideologically pure (such
as good income distribution) or tainted (industrialisation). Without willingness to embrace issues treated with distaste in the past,
including benefits of urbanisation, NGOs will contribute to the
constraints faced by the poor.

Haiti offers a useful case in point: industrialisation and growth
may bring problems of their own, but they offer a positive alternative compared to the drive by donors to turn food production areas
into cash-crop land. Erosion of food security and increasing dependency on food aid are a neo-liberal solution to the problem – one
NGOs should challenge by seeking real investment for alternative
sources of exports.[59] The reality is that development issues of the
next decades will stem from problems that scaling up alone will
not solve. Constructive calls for urbanisation to be accompanied
by effective urban policy, and industrialisation by environmental
reform, are the best accompaniments to a renewed commitment to
seek growth.

Civil society and political society as a whole, Southern and Northern, can do much to promote such policies while holding states
accountable for the quality of their implementation. The history of
ostensibly well-meaning state intervention is littered with terrible
failures. Yet it is also the interventionist approach, when pursued
well, which has produced the best developmental results. Tanzanian politician Nguyuru Lipumba, in mapping out a fairly traditional proposed path of macro-economic stability for Africa's future, nevertheless concluded:

> It is ahistorical to assert that the necessary and sufficient condi-
> tion for the initiation and acceleration of economic growth and
> structural transformation is to have sound money, open mar-
> kets and the protection of property rights. . . . For latecom-
> ers, a necessary condition for industrialization is a systematic
> and well-coordinated government intervention to promote
> manufacturing investment and supportive infrastructure.[60]

As NGOs and citizens, we can recognise that the state is an important vehicle for development, but a flawed and risky one. Amongst our greatest challenges as advocates and development actors is the need to call for those actions on the part of the state, and its critics, which create the conditions for genuine pro-poor growth.

NOTES

[1] *The Economist* (December 11–17, 1999).

[2] David C Korten, *When Corporations Rule the World* (West Hartford, Conn.: Kumarian Press, 1995); Susan George, *The Debt Boomerang* (London: Pluto Press, 1997).

[3] The tone of many of the documents distributed at the NGO centre or within the media room is shown in published works such as Public Citizen's *Whose Trade Organisation* (Washington, D.C.: Public Citizen, 1999).

[4] See Jean Dreze and Amartya Sen, *Hunger and Public Action* (Oxford: Oxford University Press, 1991); Amartya Sen with James E Foster, *On Economic Inequality* (Oxford: Clarendon Press, 1997).

[5] Bill Warren, *Imperialism the Pioneer of Capitalism* (London: Verso Books, 1981); Nigel Harris, *The End of the Third World* (New York: New Amsterdam Books, 1987).

[6] Stephen Haggard, *Pathways from the Periphery: The Policies of Growth in the Newly Industrialising Countries* (Ithaca, N.Y.: Cornell University Press, 1996), 231.

[7] Rhys Jenkins, "Capitalist Development in the NICs," in *Capitalism and Development*, ed. Leslie Sklair et al. (London: Routledge, 1997), 74.

[8] See UNIP, *Human Development Report 1999* (New York: Oxford University Press, 1999).

[9] See Iyanatul Islam and Anis Chowdhury, *Asia-Pacific Economies: A Survey* (London: Routledge, 1998), 106.

[10] Ibid., 120.

[11] Amartya Sen, "Economic Policy and Equity: An Overview," in *Economic Policy and Equity*, ed. Tanzi et al. (Washington, D.C.: International Monetary Fund, 1999), 30.

[12] Alan Whaites, "NGOs, Civil Society and the State: Avoiding Theoretical Extremes in Real World Issues," *Development in Practice* 8/3 (August 1998).

[13] See Michael Bruno, Martin Ravallion and Lyn Squire, *Equity and Growth in Developing Countries: Old and New Perspectives on the Policy*

Issues, Policy Research Working Paper 1563 (Washington, D.C.: The World Bank, 1995).

[14] See Roland Benabou, *Inequality and Growth*, National Bureau of Economic Research Working Paper W5658 (May 1997); Oded Galor and Joseph Zeira, "Income Distribution and Macroeconomics," *Review of Economic Studies* 60 (1993), 35–52.

[15] *The East Asian Miracle: Economic Growth and Public Policy* (New York: The World Bank/Oxford University Press, 1993), chap. 1, particularly 28–30.

[16] Danny M Leipziger and Vinod Thamas, *The Lessons of East Asia: An Overview of Country Experience* (Washington, D.C.: World Bank, 1993).

[17] See Bruno, Ravallion and Squire, *Equity and Growth in Developing Countries.* See also, K Griffin with Amy Ickowitz, "The Distribution of Wealth and the Pace of Development," in *Macroeconomic Policies, Growth and Poverty Reduction,* ed. Terry McKinley (London: Palgrave, 2001).

[18] Klaus Deininger and Lyn Squire, "New Ways of Looking at Old Issues," *Journal of Development Economics* 57 (1998).

[19] Griffin with Ickowitz, "The Distribution of Wealth and the Pace of Development."

[20] An approach found to be important by Mattias Lundberg and Lyn Squire, "Growth and Inequality: Extracting the Lessons for Policymakers" (The World Bank, 1999), unpublished paper.

[21] See Michael Lipton, "Successes in Anti-poverty," Discussion Paper 8 (Geneva: International Labour Organization, 1998), 111–18.

[22] Ravi Kanbur and Lyn Squire, "The Evolution of Thinking About Poverty: Exploring the Interaction" (1999), unpublished paper, 14.

[23] Kamal Malhotra, *East and Southeast Asia Revisited: Miracles, Myths and Mirages,* Focus Papers, Focus on the Global South, (Bangkok, 1997), 11–15.

[24] See Amiya Kumar Bagchi, "Problems of Effective Demand and Contradictions of Planning in India," in *Economy, Society and Polity: Essays in the Political Economy of Indian Planning,* ed. Amiya Kumar Bagchi et al. (Calcutta: Oxford University Press, 1998).

[25] *World Development Report 1989–99* (Oxford: The World Bank/Oxford University Press, 1999), 198–99.

[26] Jenkins, "Capitalist Development in the NICs," 75.

[27] Organization for Economic Co-Operation and Development (OECD), *Towards a New Global Age* (Paris: OECD, 1997).

[28] See *Offering Hope Not Despair* (Milton Keynes: World Vision UK, 1996).

[29] See Kimberly Ann Elliott, *International Labour Standards and Trade: What Should Be Done?* in *Launching New Global Trade Talks,* The Institute for International Economics, Special Report 12 (September 1998).

[30] Jorge Hardoy and David Satterthwaite, "Urban Growth as a Problem," in *Sustainable Development*, ed. John Kirkby et al. (London: Earthscan, 1995), 197.

[31] Ibid., 197–98.

[32] Ibid.

[33] Robert Bates, *Markets and States in Tropical Africa* (Berkeley and Los Angeles: University of California Press, 1981).

[34] Peter Uimonen, "The Environmental Dilemmas of the World Trade Organisation," in *Launching New Global Trade Talks*, The Institute for International Economics, Special Report 12 (September 1998).

[35] Nick Robins and Alex Trisoglio, "Restructuring Industry for Sustainable Development," in Kirkby et al., *Sustainable Development*, 162.

[36] Islam and Chodhury, *Asia-Pacific Economies*, 101.

[37] See The World Bank, *World Development Report 1997*.

[38] Sam Jones, "Stolen Sovereignty: Globalisation and the Disempowerment of Africa" (Milton Keynes: World Vision UK, 1997).

[39] Jean Francois Bayart et al., "The Criminalisation of the State in Africa," *Africa Issues* (1998).

[40] Christopher Clapham, *Africa and the International System: The Politics of State Survival* (Cambridge: Cambridge University Press, 1996); Patrick Chabal and Jean-Pascal Daloz, *Africa Works: Disorder as Political Instrument* (Oxford: The African Institute/James Curry, 1999).

[41] See Whaites, "NGOs, Civil Society and the State"; Christy Cannon, "Dancing with the State: The Role of NGOs in Gap-filling," paper presented at NGOs and Development Conference (June 1994).

[42] The World Bank, *Everyone's Mircale?* (Washington, D.C.: The World Bank, 1997), 59.

[43] Peter Boone, *The Impact of Foreign Aid on Savings and Growth* (London: London School of Economics, 1994).

[44] Craig Burnside and David Dollar, "Aid, Policies and Growth," The World Bank, Policy Research Department, Working Paper No. 1777 (June 1997), 2–3.

[45] Ibid., 4.

[46] See Richard E Nelson and Howard Pack, "The Asian Miracle and Modern Growth Theory," The World Bank (October 1997).

[47] Robert Lensink and Oliver Morrissey, *Uncertainty of Aid Inflows and the Aid-Growth Relationship*, CREDIT Research Paper No. 99/3 (University of Nottingham, 1999).

[48] Michael Edwards, *Future Positive: International Co-operation in the Twenty-first Century* (London: Earthscan, 1999), see chap. 7. particularly 137–40.

[49] See Jean Francois Bayart et al., *The Criminalisation of the State in Africa* (Bloomington, Ind.: Indiana University Press, 1999); Clapham,

Africa and the International System, see Section III, particularly chap. 9; also Chabal and Daloz, *Africa Works;* Alan Whaites, "Let's Get Civil Society Straight: NGOs, the State and Political Theory," *Development in Practice* 6/3 (August 1996), also in *Development, NGOs and Civil Society,* ed. Deborah Eade, A Development in Practice Reader (Oxfam, 2000).

[50] UK Department for International Development, *Eliminating World Poverty: Making Globalisation Work for the Poor* (December 11, 2000).

[51] Brett Parris, *Trade for Development: Making the WTO Work for the Poor* (Melbourne: World Vision, 1999).

[52] Alan Whaites, "Conflict, Repression and Politics: Dare NGOs Hope to Do Any Good?" in *Complex Humanitarian Emergencies,* ed. Mark Janz and Joann Slead (Monrovia, Calif.: World Vision, 2000). For a classic discussion of the kind of stagnation which can result from dependence on organised sections of society (whether ethnically/religiously based and clientelistic/patrimonially driven or the OECD variety of "interest" groups), see Sam Beer, *Britain Against Itself* (New York: Norton, 1982).

[53] Mick Moore and James Putzel, "Politics and Poverty: A Background Paper for the World Development Report 2000/1" (September 1999), 9.

[54] Whaites, "Conflict, Repression and Politics."

[55] Moore and Putzel, "Politics and Poverty," 11.

[56] For a useful discussion of the links between civil society and political society in the struggle for participatory government, see Alfred Stepan, *Rethinking Military Politics: Brazil and the Southern Cone* (Princeton, N.J.: Princeton University Press, 1988).

[57] Alan Whaites, "The State and Civil Society in Pakistan," *Contemporary South Asia* 4/3 (1995); idem, "Let's Get Civil Society Straight."

[58] Interestingly, the honourable exceptions have often come from those who have branched out from the NGO world. See Stephen Commins, "NGOs: Ladles in the Global Soup Kitchen" (1998), unpublished; Michael Edwards, *Future Positive: International Co-operation in the Twenty-first Century* (London: Earthscan, 1999).

[59] Laurie Richardson, *Feeding Dependency, Starving Democracy: USAID Policies in Haiti,* a report by Grassroots International, 7–9.

[60] Nguyuru H I Lipumba, "Globalization of Finance and Development Prospects in Africa," in *Rethinking the International Financial System: Views from the South,* UNDP Co-operation South Journal No 1 (June 1999).

3.

Business or Benevolence?

Examining Corporate Motives
for Engaging in Global Initiatives

KELLY RUSSELL CURRAH

*Tis e'er the wont of simple folk to prize the deed
and o'erlook the motive, and of learned folk
to discount the deed and lay open the soul of the doer.*
— John Barth, *The Sot-Weed Factor* (1960)

*We should often be ashamed of our finest actions if
the world understood all the motives behind them.*
— François de la Rochefoucauld

As all followers of Sherlock Holmes or Hercule Poirot already know, the key to understanding people's actions rests on their motives. In the intriguing case of the recent plethora of corporate alliances in international development initiatives, the motives of the private sector must also be thoroughly understood. It turns out that the particular corporate rationale for participation – and the knowledge of that motive on the part of the project planners – can actually determine whether or not alliance-based initiatives will be successful.

The trend toward these global initiatives started in the mid-1990s, when UN agencies began adopting an apparently more comprehensive approach to development problems. The logic of expanding the actors involved beyond development banks and governments to NGOs and corporations was that all the actors involved in development – regardless of whether their particular mission revolved around enhancing corporate profits, providing crisis relief, or forcing long-term structural adjustment on the local economy – had to be part of the solution. Consequently, the United Nations and the World Bank are now attempting to mobilise all elements of society to become activists in support of various global causes, from the environment to health and education to human rights. Some of this new trend reflects the big fund-raising initiatives of the 1980s, like BandAid. This international event mobilised on an global scale a new generation of activists with an increased consciousness of third-world poverty. The fate of the poor was moved into the mainstream and gave a role to the concerned citizens in the industrialised world – to ameliorate poverty.

There is a significant problem, however, when it comes to mobilising the corporate sector: the success of capturing corporate interest varies considerably from initiative to initiative. For example, the Global Compact, a UN-produced set of principles on labour, human rights, and the environment, has not been able to attract the large number of transnational corporations that were originally predicted, while in the United States and the United Kingdom, national initiatives which examine the impact of corporations in developing countries have been quite successful in attracting corporate partners. What are the factors that make one initiative more successful in capturing corporate support than other, equally significant and valid programmes?

This essay argues that corporations engage in such initiatives for complex reasons, each linked, however, with their basic corporate missions. Consequently, designers of these initiatives must not overlook or neglect the motives of the corporate sector in participating in these projects. Because at any moment there are vast numbers of "feel good" development initiatives in which corporations can choose to participate, it is clear that there must be other factors beyond benevolence that dictate a corporation's involvement in any particular issue. How does a transnational corporation choose, for example, between initiatives aimed at helping refugees, or children, or diseases of the poor, or human rights, or conflict, or development – all initiatives calling on the private sector to become a partner? What factors go into the business decisions about which initiatives they should devote valuable time and resources to; in the for-profit sector, employee labour/time and resources are indeed valuable commodities, not to be given away lightly. Cleary, the drivers for engagement are actually much more complicated – usually profit-oriented and often politically nuanced – than the typical celebratory press releases announcing corporate involvement in an initiative would indicate.

A more detailed analysis of corporate engagement in development initiatives would reveal motives closely connected with profits, market position, and fear of regulation. Corporations think through their involvement in these projects in relation to long-term planning and growth strategies. This is not to say that corporations *only* cynically use corporate social responsibility strategies to enhance profit. From the perspective of the logic of the profit-seeking corporation, they are actually behaving rationally by carefully undertaking long-term strategies that allow for the possibility that consumer objections to socially irresponsible corporate behaviour could damage profits, and even bring on unwanted regulations.

Therefore, when designing and evaluating corporate motivation and participation in development initiatives, two important and competing perspectives on corporate practices and development should not be forgotten. First, the most effective way to advance social justice and equity in development is through increased international regulation. Second, by their very nature corporations must always consider their own bottom line. However, considerations of the bottom line are not necessarily just about increasing profit. They are often concerned with preventing losses, including holding onto market share and keeping production costs down. Corporations must follow their bottom-line profitability to survive, and especially during times of recession, corporations are likely to be nervous about consumer awareness of irresponsible corporate behaviour and similarly very hostile to the idea of increased regulation. Thus it is entirely possible that corporations become involved in development projects for the very purpose of using the good public relations (PR) generated by the projects to act to *prevent* losses based on negative consumer brand preferences and increased regulation of their products and operations. While the associations between NGOs and corporations are effective in a small, limited number of ways, any real advances will be made by changing the norms through which goods are produced. Such change is certainly a complicated business involving increasing regulation of corporations, using consumer pressure to change corporate behaviour, and at the same time demonstrating through pilot projects that changes to corporate practices need not reduce profitability in the long term. Although the current vogue is to view the corporate-NGO or corporate-government partnership as the most important mechanism for this kind of change, in fact such changes will come about only when shared objectives emerge from a rational appraisal of the very different motives for partnering, and when partnerships are designed with those unavoidable tensions in mind. These factors are absent in many partnerships. Many practitioners see the creation of the partnership itself as evidence of shared objectives rather than as the vehicle for *experimenting* with the possibility of profit-based corporate social responsibility.

In order to make more effective use of these partnerships, NGOs and multilateral institutions need to be aware of the motivations that influence the corporate sector to participate. The explicit explanation for corporate involvement in these coalitions is the good deed of bringing cash and in-kind resources to bear on a pressing development problem. In fact, the motives are complex and multifaceted, and it is the apparent polarisation of the two positions, business versus benevolence, that is hampering the successes of such initiatives. Those supporting the business cause through reasons of benevolence do not understand some of the corporate motives, while those dismissing the initiatives as corporate spin fail to see the levers that can motivate corporations to join. Instead of taking at face value the *explicit* corporate rationale that their involvement is simply benevolence, instead of accepting such vague statements as "it is good for business," leaders of these initiatives need to seek out the corporate motives beyond those detailed in flowery prose in glossy four-colour corporate reports. By using pragmatic analysis of the motives of the corporate sector, planners of global initiatives can be more successful in capturing productive corporate support.

Moreover, by understanding the long-term interests of capital, creators of these partnerships can design them with an eye to the divergence of the motives of the partners. The issue of the moment, then, is not the particular concerns themselves – whether child poverty, health, or education, that is, the precise content of any one partnership – but about the means of engagement between corporations and civil society and the implicit power relationship.

THE NECESSITY OF THE CORPORATE ROLE
IN DEVELOPMENT

Most of the development community recognises the enormous role business can play in tackling poverty in the era of globalisation. Because more and more companies source their products from developing countries and because foreign investment has increased, the corporation has become a unique player in the development paradigm. The level of foreign direct investment reached an all-time high of US$800 billion in 1999.[1] Although the bulk of these financial flows were between developed countries, developing countries received US$208 billion in total. Total aid flow in 1999 from OECD (Organisation for Economic Co-operation and Development) countries was US$56 million,[2] so the increase is significant. Also, fans and critics of globalisation alike note the incredible economic size of corporations relative to many of the national economies in which they have operations. For example, the rostrum of large corporations includes General Motors, which has a turnover greater than Norway's Gross Domestic Product (GDP). Even individual business leaders are bigger than many economies. Bill Gates, co-founder of the software giant Microsoft, for example, has a personal wealth greater than the GDP of Peru.[3] While these figures do not necessarily accurately reflect the corporate power vis-à-vis state power, corporations are certainly well placed to make substantial contributions to the development mix. This is well recognised by leaders in the developed world. When the head of the Bill and Melinda Gates Foundation travelled recently to Africa on a tour to allocate funding, she was met by the head of state of the countries she visited. Where the NGOs were once seen as the mainstay in any development strategy, now corporations are cast as the critical players.

Significantly, the trend among development agencies and NGOs to find corporate partners has not, so far, produced any uniformity of structure. In fact, these ventures so far have come up with many different ways to bring corporations on board, from the United Nations's Global Compact to the World Bank's Business Partners for Development to movements of smaller agencies like the World Health Organisation (WHO) and UNICEF that require private sector buy-in to a project.

One type of initiative asks corporations to sign on to development principles. For example, as corporations are increasingly heralded in their new development role, more and more critical civil society groups shine an unwanted spotlight on the often unseemly operations of corporations in developing countries. These groups believe that corporate power corrupts traditional state-society ties and allows the infringement of basic human rights in many countries. The apparel and oil and gas industries have felt the sting of these groups' campaigns, including corporations such as Nike, GAP, Wal-Mart, Shell in Nigeria, BP in Angola and China, and Talisman Oil in Sudan. As a result of these campaigns, there are now a number of initiatives and codes of conduct, such as Amnesty International's Business Code, the Global Sullivan Principles of Corporate Responsibility, the Caux Roundtable Principles for Business, the OECD Guidelines for Multinational Enterprises, the Global Compact, and the list goes on.

In addition, there are a number of multi-partner associations among civil society, international organisations, national governments, and the private sector. Any global initiative that looks at addressing the problems of the poor in a holistic way must include the private sector – it is now *de rigueur*. As a result, the private sector has been flooded with initiatives it must consider joining. From national associated alliances like the Ethical Trading Initiative in the United Kingdom and the Fair Labor Association in the United States to international sectoral alliances such as WHO's new initiative to tackle the diseases of the poor,[4] the United Nations High Commander for Refugees (UNHCR) business forum and the United Nations's Global Compact. All these initiatives have been formed to include the business sector as one of the four main pillars; the other pillars usually include a UN agency, civil society groups, and national governments.

In addition to global alliances, corporations are partnering with individual aid agencies, like World Vision, CARE (Co-operative for Assistance and Relief Everywhere), Save the Children Fund, amongst others. These partnerships are part of a trend of transformational or strategic giving. While in the past corporations gave to charities for philanthropic reasons, now they give because it is considered part of good business practice. Most partnerships revolve around a project or particular problem that the corporation perceives as needing an outside partner to resolve.

THE CORPORATE SOCIAL RESPONSIBILITY DIVIDE:
FRIEDMAN *VS*. ELKINGTON

Possibly the most famous quote on the role of business in society has come from the economist Milton Freidman, who stated in an early 1970s *New York Times* article that "the social responsibility of business is to make profits." Thirty years later, this statement continues to resonate. However, in the partnering 1990s, corporate gurus like John Elkington espoused a more gentle and compassionate form of corporate behaviour.[5] This approach suggested that corporations could both maintain profitability *and* engage in good practices. In this "win-win-win" or "triple bottom line" scenario, the winners are the corporations, the community, and the environment.

These two very different philosophies are still competing today, and the tension between them can help evaluate the motives that attract a corporation to do good works. Have corporations really accepted that they are major players in the development of communities and the environment and therefore should adapt their business strategies accordingly? Or is corporate social responsibility a result of outside pressures and, more important, the threat of outside pressures?

The suggestion that good work in the development field automatically translates into good business practice is not always seen in the figures. According to Anita Roddick, former CEO of the Body Shop, the various campaigns waged by the company hit profits: "Every time the Body Shop runs a major campaign on human rights, we had a major dip in sales."[6] While few companies advocate for human rights as aggressively as the Body Shop, it is telling that Anita Roddick left the day-to-day overseeing of the company.

CORPORATE MOTIVES FOR ENGAGEMENT

Corporations engage in development initiatives for a number of reasons. While the following examples are not in any way exhaustive, they do illuminate many of the motives that lead corporations to participate in socially responsible partnerships.

The Soros Syndrome

Often a corporation will get involved in development issues because of the visions and leadership of its founder. These strong farsighted leaders are usually widely known individuals who have a particular calling. They include the Body Shop and its co-founder, Anita Roddick; the founders of Ben & Jerry's Ice Cream[7]; and Levi Strauss's CEO (grandson of the founder), Walter Haas Jr.[8] These individuals have forged ahead in the field of corporate social responsibility and have shown that corporations can operate in ways that benefit society globally. Interestingly, many times these corporations do not get involved in global initiatives but decide to run their own projects instead. And it is also significant that many of the individuals who have taken strong stands on corporate responsibility are, or were, majority stockholders when they took those stands.

Other business leaders keep a strict separation between their own business's practices and their work in development. For example, Bill Gates, co-founder of Microsoft, is involved personally in many international initiatives, including financing of the WHO's Global Vaccine Initiative. George Soros, the infamous money trader who made a fortune during the United Kingdom's withdrawal from the European Monetary System, has established the Open Foundation and funds much work in the transitional economies of Eastern Europe. Both Gates and Soros, however, have maintained a separation between their businesses and their personal philanthropy. Gates has established the Bill and Melinda Gates Foundation; George Soros has founded the Soros Foundation. While Microsoft participates in some UN activities, like the UNHCR refugee programme, it is aggressive in its own field. George Soros continues to operate in global capital speculation despite his writing against such speculation.

It is difficult to maintain good business practices once the visionary leader leaves. In Levi Strauss's case, once the Haas family retired, the corporation found it difficult to maintain such social principles in its day-to-day operations. When concerned about human rights abuses in China involving its workers, the company made a bold statement in withdrawing its sourcing from China. However, when it realised that its competitors were investing in China on a greater scale, Levi's returned to China in order to be competitive.

Public relations excursus

While most people involved in these initiatives argue that corporations do not get involved solely for PR reasons, the fact remains that PR is the main driver for most corporations. By participating in alliances and associations with international institutions like the United Nations and NGOs, corporations can use those alliances for self-promotion, promotion that may go a long way in increasing consumer loyalty and forestalling regulation of their non-domestic production. Unfortunately, because such motives are seen as "impure," they are not often discussed by those in the development field. Yet seminars on international issues run by corporations themselves refer to PR as a good motive for participating in these ventures.

For example, the Japanese electronic giant Sony conducted a review of its NGO strategy in the summer of 2000. The seminar covered many of the usual issues – environmental groups and activists and the threat they pose to the industry as a whole and Sony specifically. According to the group leading the review for Sony, part of the solution is to get involved in partnerships with "reliable NGOs." And, as an extra incentive, presenters noted that tax rebates on the costs of such initiatives are available in some countries.[9]

In another corporate get together, this time hosted by the Edelman PR agency, participants were told to consider the power of NGOs in the global marketplace. Lord Hurd, former foreign secretary of the United Kingdom, bluntly suggested that corporations ally with NGOs for "protection": "I rather think the way that companies and ministries now surround themselves with NGOs is an attempt to keep out one lot of barbarians, by employing another lot of barbarians."[10]

It is critical for NGOs to understand the role they and other institutions play in helping shape a positive public image for corporations. From the corporate perspective, the concrete results of the alliance are often secondary to the initial benefit from advertising the role. For example, the Phillip Morris Company has invested an enormous amount in philanthropic initiatives over the past few years in order to compensate for the bad publicity of a number of litigations over tobacco deaths. Some critics have even claimed that the US$100 million a year Philip Morris spends on advertising its philanthropy is greater than the amount it actually donates to good causes.[11] The degree of relevance of public relations will differ from industry to industry and corporation to corporation, but it is one of the main underlying reasons for corporate engagement in socially responsible initiatives. Global initiatives also suffer from not taking place in the largest economies, where the main market of corporations resides. An initiative that takes place in downtown Los Angeles will attract much more corporate sponsorship and support than one happening in downtown Luanda.

The importance of PR in these global initiatives is underlined by so-called front-loading initiatives. Partnerships typically celebrate the launch of the initiative, not its execution afterwards. Indeed, press and media attention to the project is at its height during the launch. However, the follow-up actions announced at these launches usually languish from lack of interest. Instead of lauding the commitment, there needs to be more attention to the results of the initiatives.

Deflecting possible regulation

Corporations spend a great deal of money each year on employing expensive lobbyists to push their agenda to national legislators. Consequently, they are very aware of any potential legislative or regulatory changes that might affect their industry and are very capable of taking action to postpone or deflect possibly damaging legislation.

For example, often a corporation will voluntarily take the lead to show the concerned public and legislators that there is no need for codifying in law something it is already doing. Hence, there are many corporate initiatives in areas where there is much lobbying by strong, socially responsible campaigning groups, such as Friends of the Earth and World Wildlife Fund for Nature, among others.

When corporations see that legislation is inevitable in a certain field, they will begin to make adjustments in anticipation of the legislation and to take on development partners to make these moves more credible. The advent of environmental reporting was fought for a number of years by the corporate lobby, but it was unsuccessful in fully preventing the legislation demanding corporate environmental auditing. Corporations now see social auditing heading in the same direction. For example, corporate auditors Price Waterhouse Cooper believe such reporting will be mandatory in the next decade and are working alongside their corporate clients in pioneering the process so they can be the leaders in social auditing.[12] Consequently, the company is looking for civil-society partners to help carry out audits successfully – and to add legitimacy to its own position about the requirements of socially responsible auditing.[13]

Experimenting with new initiatives

Corporations often enter alliances and relationships to experiment with new ideas and projects that may become the norm in a number of years. These projects tend to be focussed on changing consumer tastes and issues rather than "watch-dogging" to ensure that they are up with the industry norm. Such initiatives are often responses to increasing consumer concern with the social and environmental conditions surrounding production.

Collective unity

It could be suggested that many corporations join partnerships simply because their competitors have. These alliances tend to be industry specific. The Ethical Trading Initiative (ETI) has been successful because it has focussed on supermarket produce in the United Kingdom. Other such alliances include Rugmark, the Forestry Stewardship Council and the Fair Labor Association.

The motives listed above can be categorised as public relations, avoidance of regulation/legislation, experimentation, and good association. These factors could be viewed as at the basis of most corporate engagement, beyond the particular wishes of a strong corporate leader. Groups looking to foster corporate support for international initiatives should be aware of these motives when designing and building corporate involvement into their initiatives.

ANALYTICAL ASSESSMENTS

Given the various motives described above, it is easier to see why certain initiatives have been more successful than others.

The Global Compact, launched originally by UN Secretary General Kofi Annan in January 1999 at the annual meeting of the World Economic Forum in Davos, was relaunched the following year in New York. Between the original launch and the subsequent relaunch, no individual corporation had come forward; only a number of corporate umbrella groups like the International Chambers of Commerce (ICC) had joined. Since the summer of 2000 approximately 300 corporations have signed up as well as a small number of NGOs including Amnesty International and World Wildlife Fund for Nature. This falls far short of the original target of over 1,000 corporations. As a result, the United Nations has asked for professional advice from Edelman, a US PR agency, to help it "sell" the Global Compact to corporations.

The reasons for the Global Compact's failure become clear when one takes into consideration corporate motives for engagement. First, the Global Compact offers no projects or concrete objectives for the corporate sector. Corporations are asked only to post some of their good works on the Internet site (www.unglobalcompact.org) and to abide by nine principles that have been drawn from international treaties from three UN agencies: the International Labour Organisation, the Office of the High Commissioner for Human Rights and the United Nations Environmental Programme. The principles are divided into three categories: human rights, labour and the environment.

Human Rights
1. Businesses should support and respect the protection of internationally proclaimed human rights; and
2. Make sure they are not complicit in human rights abuses.

Labour
3. Business should uphold the freedom of association and the effective recognition of the right to collective bargaining;
4. The elimination of all forms of forced and compulsory labour;
5. The effective abolition of child labour; and
6. Eliminate discrimination in respect of employment and occupation

Environment
7. Businesses should support a precautionary approach to environmental challenges;
8. Undertake initiatives to promote greater environmental responsibility; and
9. Encourage the development and diffusion of environmentally friendly technologies.

There is no real association with NGOs or even the United Nations itself, although the Global Compact encourages corporations to forge partnerships with various UN agencies. The lack of concrete projects that can be feted and promoted by corporations means that few PR benefits would accrue for their participation.

Also missing is the threat of regulation. The United Nations no longer has any agency specifically working on the subject of transnational corporations. (The Centre on Transnationals was merged into UNCTAD in the early 1990s.) Therefore, the United Nations can no longer press for international conventions that would regulate corporations with international standards. Indeed, the ICC was adamant when negotiating over the terms of the Global Compact that there be no monitoring or verification of corporate activities under the Global Compact. Maria Livanos Cattiua, the secretary general of the ICC, stated: "Businesses would look askance at any suggestions involving external assessment of corporate performance, whether by special interest groups or by UN agencies. The Global Compact is a joint commitment of shared values, not a qualification to be met. It must not become a vehicle for governments to burden business with prescriptive regulations."[14] While the United Nations has avoided upsetting the corporate community by not incorporating such regulations within the Global Compact, it has also relegated itself to the sidelines due to the absence of such regulations.

The Global Compact has not been nearly as successful as other initiatives involving corporate partners. The ETI in the United Kingdom began as a Department for International Development–supported forum for NGOs, businesses and trade unions to work together to solve some of the problems of sourcing products in developing countries. The ETI has successfully focussed on the supermarket trade and associated food products. In doing so, it has brought together all the major supermarket chains in the United Kingdom as well as many of the main UK development NGOs, including Save the Children, Oxfam, Catholic Agencies for Overseas Development and Amnesty. The ETI has forged a code of conduct agreeable to all participating parties and has initiated a number of pilot projects to experiment with the code in order to see if it can be used more extensively.

The ETI has been successful in incorporating business because it has centred its work on a single industry – the supermarket trade. It has the support of the government, which is happy to sponsor a voluntary initiative rather than having to respond to pressure from the NGOs to enact legislation. Corporations are willing to support it because they can share with their main competitors and NGOs the responsibility of experimenting with ways of changing business habits without the risk of failure being highlighted by campaigning groups. While the ETI has had problems, mainly coming to agreement on methodology, it has successfully captured corporate involvement.

Another successful initiative has been the US's Fair Labor Association. This association was supported by the White House under the Democratic administration of the time. Similarly, it is voluntary and includes pilot projects working with NGOs to find innovative ways to solve some of the most deep-seated problems in clothing manufacture in developing countries: child labour, poor wages, and health and safety conditions. Corporations have flocked to this initiative because it has, or had, the support of the federal government and was also a means to prevent regulatory legislation in the United States.

Other global initiatives, such as the WHO's Massive Effort Against the Diseases of the Poor, have attracted certain corporate support because they focus on the pharmaceutical industry. At the launch workshop in the fall of 2000, many of the major drug companies were eager to get involved, as were many international medical and development NGOs. While WHO is not a forum for legislation, it has shown it is capable of taking on large industries like the tobacco and milk-substitute companies and of setting up internationally acceptable regulations (voluntary) that companies need to follow. The motivation for this corporate involvement is not merely to show a willingness to be involved in finding solutions to diseases associated with poverty, but also to participate in an initiative that may conclude with informal regulations and international norms setting. From the vantage point of the corporation, such involvement "up front" might forestall unwanted legislative regulation of pharmaceutical market-based operations in the developing world.

Newer UN initiatives, however, have not been as successful. They have lacked adequate reward for corporate participation, given the actual corporate logic involved in deciding whether or not to sign on. For example, UNICEF's Global Movement for Children aims to change the way all of global society considers children, and it includes business as an important actor. Although UNICEF has been one of the most successful UN agencies in attracting corporate support, this has been because the agency heavily emphasises promotion of participating corporations in these projects. For example, one of its most successful sponsorships has been with the British Airways Change for Good programme. British Airways has certainly been very proud to announce its support for UNICEF, advertising the relationship with the UNICEF logo on its aircraft. Translating this sort of support into a much wider initiative, such as Global Movement for Children, that hopes a large number of corporations will sign on will be a much harder task. Given the number of similar corporations participating, there is less of a PR motivation for any one corporation to sign on. UNICEF has no threatening legislative or regulatory power that corporations need to worry about. Thus for the Global Movement to be successful, it will have to highlight a particular aspect of children's involvement with business and then design initiatives that require all actors, including NGOs, to build relationships with the corporate sector. In this way the Global Movement for Children can become an active forum for experimenting with pro-child initiatives rather than another forum for promises, displays and press releases.

CONCLUSION

Undoubtedly, globalisation has raised the profile of corporations in the development paradigm. Their importance has been recognised since the 1950s, with its "What is good for General Motors is good for America." This has been stretched to include developing countries. The role they can play in achieving many of the United Nations's development targets, including reducing the number of people in absolute poverty by half by 2015, is now central to many of UN initiatives. However, the United Nations, other agencies, and NGOs must not assume their objectives are the same as those of corporations. While there have been some gains in changing the norms of business, the basics remain those that Adam Smith would have recognised: the business of business is to survive given the conditions and regulations surrounding a particular industry. In order to obtain the buy-in of corporations, then, the United Nations and NGOs must analyse and address the real motives businesses have for engaging in these initiatives.

It is certainly true that the United Nations is good at envisioning long-term solutions. The Universal Declaration of Human Rights (1948) was prophetic in its vision, but it is only now, over fifty years later, that the ideas and underlying concepts are accepted by the majority of countries and organisations. The next fifty years will be spent ensuring that these rights are made real in all parts of the world. While global initiatives like the Global Compact and the Global Movement for Children will have an impact on changing norms, some attention must be addressed to the very different long-term profit-driven concerns that underlie corporate involvement.

NOTES

[1] United Nations Conference on Trade and Development (UNCTAD), *World Investment Report 2000* (Geneva, 2000), 7.

[2] OECD, *OECD in Figures* (Paris, 2001), 65.

[3] *Forbes* (9 October 2000).

[4] This initiative is provisionally titled Massive Effort Against the Diseases of the Poor.

[5] See John Elkington, *Cannibals with Forks* (Gabriola Island, BC: New Society Publishers, 1997); see also, the SustainAbility's website at www.sustainability.com.

[6] Anita Roddick, "A Different Bottom Line: Collaboration or Confrontation; The Way Forward for Business–NGO Relations in Sustainable Development," in *Buy in or Sell out: Understanding Business-NGO Partnerships*, World Vision Discussion Paper No. 10 (Summer 2000), 6.

[7] Ben & Jerry's has since been sold to the conglomerate Unilever.

[8] See Karl Schoenberger, *Levi's Children: Coming to Terms with Human Rights in the Global Marketplace* (New York: Atlantic Monthly Press, 2000).

[9] Andrew Baynes (Sony), "NGO Strategy (Presentation to European Environmental Conference 2000, Corporate Group, Brussels, 12 July 2000).

[10] Lord Hurd (Presentation made at the Relationship Between NGOs and the Corporate Sector seminar, 7 December 2000, London).

[11] The $100 million a year publicity campaign figure was taken from Daniel Rogers, "Killing Them Softly," *Financial Times* (24 July 2001).

[12] Conversation with Price Waterhouse Cooper (18 January 2001, Los Angeles, California).

[13] Price Waterhouse Cooper, "Building Relations with Civil Society," Discussion Paper (20 November 2000).

[14] Maria Livanos Cattaui, "Yes to Annan's Global Compact if It Isn't a License to Meddle," *International Herald Tribune* (26 July 2000).

BIBLIOGRAPHY

Baynes, Andrew. 2000. "NGO Strategy." Presentation to European Environmental Conference 2000, Corporate Group, Brussels. 12 July.

Cattaui, Maria Livanos. 2000. "Yes to Annan's Global Compact if It Isn't a License to Meddle." *International Herald Tribune*. 26 July.

Currah, Kelly. 2000. "Activating the Self-Correcting Mechanism of Civil Society: A Critical Analysis of TNC-NGO Relations." *International Journal of Public-Private Partnerships* 2/3. May.

Financial Times. 2001. Editorial page. 31 January.

Hurd, Lord Geoffrey. 2000. Presentation made at "The Relationship between NGOs and the Corporate Sector" seminar, London. 7 December. London. Transcript at www.edelman.com.

Husselbee, David. 2000. "NGOs as Development Partners to the Corporates: Child Football Stitchers in Pakistan." *Development in Practice* 10/3 and 10/4. August.

OECD. 2001. *OECD in Figures*. Paris: OECD.

Price Waterhouse Cooper. 2000. "Building Relations with Civil Society, Discussion Paper." 20 November.

Roddick, Anita. 2000. "A Different Bottom Line: Collaboration or Confrontation; The Way Forward for Business-NGO Relations in Sustainable Development." In *Buy in or Sell out: Understanding Business-NGO Partnerships*. World Vision Discussion Paper Number 10. Summer. 2000.

Schoenberger, Karl. 2000. *Levi's Children: Coming to Terms with Human Rights in the Global Marketplace*. New York: Atlantic Monthly Press.

UNCTAD. 2001. *World Investment Report 2000*. Geneva: UNCTAD.

4.

Development Work
in Restrictive Contexts

DAVID CHANDLER

This chapter describes approaches to entering and implementing effective development programmes in sensitive working contexts. That is the opening premise of this discussion. Most readers are aware that Non-Governmental Organisations (NGOs) are independent, privately funded organisations that provide services to people and communities in need. These services include relief interventions such as providing blankets, food and shelter in emergency conditions. They also include community development, medical interventions, and a wide range of other forms of assistance. Traditionally, successful NGOs must have two distinct sets of professional skills. The first are those skills required to raise, manage and account for their money. The second are those technical skills needed to design, implement, monitor and evaluate the agreed-upon intervention, assistance, or services. The successful NGOs have acquired a high degree of expertise in both of these broadly defined areas.

Having worked in a highly sensitive context, I have come to believe that the human experience is undergoing a profound transition. In this age of the Internet, personal computers, intercontinental jet transportation, cell phones and other useful tools, humankind has greater capacity to achieve a rapid and more efficient flow of information, higher levels of awareness and quicker response times to crises. In essence these tools are driving humankind rapidly towards globalisation. In light of this, I suggest that a third set of skills must be added to the required skills list for NGOs. I will call this set of skills *responsible information management*. This is not the processing and manipulation of information for its own sake. It is the use of information as a tool to inform, influence, implement and empower all of its stakeholders (that is, beneficiaries, donors, local governments, donor governments, media, the international community and so on) in a way that builds a sense of community and actively serves the common good.

PREAMBLE

In my time as a country director for a large international organisation, I was happy when my time and energies were focussed only on fund-raising, and programme management. They comprised my job description, and they kept me very busy. However, I found that much of my time was also spent exchanging information. Perhaps as much as half my time was spent informing, persuading, preparing and preventing. Many visitors would knock unannounced on my office door, and if I could create the time, I adopted the practice of meeting with anyone who dropped by. The list included other NGOs, media, diplomats, representatives from multi-laterals, representatives from corporations, church delegations and private individuals. They embodied an extremely broad array of interested parties or stakeholders. Instinctively, I knew these meetings were very important – and unavoidable. I also noticed that these groups tended to be much more interested in my observations, insights and recommendations when my message was based on a well-formulated strategy, plan of action and documented results. This information meant as much as a field trip to show solid programme work. Visitors always liked seeing the projects, but they also appreciated receiving all the reports, the quarterly reports, midterm evaluations and audited financials that are the foundation of a strategy, action plan and documented results. On top of the usual reports and information that most projects produce, I routinely supplemented these data with:

- A clear mission statement, operating values and a policy statement that anticipated the most commonly asked "difficult" questions;
- Preliminary research into a concern or issue, in-depth surveys, baseline surveys and articles compiled from our research and experience; and

- Examples of the comprehensive monitoring and evaluation component, which was fundamentally part of all programmes and initiatives.

Visitors always seemed impressed to see and receive stacks of our documents. However, the scrutiny we received was continuous and seemed to go far beyond the need to verify the viability of our projects or even the professionalism of our organisation. For a long time I attributed this intense scrutiny to the fact that I was heading up a programme in what was considered a highly sensitive and restrictive working environment. It was true that many organisations considered our programme controversial. Some vehemently disagreed with our organisational decision to enter the country and start up a development-focussed programme. So, to end the controversy over our presence in that country, we worked very hard to build a well-conceived, carefully developed, high-performance programme, and we documented our efforts. But the spotlight continued to be focussed on us long after we had convinced our most demanding critics. In some cases the same critics would visit, leave convinced, and return a few months later needing to be convinced again.

I had enough experience to realise that this behaviour was unusual. It frustrated me. But I also had the nagging suspicion that this intense scrutiny was not going away. So I began to try to understand it. I began with a study of the country. This helped improve the quality and efficiency of our programmes, but it did not explain why the scrutiny of our programmes was so intense and prolonged. Then I began to study more about the history and role of NGOs; I also read about globalisation. In the end I believe the answer was very simple. The more rapid and efficient information flow of today's world creates a vacuum around those issues and rare countries that capture the imagination and about which little is known. So the demand for information is great. In addition, the information that people received from our programme about working in that particular country often went against conventional wisdom. This was significant because, sadly, it seems that those following conventional wisdom tend to hold it dearly and close to the heart.

We responded by implementing a form of responsible information management. We built relationships with the people who took the time to visit us. Visitors would see our programmes and the studies generated from them, be impressed and go away. Once home and confronted by multiple questions they were not equipped to answer (having only visited the country for a short time), they questioned the truth of what they had seen. As we continued to build a consistent track record of performance, we had repeat visitors. Each time they visited, they were impressed, and each time they learned a little more about the programmes our organisation implemented and about the country. Over time we built strong relationships of trust and mutual respect with a number of people. Quietly, and little by little, these same people re-examined conventional wisdom and began to question it. But this took time, mutual trust and a great deal of effort from our entire programme team. I found that responsible information management requires strict adherence to the organisation's core values (whether those values are defined or implicit) and decision-making based on the achievement of long-term strategic goals.

As a result of this experience, I became impressed with the power of responsible information management. Good information is rare and therefore very valuable. Results coming from the use of information are even rarer and more valuable. For this reason I became convinced that NGOs that are poised to utilise the power of information quite effectively could have a profound global impact. But how do NGOs reach this level of potential great influence? And how do they manage the challenge of being significant actors in this role? In the following background section I share my detailed analysis of the evolving nature of the world. It is my interpretation and not necessarily shared by the organisation or the people with whom I worked. However, I believe this analysis is important. Not only does it provide the basic foundation for my presentation on working in sensitive contexts, but it also suggests that the role of NGOs is evolving, that the stakes they are working for are increasing, that more and different stakeholders are involved in the monitoring of NGO efforts, and that the spotlight of scrutiny is beginning to broaden and will eventually bring all NGOs into its bright light. If the insights I offer do reflect a global trend, then the various paths I suggest are applicable to most NGOs, not just those considering opening offices in sensitive or challenging countries.

BACKGROUND

With the end of the Cold War, circumstances for NGOs changed. Before, the balance of power rested on the shoulders of the West and the Soviet Union–led Communist bloc. NGOs, for better or worse, were identified as part of the total aid package offered by the West. It was rare for them to work outside of the foreign-policy framework defined by the political leaders of the West and the parent country. In practical terms, this meant that most sensitive countries were out of bounds, as many of them were associated with the Communist bloc nations. Often these so-called closed countries did not welcome NGOs. At this time the Communist bloc viewed NGOs as political subversives. On the other hand, leaders of Western countries saw NGOs as providing extra material resources but not as participants in the mainstream aid efforts. Generally, they were classified as "do-gooders" whose impact was thought to be marginal and nominal at best. Politically, they were a non-issue, thought to be harmless, but often a good source of reliable grass-roots information.

In the late 1970s and 1980s these traditional NGO affiliations began to unravel. In Southeast Asia the unravelling started when some NGOs entered Cambodia, Vietnam and Laos against prevailing opinion and before the U.S. Embargo was lifted. This unravelling gained momentum with the fall of the Berlin Wall in 1989 and the collapse of the Soviet Union in the early 1990s. This was a time of great uncertainty for NGOs. Their role was being redefined by circumstances as well as by the activity of a few NGOs. The U.S.–led embargo of Vietnam, Laos and Cambodia did in fact deter many NGOs from working in those countries, even when they began requesting NGO assistance. But on the global front, the tide had turned. NGOs and people's movements inside Europe and the United States were expressing well-defined and well-documented opinions that were shaping policy. With increasing NGO independence in the field, and growing influence domestically, the dissociation of NGOs from the foreign policies of the Western nations occurred. The emergence of NGOs as a legitimate force of independent thought and action based on their own set of core values began to be understood and recognised.

While NGOs were working with greater independence, they were also gaining recognition for their ability to implement small-scale village-level aid programmes that often became self-sustaining. A valid and useful "NGO approach" was emerging and was being expressed in development journals and other academic publications. Increasingly, the competent NGOs were seen as useful sub-contractors for aid budgets that governments realised they could not place as effectively themselves. Therefore, increasing sums of money were made available to NGOs through government channels.

The end of the Cold War caused a shift in the global balance of power. With only one official "super power" left, there was a vacuum to be filled. Much upheaval and disruption bubbled up all over the world, including in Yugoslavia, Kuwait, Somalia, Rwanda, Burundi and Kosovo. In the 1990's the UN began to assume a much broader role in global affairs as part of its response to this turbulence. It was, perhaps, the only global non-partisan multi-lateral organisation whose mandate encompassed these emerging needs. So it rushed into the breach. NGOs benefitted from this indirectly. First, they became sub-contractors. Second, NGOs were a good source of competent and experienced staff thereby establishing closer ties to local communities. Third, NGOs complemented the UN; their expertise in providing efficient, effective and sustainable assistance at the village level dovetailed nicely with the broad-based macro-level programmes typical of the UN. With the increase in UN staff knowledgeable about NGOs, these grass-roots organisations were accorded more opportunities and more respect. This development, in turn, pushed the re-shaping of the identity of NGOs. Although they are not accorded full status as multi-laterals, the trend is that NGOs are seen more as independent international players with resources and expertise of their own, rather than as a component of the foreign policy of Western governments.

This shift in identity elevated NGOs to acknowledged players in the global arena. The impact of this shift included responsibility to help shape foreign policy on the home front, as well as a commitment to on-the-ground involvement wherever there is need in the world. The modes of NGO involvement globally have expanded to include assisting (and playing significant roles) in international peacekeeping activities, implementing development projects in restricted countries, becoming a "watch dog" for human rights violations, as well as continuing to implement top quality programmes at the village level over longer periods of time (varying from five to twenty years) than governments will typically sustain in their aid programmes.

The end of the Cold War changed the role and identity of international NGOs. However, it is clear that this process is ongoing because the balance of power and the roles of several key global players are still being defined. The traditional power base controlled by the nation-state system is now being challenged by the active efforts of potential super powers (such as China, India, and the European Union), emerging nation states, the multi-laterals, and, more than ever before, transnational corporations (TNCs). This evolution of the balance of power and the shift in the role and identity of NGOs have placed them under greater pressure. With NGOs having the acknowledged capacity and networks to provide the on-the-ground know-how and connections to supplement the efforts of these "macro-organisations," there continue to be unprecedented opportunities for NGOs. However, the risks are great. As the NGO movement enters a new phase of growth and influence, the values by which NGOs operate take on greater significance. These values will help establish the movement's credibility and effectiveness during the uncertainty of this period of global transition. Each NGO's values are expressed and borne out by how it manages information, raises money and provides its services. NGO behaviours are being closely monitored and will be the true test of whether each organisation can stand up to the stresses and be an integral part of this emerging global reality. Therefore, several questions arise that are fundamental to the health of any organisation. They are:

- What is our mission?
- What are our core values?
- What is our long-term vision?
- What are our strengths and capacities, our weaknesses, our opportunities, and our constraints (SWOC analysis)?
- What additional strengths and capacities are necessary in order to achieve our long -term strategic objectives?
- How much dependence should we have on the macro-organisations as a funding source?
- How much independence from the macro-organisations should we retain?

- How do we share our privileged knowledge and our programme findings with our donors, interested parties and the international community?

In this age of transition, rapid change, electronic communication and globalisation, it is even more important for the survival and growth of any NGO to be extremely dutiful and precise in engaging in the appropriate processes to answer these questions. In fact, the more accurate and precise the answers, the greater the control each NGO will have over its own future. The prepared NGOs will be better equipped to determine which opportunities are most likely to lead it, and the world, into the bright future we hope lies ahead, out of sight, but just around the corner.

WORKING IN SENSITIVE COUNTRIES

Should any NGO work in sensitive countries?

Most NGOs pursue the humanitarian principle that their function is to save and improve lives. However, this general mandate does not describe the ways in which this principle is pursued. As stated above, in this fluid and dynamic environment for NGOs, it is essential that organisations take the time to define their mission, vision, core values, long-term strategy, and short-term goals and objectives with great precision. For the purposes of this chapter, we will assume that these questions have been appropriately answered. Now we will examine one particular area of long-term strategy – should any NGO work in sensitive contexts? And if so, what are the guidelines to help NGOs determine whether or not that particular organisation is appropriate for a given country? Once an NGO decides to work in a sensitive area, what are some of the basic guidelines for establishing an organisation in order to help minimise danger to all participants and enhance opportunities for success?

Case #1

An agency concerned with the preservation of wildlife and rapidly dwindling habitats around the world becomes aware of a section of tropical rainforest that has great diversity of animal and plant life and is still relatively untouched. It finds that the professionals from the Ministry of Forestry with whom it has come in contact are quite knowledgeable and open to new and different ideas for the management of these habitats. The country within which this rain-forest tract is located happens to be ruled by a military regime that is considered one of the worst globally in regards to human rights. There is an active opposition movement both inside and outside the country. However, it has faced dramatic defeats in recent years. In fact, the area of tropical rain forest that has attracted the interest of the wildlife preservation agency happens to be located in the border area of this country and has long been a traditional stronghold for a large ethnic group that has maintained a guerrilla-type struggle against this military regime for decades. The group uses this tract of rain forest to "disappear" and then surreptitiously cross over to camps across the border in the neighbouring country. The military government is currently involved in a final push to "eliminate all opposition" in the area. It has also initiated talks with the bordering nation's government regarding the expulsion of all "illegal immigrants" squatting on the border. Fighting has been intense, and no quarter has been given. The situation has been particularly brutal to vulnerable groups, such as women and children maintaining a subsistence-level existence in villages scattered throughout this area.

There are several international business groups that have initiated a huge infrastructure project contiguous to this tract of tropical rain forest. This project has also been controversial because it is viewed as providing substantial amounts of hard currency and a future income stream to the military regime, which is struggling to meet its balance of payments and is in arrears with several of the multi-lateral organisations (including the World Bank and the IMF). Recently the international media scrutinised activity in this geographic area. Reports emerged from several human rights organisations citing a number of human rights violations that occurred because of the infrastructure project. The international business consortium was accused of sanctioning significant human rights violations committed by the military government as part of providing security for the project as well as using forced labour for supplemental work projects that the military government considered essential to support the construction of this infrastructure project.

International media have taken an interest in this struggle for political freedom because the retaliatory responses of the military government have been so heavy-handed, and one of the main opposition leaders is a charismatic and appealing figure who won the Nobel Peace Prize within the last ten years. The news of this struggle has been steadily reported for years. It has periodically jumped on and off the radar screens of the international media when specific events of international interest occurred. The opposition leaders understand the power of the media and recognise that it is crucial to swaying international opinion in their favour. They know that periodically their cause has to jump to the fore of media attention or else it will permanently drop off the agendas of political leaders, who have enormous numbers of other causes to represent.

The NGO, which represents one set of concerns and interests, has expressed interest in creating a wildlife preserve in this disputed rain forest. The military government, which represents a second set of concerns and interests, is in the midst of clearing this land of all guerrilla activity so that the infrastructure project can be built unopposed. Furthermore, the establishment of a wildlife preserve in this geographic location would allow the military government to keep the area completely clear of human habitation, making the task of maintaining the security of its future income stream much simpler. The opposition groups have their backs against the wall and need a way to bring enormous media coverage to bear in an effort to offset their military losses and maintain international pressure on the military government. The international media are always seeking a good story. Furthermore, they like this issue and like to bring the spotlight of attention to bear on the military government. They are always happy when there is a story that can draw immediate attention. Interested parties from local embassies and multi-laterals take interest because if a story gets significant media coverage, it will affect the *positions of their superiors back home towards* this country with its military regime. With greater attention brought to bear, the *ability to move their own agendas forward* will either be made harder or easier.

Actions in one system often have a spill-over affect in other systems. Yet, typically, these issues are not discussed among the participants representing the various systems. Such issues as a military push, a human rights report that is being released, the opposition launching its own campaign to embarrass the military government, or the media seeking a story that could re-focus the spotlight on this military regime all affect the other players from other systems. Strategy and plans are deliberated within the respective systems but are not discussed between the systems. Furthermore, no specifics of strategy or plans that may affect other systems are ever discussed between the systems. The result is that the efforts of many of the systems to bring political freedom, peace and prosperity to this nation ruled by a military regime sometimes are at odds with each other. As a result, there can be much waste and loss of opportunity for mutual benefit.

In this case we can see that the environmental NGO is not aware of the other dynamics at work here. It is extremely vulnerable and about to be embarrassed. A few weeks later a substantial story was published in the Sunday *New York Times* entitled "NGO and Military Government Kill People to Save Animals." Obviously, the environmental agency will take a long time to recover from a mistake of this magnitude. However, if it were conscious of different systems at play, there could be powerful synergy generated to marshal resources towards achieving the common good of the people within the country as well as the tract of virgin rain forest.

The context for viewing this case has two major elements:

1. Discussion of the philosophical and ethical basis for NGOs to provide humanitarian assistance to sensitive areas; and
2. Practical guidelines for moving ahead should an NGO decide to initiate a programme or find itself operating in a restricted area.

PHILOSOPHICAL AND ETHICAL BASIS FOR NGO INVOLVEMENT

Rationale:

Is it necessary for NGOs to concern themselves with human rights, politics and those larger issues, or should they simply provide humanitarian assistance wherever it is needed – as is their mandate?

For some, the question of whether NGOs should provide humanitarian assistance in restricted country is a non-issue. They believe that NGOs have a mandate to work for the poor, providing comfort and assistance wherever it is required and whenever the need arises. Access to food and basic services, they believe, is a fundamental human right. Therefore, an organisation must respond to needs as they are uncovered or emerge. Furthermore, they believe that spending time and money on feasibility studies and advocacy issues drains precious resources that could be used more effectively saving lives.

Others believe that NGOs often go tromping about where they have no business. In the past they have entered countries without knowledge of the local context. Their approach was stereotyped as single-minded "do-gooding." Their interventions were thought to be standard "cookie cutter" programmes that had worked well elsewhere but were not necessarily effective in the new country. Even in the best of circumstances, it is very difficult to work with the poor in ways that promote self-sustaining development activities. NGOs new to restrictive countries often were not up to speed with the interlocking issues that were causing the problems, and they were not taking the time to learn. Therefore, they were thought to be ill-equipped to conduct precise assessments, make the necessary subtle differentiations, identify the key issues and design well-crafted interventions to address those key issues effectively. They had proven themselves effective in logistically complex situations. But in contexts that were dynamic and complex culturally and politically, they were thought to be naïve. In their ignorance NGOs sometimes unknowingly implemented programmes or efforts that indirectly supported the very injustices they sought to rectify. At the very least, they muddied the waters for the "professionals." At the worst, they set back or even damaged the efforts of the "legitimate" change agents.

There is truth in both perspectives. Some NGOs do take the hard-nosed crusader approach. They will go anywhere there is a major problem, sometimes where they have no business going. But the global environment has changed. Ignoring or avoiding this reality will only lead to atrophy and the demise of NGOs. So let's take a harder look at what is really happening. Currently, there is a vacuum that is being filled by the NGO movement. This vacuum is the gap between macro-level policies and the micro-level needs of people at the village level. NGOs are the entities best equipped to fill this vacuum, perhaps partly because they *have* gone tromping around unfamiliar places. They have built the knowledge and expertise to work effectively at the grass roots. They have information that must be managed responsibly. Through their networks, process methodologies, strategic initiatives and independent resources, NGOs can knit together communities out of the threads of mistrust, uncertainty and chaos. I believe NGOs are well positioned to achieve this without undermining concurrent change efforts and without compromising their own organisational integrity. But it requires a shift in their operational paradigm that I believe is already happening.

So my answer to the rationale question is yes, NGOs should work in restrictive and repressive countries. I believe they have the ability to do so in a way that contributes to the solution rather than adding to the problem. If the NGOs are clear on their goals and objectives; if they know their mission and their strengths for achieving those missions; if their strategies are well tailored to their mission and their strengths; and if they have organisational integrity, then I believe NGOs can be extremely effective. They can begin to help the policy-makers communicate with the grass-roots population. I believe bridging this gap is a crucial first step even if all the political pieces are not yet in place because it begins the process of including all the stakeholders in the process of creating communities.

Complexity

The paradigm shift that I believe is already happening is the ability to handle complexity. Perhaps the best definition of complexity is the utilization of multiple means to achieve multiple objectives while serving multiple stakeholders and adhering to a clearly defined operational framework and commonly accepted long-term goal(s). NGOs are developing methods of achieving this and still being able to implement effective programs. Old tools need to be used in new ways if organisations such as NGOs, multi-laterals and the like are to be successful in this dynamic and fluid operational environment. By recognizing the need for a paradigm shift, NGOs can be part of the solution while remaining true to their mandate. But doing so requires acknowledging complexity and working with it; it requires the effective use of process; it requires an honest attempt at understanding and then meeting the often-conflicting requirements of multiple stakeholders. It requires leadership by consensus, high levels of communications, and a focus on long-term strategic objectives. It requires organisational integrity. It requires creative problem solving rather than conventional solutions with surface level dressing to accommodate a new situation. It requires enormous efforts towards achieving mutual understanding, reconciliation and ultimately trust. It requires time and patience; it requires a commitment. It requires the ability to build networks, coalitions and allies. It requires open-endedness (the ability to take action before knowing the outcome). It requires a high tolerance for ambiguity. It requires a shift in mindset to adapt to the new world order. Here's why.

Multiple stakeholders

The global power structure is in transition. There is only one super power. There are several other entities striving to achieve super-power status. In addition to military might, other significant factors affecting the outcome of this shuffle of the global balance of power are economic power, political influence and information flow. Multi-laterals such as the World Bank and the UN are playing larger roles. Through the use of economics, politics and information, TNCs, media organisations and elements of the NGO movement all wield much greater influence than ever before. One glaring omission in this discussion, however, are local stakeholders. This includes the local government, and, most conspicuous by their absence, the poor. There is no institution that effectively exercises clout and influence on behalf of the local stakeholders in redefining the global power structure, designing macro-level policies, or even in shaping local programs. However, a number of indigenous institutions are emerging that, in their maturity, may assume that role for the poor. They include micro-credit programmes best exemplified by the Grameen Bank. There are other, people-focussed organisations, and there are significant leaders in multi-lateral organisations and NGOs that can wield some level of influence on behalf of the poor. Finally, there are NGOs that are developing procedures to facilitate the participation of local stakeholders. None of these institutions, as yet, has matured to the point that it effectively wields the economic, political and information factors previously cited while sidestepping the use of the military factor. Several potential institutions are appearing on the horizon and offer great promise. They need to be nurtured. In the meantime, the needs and concerns of the poor are represented by the UN (through its crafting of macro policies), and NGOs (through their ability to provide sustainable assistance at the village level). Though many NGOs, the UN and other multi-laterals profess to represent the poor in forums and programmes implemented around the world, they remain one tiny disenfranchised voice amidst a puzzling array of seemingly irreconcilable players and stakeholders holding court on the global stage. For NGOs, our hearts tell us that the poor should be the most important stakeholders, but realities force us to think about the local regime, the donor(s), the media, other NGOs – the organisations that wield economic, political and informational/media influence.

With that said, the discussion of multiple stakeholders still points towards interesting challenges and developments for NGOs. The level of complexity has increased dramatically. One way to address this increased complexity is to characterise the shift in the global power structure as many voices clamouring to be heard and heeded. For NGOs and other "actors" working in sensitive countries, this shift is key. The challenge is to help these many voices become harmonious. To achieve this, NGOs must acknowledge that the group of stakeholders to whom they are held accountable has expanded significantly. In the past, stakeholders have been defined for the most part as donors. This has always been a given for fund-raising organisations in order to keep the funds coming in and to pay the rent. However, because of the on-going shakeout in the global power structure, stakeholders are no longer only those who have financial assistance to dispense. Increasingly, stakeholders include vocal constituencies that monitor and track any newsworthy or noteworthy situation and have access to information networks. In other words, they wield information. This manipulation of information can enable organisations and/or movements to influence the policy of one or more governments in the allied West. Any organisation that seeks to work in a sensitive area must recognise this increase in constituents to whom it is accountable. Stakeholders are no longer simply donors. They include those with access to significant information flow as well as cash flow.

Let me give one illustration of the power of information networks. Ten years ago, if a human rights organisation wanted to raise the profile of a certain issue, it had to conduct research, publish, circulate its information to a wide and influential body, then take those reports and advocate in the capitals of powerful nations. The cost of publications, postage and travel to the power seats of several governments was great and daunting. Today, with the advent of the Internet, an activist organisation can develop materials relatively cheaply through desk-top publications software and circulate them to an extremely wide audience at close to no cost. Information can flow easily to and from agencies as well as government bodies. Furthermore, the rapid communication by email enables low-cost logistical organising by these relatively small groups at an extremely sophisticated level. Elements of this were in evidence at the protests staged so effectively at the November 1999 World Trade Organisation meetings in Seattle, Washington.[1]

The fact that stakeholders are no longer defined as only donors creates a volatile but also dynamic working environment. It means, for example, that the number of stakeholders to be accommodated has increased dramatically. This increases the likelihood that whatever solutions emerge from the resulting complex process will be extremely well-crafted with many elements and aspects of the challenges carefully considered. This in turn should increase the likelihood of success.

When resolving disagreements, the smaller the number of stakeholders the easier it is to agree on an operational framework and move ahead. Obviously the larger the number of stakeholders, the more difficult it is to reach agreement. With too many stakeholders at work representing different positions and holding fast to them, a workable change process may become impossible. In these instances an atmosphere of complete mistrust develops. No initiatives can be formulated, pilot tested, and carefully nurtured. No tentative alliances can be struck before they are attacked. No single stakeholder (whether for the common good or not) can develop a critical mass of influence. At best a plurality is achieved, when a majority is needed. Unfortunately, this tends to play into the hands of totalitarian governments because, unlike democratic governments, they are able to function with a plurality as long as it includes the military.

The reality of multiple stakeholders definitely makes the entire change process far more complex and difficult. But this volatile situation is not hopeless. I believe, in fact, that successes forged within this intense crucible are more comprehensive in their conception and therefore more durable. To help develop change processes that stand the test of time is a worthy challenge. There are a number of interesting characteristics that must be managed in order to weight probabilities on the side of success:

1. *Respect all stakeholders.* By the time NGOs are on the scene, the stakeholders have classified all the players and each other as "good guys" or "bad guys." The incoming organisation tends to accept those labels without making the effort to validate or at least understand the process that resulted in those classifications. Even if identifying the "good guys" and the "bad guys" is quite straightforward, whenever a conflict seems insoluble, the place to start with each stakeholder is a point with each stakeholder of agreement, a place you can work together agreeably. Out of this comes a working relationship, and, it is to be hoped, some degree of mutual respect. This respect, however, *must* be given without fundamentally compromising the mission and objectives of the organisation as well as the larger humanitarian objectives espoused in various UN documents, such as the United Nations Declarations for Human Rights and the Convention for the Rights of the Child. For example, in one country the initial project was with the Ministry of Health. It was clearly documented in all the literature that there was very high infant and child mortality rate because of poor hygiene, water-related diseases and inadequate immunizations. In its official literature and studies, the ministry claimed to be grappling effectively with these problems. In reality, there were too few doctors, and they were poorly paid. Equipment was inadequate, and there was not enough medicines and other consumables. Twenty years previously the medical profession had been world class due to its student selection process and indigenous medical schools. Decades of ineffective government had nearly destroyed what was once a glorious tradition. There was still a great deal of capacity as well as pride among the senior officials of the ministry. In offering assistance, the expatriate team leader did not want to offend the officials with whom he and his team had to work. At the same time the NGO could not be seen by the international community as openly collaborating with and

supplying the Ministry of Health with supplies and equipment that the government itself should be supplying.

The initial strategy was to provide essential medicine and equipment to projects that were jointly operated. The local medical officer had precedence because the hospital and clinics were his. However, the team maintained a presence and provided assistance, working hard to win respect and trust. Over time, the busy medical officers began to allow the NGO medical team to work autonomously. By using the NGO medical team's expertise as well as their access to additional resources, the medical officers could generate many more activities and meet more expectations. Over time, they could demonstrate progress to their superiors. After a few years the NGO medical team evolved the project design so that it required more hands-on and grass-roots activities on the part of the NGO medical team in order to achieve even greater success while implementing detailed monitoring and evaluation programmes. The plan was medically sound, and the NGO medical team had demonstrated that it could work on the ground without creating problems for the government medical officers. The new projects were all approved. In this way the NGO was able to respect all stakeholders and operate within its mission and objectives without compromising the integrity of the organisation.

2. *Develop an understanding of the historical and cultural contexts.* Perhaps the best starting point for developing respect or at least a functional understanding of each of the stakeholders is the historical and cultural contexts. Wherever there is deep-seated conflict, the problems are rarely black and white. Often they have existed for a period of time. If this is the case, the problems are usually layered and quite complex. Actual knowledge of the uniqueness of the situation not only demonstrates genuine commitment (which, of course, is the first step to engendering trust), but it also enables the organisation to:

   • Establish communication links and build relationships with the key players, so they can believe that the stated agenda is one they agree with and that it is in fact the organisation's actual agenda;

- Engage the key players in activities that may lead to the process of structuring their own solutions (which enhances their potential for success and sustainability); and
- Enable the intervening organisation to discern with some confidence which steps, programs, and approaches are least likely to offend any of the stakeholders but will at the same time move the engagement process forward.

For these reasons, having an understanding of the cultural and historical context of all of the stakeholders is essential. It is useful to realise that all stakeholders are imperfect and have a "shadow side." All stakeholders have been involved in events or circumstances of which they are not proud. This history may be months old, or it may be centuries old. This perspective helps in creating an effective approach to developing a framework within which all stakeholders can enjoy a sense of acknowledged legitimacy and begin to communicate.

3. *Maintain a pragmatic balance between short-term integrity and long-term strategic objectives.* This is perhaps the most difficult balance to maintain. In any human interaction there is give and take. The organisation must be able to make appropriate compromises without subverting its essential integrity. In this way an organisation develops the flexibility and operational range needed to initiate essential long-term change processes in a situation that is otherwise closed up. This is why core values are so important. They provide a framework with which stakeholders can utilise greater precision without jeopardizing their integrity. For example, the situation mentioned previously described an NGO medical team trying to initiate high quality, grass-roots health programmes within a repressive country. In the beginning the team had to work with the Ministry of Health in order to have official permission to work in the country. At the same time, it ran the risk of being seen as supporting or even legitimising the government. The pragmatic balance the team maintained was to take the time to build relationships and trust levels by designing a project that was less than ideal for the long-term objectives of the community served and of the NGO. However, by working under the conditions it was given, the NGO could then demonstrate the mutual benefits of granting it greater working

autonomy. Over time, this approach led to its being able to develop a number of innovative programmes and operate in the country in the way it had originally envisioned.

It is clear that the presence of multiple stakeholders makes the process of working in sensitive countries far more complex and challenging. However, the positive aspects of this changing reality are several:

1. Any solution that emerges has a greater chance of standing the test of time and circumstances.

2. Multiple stakeholders generate scrutiny and concern that have de facto become part of the global conscience. Furthermore, this global conscience is resting on the shoulders of a broad-based movement defined less by a particular policy, politics, or institution and more by a collective understanding that has grown up from a body of generally accepted practices and behaviours. Many of these have been captured by various UN treaties and protocols. This means that there is greater consistency in the generally accepted practices and principles. At the same time there can be greater diversity of opinion expressed within the global conscience because there are dimension and nuances as to how the global conscience is applied and monitored. In practical terms, it also means that information gathering and the monitoring of sensitive areas are conducted by a wide range of key players and constituencies. This in itself provides a range of checks and balances on prevailing opinion and is a good "litmus test" for ensuring accuracy and objectivity of the information generated.

These are all significant steps forward because with the acknowledgement of multiple stakeholders – clamouring voices – comes the acknowledgement of complexity. With the acknowledgement of complexity comes the need for an attitude of inclusion. These voices and their concomitant complexity are part of the problem, so they must be part of the solution. A key voice or key issue cannot be left out of the process or the change equation or it will fester and haunt the long-term process somewhere down the road. Once this realization has been reached, the challenge is to craft the most inclusive process possible without becoming bogged down. Balance is key. In summary, successful implementation of the change process leads to a broader range of possible solutions, creating more space and openness in the discussion environment. This in turn leads to a greater chance of developing a mutually agreeable solution.

THE NEW OPERATING PARADIGM

NGOs, perhaps unknowingly, have been edging towards a new paradigm that has short-term and long-term parts of its implementation. In the short term, this paradigm requires what the *Christian Science Monitor* called "tough-minded cooperation."[2] This is when business competitors, or in this case stakeholders, agree to work together towards shared goals or concrete objectives even though their philosophies or ultimate goals may be different; for example, the joining of a reputable human rights organisation and an investigative reporter with great research skills but a reputation for "shooting from the hip." Both want to know the truth of a situation, but the human rights organisation stakes its reputation on substantiated proof, whereas the reporter is more concerned about a timely scoop. For a short time they could work together, pooling their resources and skills by setting out clear operational guidelines. Or it might be appropriate in some instances for a development NGO to work alongside a government with a terrible record on human rights if such effort were to achieve the relief of human suffering and build a foundation leading towards fundamental change over the long term.

Traditionally, making these fine distinctions was not necessary. There were, by and large, two official sides to the story. It was easier and certainly safer to follow the KISS rule (Keep It Simple Stupid) and not risk entanglements or the perception of entanglements that could greatly damage the programme, the organisation, or individual careers (which unfortunately is a consideration that often creeps into the decision-making mix). In this day of globalisation and multiple stakeholders, adherence to obvious distinctions and the avoidance of complexity are luxuries organisations can no longer afford. If NGOs want to fulfil their potential for influencing the human condition and moving the world towards the common good, then they cannot shy away from the risk of managing complexity. Those that do will simply fall by the wayside.

The long-term element of this paradigm requires the NGO to become a learning organisation. This requires the intentional nurture and professional development of local/national staff by NGOs as well as the building of a dynamic, capable, thinking human resource base on which organisations and ultimately the country itself can build their future. Many NGOs have implemented participatory strategies and planning processes in an effort to improve their development programs. They have designed exercises and procedures to enable their own management and operational staffs to contribute to organisational strategy and planning. The purpose has been to enable staff to experience firsthand the empowerment process, as well as to implement a more effective planning process. The thinking among NGOs was that if their management teams and staff, who are often nationals, have the opportunity to experience the empowerment process personally, then perhaps they can better nurture it in their project activities. Logically this makes a great deal of sense. Furthermore, involving the national staff in the planning process is better management. Those who work in the programmes and are familiar with the villages and communities know what is happening day to day. It is a better use of their knowledge and skills to involve the implementing teams in planning the on-the-ground programs, and identifying the NGO's future directions. At the same time, each team member is encouraged to be an active contributor to crafting an effective and contextually appropriate programme. Each member has, ideally, been encouraged to question and even voice opposition to ideas posed by the leader. The effect has been to encourage growth, change and continuous learning among staff. NGOs have thus begun, more or less, to become learning organisations.

Together, these two strategies, tough-minded co-operation, and the fostering of a learning organisation, are a perfect response to the challenges of today's world. They are effective because they are concrete ways to manage and distribute information. Undoubtedly more ways can and will be added to the list.

LEARNING ORGANISATIONS AND SYSTEMS THINKING

Amidst the crush of day-to-day pressures to achieve measurable results and meet deadlines, it is difficult to step outside and objectively assess one's world. The "tyranny of the urgent" can be extremely compelling. As the country director, I struggled with this. Nothing would please me more than spending time in the projects, getting to know the community members and helping my programme team members become better at their jobs. However, I rarely did this. I spent my day in paperwork, fighting fires when they sprang up and preventing fires when I could see smouldering embers. When I did get to the projects, it was almost always either as a tour guide or participant in a formal community ceremony, rarely as simply a member of the management team. In fact, the actual on-the-ground management became the de facto responsibility of the project managers. They had to build their own teams. All I could do was help them formulate their project vision, articulate the tools and values for achieving the vision, and then provide advice or guidance to the managers when asked. The closest I would come to actual involvement in the management of field programs was to know generally how the programmes were running and ask targeted questions to ensure they were operating efficiently and in line with our stated policies and strategic directions. Gradually I came to realise that my job was to understand the global issues and concerns that could affect the working environment of our in-country organisation and to manage these pressures so the programme managers had enough space in which to operate freely.

I began looking around for more systematic ways to understand and then manage this new world of multiple stakeholders and many conflicting interests amidst rapid and vast information flow. If I was going to open the door for staff empowerment, I knew I was going to have less control over the day-to-day operation of the organisation. I knew I was going to feel vulnerable and less able to show outsiders (and perhaps myself) that I had the facts at my fingertips. I needed a good conceptual framework on which to rely. I found it in the business sector. The work of Peter M. Senge of the Harvard Business School proved particularly helpful.

Over the past twenty years, a problem-solving model has emerged from the Harvard Business School. In *The Fifth Discipline* Peter

M. Senge describes systems thinking as a way to approach situations where many large processes (or systems) are working at the same time. Senge gives many examples of situations that are typical of the business world.

Applying the new paradigm

Senge's systems paradigm applies very well to development work. It is especially applicable to sensitive areas because many of the multiple stakeholders represent different systems. Part of the problem is that these systems are not interfacing effectively. As an illustration, let us look at a few of the systems at work in a sensitive context:

- The de facto government;
- The exile or opposition government (of which there may be more than one);
- The allied West and its policy mechanism. This will start churning if a danger such as nuclear threat is perceived or some egregious event(s), such as a major disaster or consistent and flagrant violation of human rights, has occurred;
- The multi-lateral organisations such as the IMF, World Bank and the United Nations will all have "positions" on the situation. These positions will need to be reviewed and updated periodically;
- The "watch dog" organisations, which include NGOs, departments and agencies of the United Nations, and elements of many governments in the global family will have their own stance and issues that they are monitoring;
- Implementing aid agencies, which again include NGOs, departments and agencies of the United Nations, other multilaterals, as well as the implementing arm of many governments. These are accountable to their own systems and donors as well as the global watch dogs;
- Economic systems (trade), a wide range of systems that include laws and practices around trade, such as trade agreements among particular countries (such as Most Favoured Nations status in the United States and in the European Union), the presence and activities of TNCs and policy responses such as embargoes that specifically target economic systems;

- Economic systems (policy), a wide range of systems that include laws policies, and practices around financial practices and protocols. These can include free-market trade of currencies, access to loans from the IMF and the World Bank, indirect government assistance through aid programs and the denial or acceptance of the non-formal economy (which in some restrictive contexts can be enormous);
- Media systems, including the collecting of information, the crafting of stories, the opinions expressed that can shape policy and the quantity of publicity and awareness that is generated. The "slant" of a story can have repercussions that influence national policy for years to come.

All of these systems (or processes) have their own sets of concerns and issues. The overpowering tendency is to focus on the immediate concerns and routines of our own particular system. For example, NGOs tend to worry about NGO operations. This involves the establishment and maintenance of programs, raising funds and accounting for those funds. As part of this process, when a development NGO decides to establish its operations in a new country, it must approach the embassies and/or representatives of the government in power, regardless of whether they are "good guys" or "bad guys." Then the organisation must seek out the cooperation of the relevant ministries in their particular area of work (such as health or education) in order to hold meaningful discussions, exchange ideas for possible programmatic interventions and ultimately to implement projects in those countries. On the other hand, watch dog NGOs worry about getting and verifying information as to what is really happening in the sensitive country. Maintaining good cooperation and communication with the government and ministries of the country they are examining often becomes a low priority (and in reality impossible) because the information the watch dog NGOs seeks is incriminating for the host government. Clearly, development NGOs and watch dog NGOs working within their own contexts (or systems) have greatly differing priorities. They are not necessarily at odds with one another because in the long term both organisations seek the same thing, that is, to help the people of a given country. But the means chosen may be different in spite of this shared end. To ensure that there are no damaging misunderstandings along the way, the interface or meeting point of the two systems (and their representative organisations) must be intentionally managed. The key in systems thinking is that sufficient communication is required between these parties to know that each is operating responsibly within its respective spheres.

It is not automatically true that all of these systems collectively work for the greater good. In fact, on close examination it makes sense that the range and variety of systems at work within the nations of today would not mesh easily:

1. *Purpose.* Systems have different roots and were designed to achieve different things. For example, it is hardly surprising that World Bank loans, which were developed in the wake of World War II as the West's response to the economic needs of the European nations seeking to recover quickly from the destruction of the war, were woefully inappropriate for the needs of a wide range of developing countries. The World Bank recognised this and has worked very hard to modify itself so that its approach and systems are more compatible with the needs of emerging nations in the post–Cold War environment;

2. *Pace.* Many of these systems work at different rates. Some, such as media, operate in terms of seconds (the sound bite), with a story lasting weeks at the most, whereas cultural and historical seeds can still be bearing fruit one thousand years after they have been planted.

3. *Perspective.* All systems reflect a worldview and a set of values. The purpose of some systems is to perpetuate that worldview and protect those values. For example the security system seeks to protect the motherland and/or the status quo, not foster the growth and potential of each individual. Perspective is key in determining how a given system will respond to an NGO and its programmes.

4. *Process.* This is the means by which systems achieve their goals. In so doing, they reflect their perspective. Some systems are designed to be people centred, and therefore they try to be participative. They seek to further the common good by attempting to satisfy the needs of the majority. Others are classified as "top down" and are often rooted in military power and/or cultural traditions. They tend to respond to and serve

the needs of the systems makers (the ruling class). In this day and age the participative processes are thought to be democratic in nature and therefore are labelled as good, whereas the top-down processes are generally labelled bad because they are viewed as satisfying only the needs of those at the top and facilitating their control by polarizing the grass-roots communities rather than seeking to bond them in a positive and productive unity.

These are the macro differences to various systems. There are countless micro or perhaps corporate-culture types of differences that cause dissension among groups that agree on essential principles but differ in practice. An effort must be made by the players within each system to find the shared, often long-term goals and avoid being judgmental. This is where tough-minded cooperation comes in. A guideline is to strive always for the common good. As much as systems seem immutable, and consuming of all that is human and personal, they always serve a need. They will evolve once that need is no longer served. I believe that Senge's message is that the usefulness of systems is best determined at the point of interface with other systems. If the systems have become dysfunctional, the interface will confirm that and provide the opening for the contextually appropriate change process. For this reason communication – on-going discussion with all the stakeholders – and endless patience are key. Otherwise, according to Senge's model, corporations lose money and opportunities. In the case of the global society, there is great waste and loss of human potential. Evidence is quite overwhelming that those who suffer the most when societal systems fail are the poor and disenfranchised.

To avoid this loss and waste, Senge talks about creating a learning organisation, an organisation made up of people who feel empowered to learn continuously, knowing that change is a constant and that there are always better ways to work or operate. If they are empowered, with guidance they will more readily recognise the potential for empowerment in others, creating a "virtuous circle." This same approach is effective in the global context as well. Societies can work in ways that encourage people to take responsibility and to grow. Societies can work in the mode of a learning organisation. If the implementing organisations are true to their deepest mandate, they must work constantly towards the creation of learning societies. They must be constantly aware of the larger strategic implications of their actions – with one eye fixed on the greater good – as they simultaneously focus on fulfilling their organisations' responsibilities by achieving their own immediate short-term obligations within their own systems. The stakeholders observing these efforts must in turn support them. This is the responsibility and challenge posed by the post–Cold War order, the diversification of economic flows and the information revolution.

Case #2

The following situation shows how different systems can work in harmony to further the common good.

An NGO is working in a country ruled by a military regime that is considered one of the worst in the world in terms of its human rights track record. Through its other programs, including HIV/AIDS, this NGO has been able to travel to interesting areas within the country and see many things the government would prefer not to become known within the international community. One of the areas that stands out most is the area of child rights and the country's lack of compliance with UNICEF's Convention on the Rights of the Child, even though the military dictatorship happens to be a signer of the convention. To date this country has several areas in which it is blatantly outside the framework of the convention; however, it continues to report back to the convention that it is moving forward very effectively towards achievement of the goals. The local UNICEF office has not expressed any concern at the lack of substance in the reports. Instead, it has applauded the reporting efforts.

The NGO is aware of many situations in which children have been recruited as soldiers, pressed into forced labour, tortured, and coerced by police and other enforcement officials into granting sexual favours. Because of its expertise, as well as the magnitude of the problem in the country, the NGO wants to become involved in implementing programmes for street children and other child populations that are extremely vulnerable and should be served by the provisions of the Convention on the Rights of the Child. However, officially there are no street children in the country. Also, the ministry responsible for services to children is the weakest and least capable ministry in the government. The NGO has been wrestling with how to secure approval for the project. If the project proposal is officially submitted and rejected, it will be very difficult to implement the programme anyway. But if the proposal isn't submitted, the NGO has no official approval supporting its implementation. The NGO is well aware that when operating in a totalitarian context, it is extremely important to have official approvals as well as the unofficial blessing of the local officials.

The NGO is trying to determine the best way to proceed. For an unrelated reason it seeks an audience with one of the officials of the ministry responsible for child services. It just so happens that when the meeting is finally scheduled, it falls in the week after this official has returned from a reporting trip to Geneva.

The meeting in Geneva was a mid-decade report on the nation's progress in achieving compliance with the Convention for the Rights of the Child. Several human rights NGOs, frustrated with the country's brazen denial of the existence of multiple problems – not to mention lack of acknowledgement of wrongdoing – came to the meeting armed with detailed reports and data painting a grim picture of children's situation in this military dictatorship. Usually in meetings of this sort, the reporting group's version of the facts is politely accepted. However, in this case the "facts" presented by the national delegation were shouted down and refuted by counter-reports. Of course this brouhaha attracted media attention. All in all it was a very unpleasant experience for the delegation.

The ministry official with whom the NGO was meeting the following week had been one of the senior representatives, and he was embarrassed by the situation. Apparently, he was ordered to do something about it as well. At the meeting the NGO representatives heard a long rendition of the impoliteness endured at this meeting. But at the end of the spiel was a plea. Can you help us? Do you have any projects you would like to submit for approval that might assist us in addressing these serious problems? The NGO director, barely able to suppress a smile, answered that the NGO did indeed happen to have a proposal that might fit the ministry's needs. The proposal was submitted, and within a month (record time in this operating context) the proposal was approved for implementation.

In this situation the facts gathered by media and NGOs, and the pressures brought to bear by both groups (working out of different systems), assisted the in-country NGO in achieving its goals and objectives. Even though these organisations may disagree on some of the implementation methodologies and specific actions, they all agree on what they would like to see happen in the country over the long term. An example of this sort shows how, with effective use of information, players in one system, doing what they do naturally, help players working out of other systems. In this way an entire range of differing groups (media, NGOs, the opposition, and so on) can use their collective strengths to move forward concretely in furthering the common good.

PHILOSOPHICAL AND ETHICAL GUIDELINES

The complexity of working with the new world order amounts to a continuous balancing act. NGO managers must juggle many different variables, with an eye always fixed on the greater good. An additional challenge is the reality that defining the greater good is ambiguous. As a result, agreement on the actual map or pathway of steps by which we achieve the greater good is difficult to obtain. Furthermore, since the journey is long and much social infrastructure to support the process is lacking, a series of well-conceived baby steps is usually essential before the process can stand on its own and move forward in any significant way. Initially these baby steps may not appear to be going in the desired direction but in fact may be the necessary groundwork for creating a social infrastructure within which much can happen.

Within the puzzling complexity and clamouring voices of the sensitive context, it seems rather simplistic and beside the point to state philosophical and ethical guidelines. Generally they do not provide tools to assist in preventing mistakes, understanding the context and determining appropriate first steps. Instead they seem to set pie-in-the-sky standards without providing a bridge to the on-the-ground reality. This is a drawback. On the other hand, they do provide a starting point as well as a framework for discussion that can include the full range of stakeholders. This, in itself, is sufficient reason for us to articulate guidelines, and for implementers to attempt to engage them. It is likely the guidelines will change and evolve, but that process of evolution requires discussion and active participation of the key stakeholders. The dialogue must begin early. As long as the process of evolving the guidelines is positive and inclusive, then their purpose has been served.

Ideally, an organisation operating in a sensitive context will seek the following:

- Do no harm.
- Conduct a feasibility study as to the appropriateness of an intervention, and then if it is called for, develop a vision, mission statement, and long-term strategy.
- Monitor, closely control, and be accountable for organisational resources. (This entails the development of effective systems and periodic financial and programmatic audits).
- Develop additional or appropriate systems to reduce or eliminate loss through institutional means. Such means include the garnishing of monetary resources through artificial exchange rates, levying exorbitant transaction fees, "taxing" village people for services received, and so on.
- Share research and other studies as much as possible. Sharing information sends a clear message of transparency to all stakeholders.
- Along with setting accountability standards and monitoring procedures, share the systems and information freely and as much as possible.
- Strategy, policy and methodologies should all be clearly stated, with accompanying rationale for the directions and approaches chosen. This should all be in writing. Supporting documents and research should be available as needed. If an organisation can clearly present its programme plans along with a strong rationale, this inspires confidence that the organisation is doing its homework and that it has nothing to hide. If the organisation then manages to accomplish its stated strategy (within reason), this establishes confidence that will serve the organisation very well over the long run, regardless of whether all stakeholders agree with it or not.
- Have a clear policy regarding staff recruitment, needs, and training. Over time this particular area will demonstrate perhaps more than anything else the depth of understanding that the

organisation has of the context and the cultural milieu in which it is operating.

- Reports, studies, policies, and so forth should all demonstrate knowledge and understanding of the context. In this way all stakeholders will know that tough decisions and all strategic directions were developed out of a careful weighing and balancing of all the key factors. An organisation can appear to be naïve if it shows ignorance of cultural or contextual nuances as it strives to fulfil its corporate mandate within its own values system. This failing can undermine years of solid work. Organisations need to demonstrate the ability to manage complexity and still forge ahead.

Such guidelines are very specific to operational issues and it is hoped SMART (**S**imple, **M**easurable, **A**chievable, **R**eviewable, and **T**ime bounded). They are stated as black and white, however, which is a problem. Specific situations are never black and white. In most sensitive contexts the intervening organisation will not be able to stay absolutely true to all the standards all the time. The challenge is to maintain organisational integrity (in relation to these ideal guidelines) so that "on balance" programme interventions continue to serve the greater good. This is very hard. That is why I started with the extremely ambiguous "do no harm."

Knowing precisely what the common good is and how to "do no harm" in a given context are subjective and unclear. Furthermore, maintaining focus in a dynamic and fluid operational environment is extremely taxing and very difficult to sustain with any level of precision. To help support this effort, the following pointers may be helpful in the effort to keep the balance required to maintain a learning approach within programmes and organisation while working in a sensitive context:

- *Do the homework*. Make an effort to understand the background and the cultural, historical and social context. In this way decisions regarding the programme or the temporary relaxing of operational standards are based on as solid a knowledge base as possible. In today's world of rampant information, it is no longer acceptable to make mistakes out of ignorance. If the NGO has done its homework, still made a mistake, and then was able to catch it and correct it, that is acceptable and a reflection of how NGOs tend to work at their best. Guesswork has been minimised and impact maximised.

- *Seek macro-and-micro system links.* Linkages between policies levied by large institutions such as the World Bank, the UN, or the local government, and the actual on-the-ground implementation are essential. Too often we believe that "trickle-down" and other kinds of transfers of benefits from the policy level to the village reality are automatic. But the ground must be prepared for this to happen. Resources targeted for the village-level people in the programme must be made available to them. I know of one programme that was providing community rehabilitation services. Much of the work was simply making arrangements for the specialist doctors in the capital city to set aside one day each month to drive twenty miles to set up a day-long clinic. They did this day in and day out for years. Much of it was possible because the NGO provided the transportation. In general making these concrete connections between policy and people requires cooperation and coordination between the various stakeholders; awareness of the kinds of programmes and policies that tend to promote trickle-down; and continuous (often tediously repetitive) reminders that the purpose for being in the country is to help the village-level people throughout the country. When people are heatedly deliberating a policy issue, this reminder helps keep the discussion focussed in a constructive way.

- *Utilise the pre-existing informal mechanisms as well as formal ones.* In most top-down totalitarian contexts, there are too many issues being deliberated for the system to cope. Wide-ranging informal networks naturally develop. Often they arise among the assistants and aids of senior decision-makers. They also can arise through a collegial trust that can develop between organisational staff and local government administrators. This informal system is essential to the operation of totalitarian governments. It is completely appropriate for an outside organisation to utilise these informal networks while working the formal networks, as long as the organisation's integrity is not jeopardised through graft or under-the-table payments. An example is the application process for project approvals. The proper procedure in one country was to develop a proposal, answer some questions, and submit the package for the approval of the council, which met once a month. The NGO took all these steps. It also worked with its facilitator within the government to make sure he understood exactly what was requested and that there was no hidden threat. He then spoke to the assistants and support people of all the principals on the council. When the council met to deliberate the issue, approval was a foregone conclusion. But that approval was due to the correct management of the informal systems as well as the formal ones.

The key objective in this entire effort is to develop methodologies and approaches that go beyond rhetoric and begin to build practical mechanisms and systems that help village-level people to create their preferred reality. Humanitarian assistance can facilitate this by taking actions and designing interventions stimulating discussion and interaction that may ultimately lead to movement where previously there was none. My own opinion as to the most appropriate first steps for an intervening organisation is to facilitate the growth and effectiveness of the NGO's operational team, as well as the village people, so both can begin to develop decision-making skills and action steps that are specifically shaped to the context. Once the staff and project participants begin to use this behavioural model in their everyday lives, there will be enormous, even transformational changes. But until that time, substantial change will be hard to track or verify.

PRACTICAL GUIDELINES

We tend to think of restricted contexts as the same. Bad governments, run by bad people who do not care for the population with whose care they have been entrusted. Even if the situation were this simple, such an analysis is neither useful nor accurate. I believe every restricted context is different, so a "cookie cutter" instruction manual is useless. A case-by-case approach seems better suited to meeting this challenge. However, there are also some commonalities among sensitive situations that can serve as a starting point. Sensitive contexts tend to have high levels of mistrust, suspicion and even fear. We see it within the sensitive contexts themselves, that is, between government officials and local people, between the government in power and the opposition, and even among the people themselves. This can be crippling. It also can carry over very quickly to the intervening agencies themselves unless they are conscious of this mistrust and include it in their calculations. NGOs are noted for their independent thinking and operations; the climate of mistrust adds fuel to this highly competitive fire. It is important for all intervening agencies to be aware of the danger of arrogance and superiority in these contexts. Listed below are just a few of the elements of the mistrust that typically develop among concerned agencies:

- Lack of agreement on the long-term objectives for the country.
- Lack of agreement on approach to the target country.
- Lack of agreement about what can be accomplished.
- Extreme polarization; that is, various stakeholders do not even acknowledge the legitimacy of others' existence.
- Intense scrutiny of every action.
- Politicization of every activity, particularly humanitarian assistance. Embargoes and other policy responses often muddy the situation without actually helping the warring parties to resolve their differences. This kind of response can seem more like a way for observing governments to say they are angry about a situation. But it tends not to be constructive, because it draws the focus away from the constructive act of resolving differences. The only way it can be constructive over the short- or mid-range term is if the embargoed countries are so upset by the imposition of the embargo that they are driven to do something about it, but this does not typically happen.
- Rumours. In a restrictive context all formal modes of distributing information domestically are controlled by the de facto government. Consequently, there is very poor access to information. Rampant rumour mills are typical of sensitive contexts as they are the only sources of information. However, there is no way of knowing the quality of information. Also, repressive governments can start and fuel rumours as part of their information distribution system. Consequently, rumour mills can be tools to divide communities in sensitive contexts. In such circumstances, they can be extremely destructive and must be treated with care.

Once the seed of mistrust has taken root among NGOs, it is very easy to justify. "We are trying to save lives." "Because they are supporting the regime (or because they are supporting the opposition), we don't have to protect them. We can talk behind their back." "They have attacked us; it is perfectly okay for us to attack back." The in-country situation of backbiting and mistrust can escalate with amazing rapidity. This is extremely dangerous. Once trust has been lost among the various intervening agencies, other stakeholders can discount the credibility of all these agencies. The people in powerful positions (government officials, donors, media people, and so on) can play the agencies off against one another. When this happens a vicious circle begins and the intervening agencies lose their ability, collectively, to promote change through example. And it is extremely important that intervening agencies set positive examples. Cooperation and coordination are key to this. One way to begin this positive process and create a "virtuous circle" is to attempt to implement a systems-thinking approach in a challenging context. This shifts the paradigm from a black-and-white labelling of agencies as "good guys" and "bad guys," to the bottom-line acknowledgement that *all* agencies are operating in a complex context, *all* seeking to serve the common good, and therefore *all* in this together. Rather than define the challenge as how to take action when there is so much disagreement among the players and stakeholders, it is better to focus on how to adopt a constructive, systems approach in an environment that is seemingly hostile and unfriendly. One effective way to begin is to seek common ground.

As each agency, including NGOs, conducts its own feasibility studies and begins to implement its own carefully conceived strategies, there are some guidelines and attitudes that are highly compatible with systems thinking and will greatly enhance prospects for success – both organisational and collective:

- *Transparency.* It is not commonly discussed, but when an agency establishes itself in a restricted context, its presence, its way of working and who it is take on a meaning greater than is intended or even suspected. Like it or not, the agency becomes a symbol – to all sides. The result is that anything the agency does is reported and interpreted by all sides of the issues. Anything written will probably get back to the authorities, so it is important not to write anything that is intentionally inflammatory.

But publish studies, findings and projects to make them clear to all. In this way rumours will have less impact. It is important to influence the rumour mill positively. Publications, efforts to coordinate and cooperate, efforts to understand the cultural and social situation, and an open attitude are all ways to develop a reputation that inspires trust among all the stakeholders. In contexts with a large number of stakeholders, trust is key. Perceived transparency by all stakeholders is how trust is built.

- *Trailblazing.* The first NGOs in the country make arrangements and agreements for their programmes and operations. These arrangements often become the standard for all NGOs that follow. It is important that the early NGOs are aware that they are negotiating for an entire industry and not just for themselves.

- *"Angels."* It is extremely helpful to have someone in the government who is willing to stand up for the idea of NGOs in general and/or for a specific NGO. This is a risky course for that individual, as well as for the organisation. If the person should fall out of favour, or if the organisation does something that is not approved by the de facto government, the safety of the angel may be jeopardised. Angels can take a variety of forms and be on several levels of the government structure. They may not be people with whom members of the NGO are socially friendly. Instead, the relationship may be on the basis of an unspoken mutual respect for what each is doing. In my experience, there were several angels who positively influenced the progress of our organisation. I have a high regard for all of them, even though we often disagreed on specifics.

- *National staff.* National staff are essential both for capacity building and insights about how programme efforts can and should be appropriately contextualised. Because the expatriate is the expert in how the international community scrutinises things, he or she is necessary to establish and maintain connections between the local and international contexts. The national staff are experts on how to operate within their own country. Both are necessary. At first it may feel awkward for both, but sooner or later the nationals and the expatriate will see that this position of equal or shared footing is developmental. There may be an initial loss of respect from the staff to the expatriate leader because the leader is not behaving in the expected manner. There may be a year or two before members of the team realise the significance of this approach to management. To maintain the model in the face of adversity takes courage and strength on the part of the leader.

- *An objective outside observer.* It is hard to maintain perspective, so it is useful to have an objective observer outside of the fray, perhaps even outside of the country, who is not swayed by the day-to-day concerns and emotions and whose judgement is trustworthy.
- *A win-win approach.* This is hard in our conventional competitive setting and in an environment of limited funding sources, but it must be done. It only takes a critical mass of agencies to work; not everyone needs to buy in right away.
- *Deep pockets.* Don't commit with the expectation that other sources of funding will automatically follow. The entering organisation has to be prepared, in the worst case scenario, to establish a track record of effective programmes on the ground. I have seen many fail. I have seen it take years for organisations that ultimately are successful.

I have a few closing thoughts and comments for this section on practical guidelines. Staff development is key. In any restrictive context in which the majority of people have been isolated from the outside world for more than a generation, it is essential to promote staff development and training. The obvious reasons for this are that the isolation has forced all members of the society to fall behind the pace of the world. They do not have access to the latest thinking or the latest materials and equipment. If a select few do gain access, they need to be trained in understanding the nuances as well as the basic operation. Development agencies can give all sorts of examples for why this is absolutely essential. Hydrologists who find water are not thought of as scientists; instead, they are seen as very powerful witch doctors. Or latrines are left unused and pristine because they must be kept perfect for visiting VIPs. Training staff in background, contextual understanding, and values implications is as important as "how to" training that teaches an individual how to run something.

Also, cultural differences between the local staff of a restrictive context and the expatriate are usually so vast that it is impossible for the expatriate to adjust to the new environment without guidance. This means that both the expatriate and the national staff will wonder about each other. The expatriate may find the nationals, for example the women, to be too shy and retiring – to the point of ineffectiveness. The national staff may believe the expatriate is too loud and demanding. They may find that the expatriate does not understand obvious non-verbal signals. The bottom line is the expatriate needs the guidance of the national staff to function appropriately within the culture of the restrictive context. Likewise, the national staff need the expatriate in order to understand the international context from which the assistance is coming. Each party needs the other. And each party is in a position to help the other. I believe it is imperative that the relationship between the expatriate starting a programme in a restrictive context and the in-country national staff that have been hired to help must be based on acknowledging this mutual need and using this acknowledgement to build mutual trust and respect. Two-way sharing of information engenders trust and makes transformation possible for all participants. In this way the first meaningful steps are taken towards enabling the clamouring voices of an intractable and restrictive context to become harmonious.

NOTES

[1] Deborah Spar, "Foreign Investment and Human Rights," *Challenge* 42/1 (January/February 1999), 56.

[2] Willaim E. Halal and Richard J. Varey, "Recognizing the Emerging Third Way," *Christian Science Monitor* (3 February 1999), 9.

5.

Searching for the Lesser Evil

Operationalising Do No Harm

ABIKÖK C. RIAK

> *[Humanitarian agencies] have not worked out what it means*
> *to be neutral in a conflict yet in solidarity with all its victims.*
> —Ian Levine, "Promoting Humanitarian Principles"

On 1 March 2000 the World Vision Sudan (WV Sudan) programme issued a statement to the effect that it was ceasing all project activities and pulling out of Sudan People's Liberation Army/Movement (SPLA or SPLM)–administered areas of southern Sudan. Unable to sign a Memorandum of Understanding (MOU) issued by the humanitarian wing of the SPLM, the Sudan Relief and Rehabilitation Association (SRRA), WV Sudan complied with the order to leave SPLM-administered areas. In the statement it was noted that "concerns about the current draft of the MOU include the requirement to work 'in accordance with SRRA objectives' rather than based solely on humanitarian principles; the right of the Sudanese to receive aid in an impartial manner; our ability to target aid according to the greatest need; and clauses that could reduce individual NGOs' ability to guarantee the safety of their staff."[1]

All NGOs operational under the United Nations (UN) umbrella, Operation Lifeline Sudan (OLS), raised concerns with the content.

The views in this chapter are those of the author alone. They do not necessarily reflect the views of World Vision Sudan or World Vision International.

However, of the approximately 40 international OLS agencies, 13 did not sign. The agencies that chose not to sign the document had different reasons for doing so. For some, the main issue revolved around the significance of signing a bilateral agreement with a non-state entity; for others, it was the restrictions placed on access to beneficiaries. The main breaking points for WV Sudan revolved around maintaining neutrality and impartiality and guaranteed security for staff. It is estimated that 75 per cent of the aid provided to southern Sudan was withdrawn in March 2000 – an estimated total of over US$31 million. In effect, this decision meant that over 1.6 million people in southern Sudan would lose their access to basic services such as healthcare, clean water and food.

WV Sudan's budget for fiscal year 1999 was over US$16 million. In the areas where WV Sudan was operational, the withdrawal meant the end of a 6,000 metric tonne (mt) food programme aimed at improving the ever fragile household food security situation in Sudan. In Yambio county WV Sudan was the sole supporter of primary health care services. For the communities of Tonj, where there were fewer than 600 functioning boreholes in an area with a population of over 200,000, this meant removing the newly acquired mechanised drilling rig that had been in Tonj for less than six weeks.

We left behind people. Not nameless, faceless generic beneficiaries, but people. People with names, faces and lives more marginal than yours or mine. In Yambio, over 400 local staff lost their main source of income. In a region where WV Sudan was the largest employer and where stability has been the norm for the past seven years and where families have been able to send their children across the border into Uganda for school, WV Sudan's withdrawal has had serious multiplier effects that will ripple through the Yambio economy for years to come.

And yet, WV Sudan made the decision to leave SPLM-administered areas. As we dissect the months leading up to the final decision not to sign the MOU, it becomes clear that there is no easy or clear-cut way to categorise the discussions or the outcomes. The decision, though presented in a brief (667 word) statement, was not easy to make; it was not made overnight, nor was it made by one person or even the Sudan programme on its own. Rather, the decision-making process was lengthy and included the advice of many people both at the field and the partnership levels.

This chapter attempts to shed some light on the process that went into making the decision not to sign the MOU, as it relates to WV Sudan's involvement with the Local Capacities for Peace *(Do No Harm)* project. First, we will analyze the operational environment in southern Sudan leading up to and reinforcing the decision not to sign. Second, we will examine the *Do No Harm* project in Sudan and explore if and how it influenced the discussion. We will look at the struggles that surrounded the decision to pull out in light of the *Do No Harm* implications and the humanitarian impact of such a decision. Some time will be spent analyzing the MOU through a *Do No Harm* lens. In conclusion, we will assess the implications of this decision on the future of World Vision in Sudan.

THE SOUTHERN SUDAN CONTEXT

The Sudan has been at war with itself for the greater part of 50 years. Independence from Britain in 1956 soon disintegrated as the ethnic and political divide provoked a crisis leading to civil war that lasted until 1972, when the Addis Ababa agreement was signed giving the south some degree of autonomy. Peace lasted until 1983, when the government in the north instituted *sharia* law, even though most southerners were not Muslim. The institution of *sharia* law led to a mutiny in the southern armies and the formation of the SPLM under the leadership of John Garang, a member of the Dinka tribe, the largest in southern Sudan.

Even from the beginning there was discord in the movement over whether the southerners were fighting for a united, secular Sudan or for self-determination and secession for the south. Not surprisingly, many of these differences were delineated along ethnic lines. In 1991, the SPLM inevitably split and a group of commanders formed the Nassir Faction, which later became SPLM United.[2] Riek Machar, a Nuer, left SPLM United to form the Southern Sudan Independence Movement, initially advocating for self-determination and secession from the south. The Southern Sudan Independence Movement is predominantly a Nuer faction. Lam Akol was left as the leader of SPLM United, which after the split was made up primarily of the Shilluk people. Both the Southern Sudan Independence Movement and SPLM United signed a peace agreement with the Khartoum government in 1997. In recent years much of the fighting in the south has been between different southern factions and rival groups.

Southern Sudan remains one of the most isolated and least developed regions in Africa. The combination of war, drought, floods, crop failure and historical lack of attention to the south has ensured that essential services in most parts of the south are virtually non-existent. In most areas populations are forced to the brink of collapse as traditional coping mechanisms have all but disappeared. Large-scale displacement of people occurs regularly. The UN and NGOs operating in southern Sudan estimate that 1.2 million southern Sudanese have died due to war, malnutrition and neglect, and that over 4 million people have been displaced over the history of the conflict. Approximately 2 million displaced people occupy camps and shanty communities around the nation's capital in Khartoum.

WORLD VISION, OPERATION LIFELINE SUDAN AND THE MOU

World Vision is a founding member of OLS, a consortium of agencies, both international and indigenous, led by UNICEF, that implements a wide variety of humanitarian activities in southern Sudan. There are also agencies that operate in southern Sudan outside of the consortium. When OLS was established in 1989, a tri-partite agreement was signed between the Government of Sudan, SPLM and UNICEF. The agreement's main purpose was to secure guaranteed humanitarian access to vulnerable populations across the entire Sudan. The UN essentially was the guarantor for OLS member agencies and, as such, OLS NGOs did not actually sign the agreement. Pursuant to the tri-partite agreement, NGOs who are members of the consortium must sign annual cooperative agreements with UNICEF.

In 1994, OLS signed a second agreement with the SPLM, referred to as the ground rules, which details the responsibilities of the SPLM with respect to humanitarian organisations, as well as laying out rules of engagement for NGOs with the SRRA/SPLM. Both the tri-partite agreement and the ground rules were considered adequate to secure humanitarian access for vulnerable populations and describe the responsibilities for all stakeholders. In reality, the Government of Sudan exercises control over the access to southern populations and must approve locations for flight clearance each month. Many areas such as the Nuba Mountains have never received clearance. This has always been a legitimate bone of contention for the SPLM and other southern movements. Many NGOs have begun to question their membership in OLS, given their decreased ability to negotiate access.[3] Several years ago the SRRA began discussions with partners about establishing project agreements with NGOs regarding their operations in the south so as to regulate NGO operations within the areas they control.

These discussions were formalised in early 1998 when the SRRA announced that it wanted to establish a memorandum of understanding (MOU) with each NGO operating in SPLM-occupied areas, including indigenous organisations. The movement has always seen OLS as the UN and the NGOs as separate entities and therefore wanted a separate agreement with them. In principle, agencies approved of an MOU, and so negotiations on the document began and a draft was produced by early 1999. Following additional negotiations, the SRRA issued an ultimatum in March 1999 that all NGOs must sign the MOU or else leave SPLM areas of administration. Following discussions among the SRRA, the UN, donors and NGOs the deadline was dropped and another round of negotiations ensued over the many inclusions in the original drafts that confused understanding among partners, given the existence of the tri-partite agreement and the ground rules. Negotiations continued and for the most part, by August 1999, there was a general sense that, with the exception of a few minor points, the agencies were ready to sign the MOU.

In August 1999 another draft of the MOU was circulated and OLS NGOs produced a list of 19 concerns over its content of the MOU. Unfortunately, these points of concern were never presented formally to the movement. Instead, what was presented was another version of the MOU called a letter of understanding. This further polarised negotiations because the letter of understanding was very different from the MOU, although equally one-sided, as the MOU was seen to be. Not surprisingly, the movement interpreted the letter of understanding as a breech of faith and the already slow negotiations grounded to a halt.

Both the MOU and the letter of understanding were presented to the highest legislative body in SPLM-held areas of southern Sudan, the National Liberation Council at the end of the year. The National

Liberation Council endorsed the MOU as the desired agreement
with NGOs. The National Liberation Council mandated the SRRA
to have all NGOs sign the document by the end of February 2000.
This was followed by a second ultimatum issued by the SRRA in
January that all NGOs must sign the August 1999 version of the
MOU or leave the country. After intense discussions and debates,
WV Sudan made the decision not to sign the MOU but to remain
in SPLM areas. After veiled threats that the movement would not
be able to guarantee the safety of World Vision staff and that World
Vision staff in Sudan would be handed over to the army for being
in SPLM held areas "illegally," the decision was made to evacuate
all staff and most assets.

At the time of writing, the movement is insisting that NGOs that
did not sign the MOU by the March 1 deadline must make a formal application to the SRRA and sign the original MOU before
anything is negotiated. In May 2000 several of the larger NGOs
which had chosen initially to not sign made an application to the
movement to re-enter Sudan and sign the MOU. By the end of
2000 eight of the original 13 had chosen to sign the MOU. World
Vision will continue to maintain its position that as the MOU stands
and without a clear process of revision, World Vision cannot sign it
and therefore chooses to not work in SPLM-administered areas.

Before the March 1 withdrawal, WV Sudan was operating only
in areas of southern Sudan controlled by the SPLA. WV Sudan was
also operational in areas of northern Sudan until 1988, when it
was expelled by the Government of Sudan along with several other
Christian relief-and-development agencies. In the past WV Sudan
has also worked in areas controlled by what was then known as
the Southern Sudan Independence Army, in collaboration with the
Relief Association of Southern Sudan, the humanitarian wing of
the Southern Sudan Independence Army. WV Sudan ceased this
collaboration several years ago because of insecurity and logistical
difficulties.

World Vision had been implementing health, water, agriculture
and social development programmes in Tonj County in Bahr el
Ghazal province and Yambio County in Western Equatoria since
1993. In 1996 WV Sudan began work in Gogrial County, which
is also in Bahr el Ghazal. In these areas WV Sudan worked with
the SRRA, which was formed in 1989 as the humanitarian wing
of the SPLM with the main task of co-ordination of relief-and-

rehabilitation activities with all NGOs working in SPLM areas. When the SPLM split in 1991, other factions of the southern rebel movements also established humanitarian organisations to work with NGOs.

SRRA's importance grew enormously after the inception of OLS, during which the SRRA was given the responsibility to facilitate and co-ordinate all aid in SPLM areas, in part as the result of do-nor and aid-agency pressure. Through its relationship with OLS, SRRA has a virtual monopoly on contacts with aid agencies and is the conduit for most resource movements into southern Sudan. In 1994 a civil structure was set up to be distinct from the SRRA. However, most co-ordination of relief-and-rehabilitation activities with NGOs is managed through the SRRA.

WV SUDAN'S INVOLVEMENT
WITH THE LOCAL CAPACITIES FOR PEACE PROJECT[4]

In the mid-1990s the Local Capacities for Peace Project (LCPP) was launched to investigate the relationship between aid and conflict. The project is a collaborative effort involving international (including CARE, Catholic Relief Services, International Federation of the Red Cross, Norwegian Church Aid, Oxfam Quebec and Oxfam US) and local NGOs. UN agencies, and European and American donor agencies (USAID, Canadian International Development Agency, Swedish International Development Cooperation Agency). Spearheaded by Mary Anderson of the Collaborative for Development Action, the LCPP set out to answer the following question: *How can humanitarian or development assistance be provided in conflict situations in ways that, rather than feeding into and exacerbating the conflict, help local people to disengage and establish alternative systems for dealing with the problems that underlie the conflict?*

The LCPP is based on the premise that when international assistance is given in the context of conflict, it not only becomes part of the conflict but also has the potential to feed into and exacerbate the conflict – even when it is effective in doing what it is intended to do. The project has also noted that aid has the potential to strengthen those connectors that can bring people together and reduce conflict. Lessons learned from the field experiences of aid

providers working in conflict situations around the world were compiled into a book and a field manual, both written by Mary Anderson.[5] Over time, the project has come to also be called the *Do No
Harm* project.

The *Do No Harm* process is iterative, involving continual reas-
sessment of the context of conflict and the way that aid affects that
conflict. It begins with an analysis of the conflict environment and
looks at the historic, current and future roles, capacities and agendas of groups in conflict, historically and potentially. During this
process, aid workers (assisted by external facilitators) identify the
dividers (or *tensions*) or *capacities for war* (for example, different
values and interests, the apparatus of war propaganda, systems of
discrimination) that separate groups in conflict and the *connectors*
or *capacities for peace* (for example, common history, language
and experience; shared infrastructure and markets) that bring them
together. The dividers and connectors are ranked according to those
that are in an agency's sphere of concern and others that are in its
sphere of influence. The focus of the conflict analysis is on local
dynamics – to understand how power is exercised at the local level
and by whom.

The different components of an aid project are analyzed in relation to different manifestations of the conflict. For example, how
does the methodology used to target food distributions feed into
intergroup tensions? More specifically, how would an agency provide services to internally displaced persons in a location where
they are hosted by a community that has had historic and deep-
rooted tensions with these same people? How does the hiring of
one ethnic group in an ethnically diverse yet divided community
feed into tensions? Through this qualitative analysis an agency is
better able to design programme alternatives that decrease negative impacts on tensions and, if possible, strengthen connectors. A
thorough *Do No Harm* analysis requires a keen understanding of
the operational environment in which an aid agency works. As
would be expected, this environment is dynamic and needs to be
continually reassessed.

The *Do No Harm* project has identified two mechanisms through
which aid can affect conflict, both negatively and positively: transfer of resources and implicit ethical messages. The term *transfer of
resources* refers to the economic dimension of aid. All aid
programmes involve the transfer of resources that can feed into,

prolong and worsen conflict. Resources refer to both tangible goods such as food and blankets, and intangible services such as training. A negative transfer of resources could include the theft or diversion of aid resources to directly or indirectly support the war effort. Aid can support a war economy as opposed to a peace one. For example, direct or indirect taxation of relief goods and services decreases the incentive for a non-war economy.

Implicit ethical messages refer to the more subtle messages that can be delivered along with the food and other resources. What is the general attitude of aid workers? How do they work with local authorities without showing belligerence and tension? How do they use project resources and manage other situations where they have power? The links between implicit ethical messages and conflict are less direct than the links between transfers of resources and conflict, but they have been identified by aid workers as important in understanding the role that aid agencies play in conflict settings.

LESSONS LEARNED
FROM THE SUDAN EXPERIENCE WITH *DO NO HARM*

In February 1998 WV Sudan, in partnership with WV Canada, joined the *Do No Harm* project to investigate the effects of its aid programme on the conflicts in southern Sudan and to demonstrate how the field-based lessons learned through the project could be used to improve the design and implementation of WV Sudan aid programmes. In the past two and a half years, through our involvement with the *Do No Harm* project, we have learned much about the impact of our aid on the conflict in Sudan and the specific mechanisms through which our aid has affected the conflict. We have learned how to analyze these impacts systematically and develop programming options to minimise negative effects and support positive ones.

In the past few years of working with the *Do No Harm* project and analyzing the impact of our projects on the conflicts in our areas of operation, three main issues have been identified repeatedly: the North-South war, ethnic tensions, and problems of governance and lack of representative civil structures. Of the three, ethnic tensions has been identified as the one with the most potential for future violent conflict in southern Sudan, especially in the advent of a peace agreement between the north and the south. Questions that we continually ask ourselves include: Is our aid equipping the different southern factions to fight each other? Is our aid reinforcing intergroup tensions between, for example, the Dinka, who dominate the SPLA/SRRA, and other groups in southern Sudan?

Carrying out a detailed conflict analysis in the areas where WV Sudan was operational deepened staff understanding of the complexity of the conflicts in Sudan and our role in them. Before using the *Do No Harm* framework intentionally in programming, World Vision staff members were inclined to fall into the trap of thinking of the war in Sudan as between the north and the south and to think of the south as one unified whole, collectively referred to as "the community" in our project proposals. From the information generated during the *Do No Harm* analysis, we were able to develop a better understanding of the tensions that existed among the army, the SRRA and the civil structure, and how our aid could feed that conflict. The team learned that the conflicts in southern Sudan were not just inter-ethnic (for example, between the Dinka and Nuer) but also intra-ethnic (for example, among the different sections of the Dinka tribe). When the WV Tonj team was leaving the town of Thiet in late February, its members were approached by some community members who told them that they were "from a different section of the Dinka tribe than the SPLM" and that they would protect World Vision staff if they wanted to stay and continue working.

The analysis has also helped the team through the process of understanding that the delivery of aid is more than just a logistical exercise. An agency with a strong Christian identity, working on one side of a war that is often over-simplified into a north-south, Arab-African, Muslim-Christian war, could be perceived as supporting one side of the war – the Christian side. It has been suggested that the best way for a Christian agency to demonstrate neutrality and impartiality in a war with a religious dimension, such as in Sudan, is to be present on as many sides of the war as possible, working to reduce the suffering of all victims.

This realization has helped us rethink our advocacy position on the war in Sudan, and it has helped us examine the dynamics of our relationship with all parties and stakeholders in the conflict. It became increasingly important for WV Sudan to present itself as not supporting any of the *parties* to the conflict but being present to support the *victims* of the conflict. It also became important for the programme team to diversify our funding base. Our heavy reliance on US government funding helped to fuel perceptions that WV Sudan was an American organisation that supported the US government position on the conflict in Sudan.

Lessons learned from LCPP implementation around the world have shown that when local authorities such as the SRRA insist on having control over agency hiring, they can control the benefits to be gained from employment. This, in turn, can increase the power of those local authorities. This is potentially quite damaging in southern Sudan because of the existing tensions among army, the local authorities (SRRA) and the civil structure. After the initial LCPP analysis of WV Sudan programmes in Yambio, it became evident that WV Sudan had hired entire families of SRRA supporters. In a process that took several months to work out, the recruitment pool in Yambio was broadened to include input from civil society structures such as the churches.

In Yambio county many of our local staff, once trained and equipped with transferable skills, would be conscripted and sent to the front line. In response, we began to train, for example, female mechanics who at the time of WV Sudan's withdrawal had not been drafted by the movement. In Tonj we made several changes to our food distribution methodology to take into consideration the needs of communities hosting internally displaced persons.

World Vision's size allowed us to achieve incredible impact but at the same time left us incredibly vulnerable to manipulation. WV Sudan's high level of funding (US$16 million; over 80 per cent from the United States), the significant size of the food programme (6,000 mt), the large number of vehicles (over 25), the intended "beneficiaries" (400,000 plus), and staff, both expatriate (over 100) and national (over 600), meant that WV Sudan has had to be extremely careful in understanding the ways that its projects could feed negatively into the conflict. For many agencies the size of their programmes or the value of the goods and services they provide will influence the degree of negative impact on conflict. For example, an agency with only one expatriate in a particular location, providing teacher training services to approximately 200 people, will have a relatively small negative impact on conflict. Likewise, the impact of signing the MOU for some of the smaller OLS agencies was quite different from the effects for the larger ones such as WV Sudan.

DO NO HARM ANALYSIS OF THE MOU

How instrumental was the use of *Do No Harm* framework and the resultant analysis in helping us make the decision not to sign the MOU?

The MOU is almost a perfect case study for *Do No Harm* because it affects all the components of a relief or development project (organisational mandate, identity and policies of the implementing agency, location and timing of programme activities, hiring and payment of expatriate and national staff, ways of working with local authorities and communities, use of vehicles) which could, in turn, influence how WV Sudan and its specific projects interact with the identified dividers and connectors in communities. Clearly, the MOU cannot be analyzed in a vacuum; it needs to be examined in relation to the context into which it was introduced.

When we look at the MOU in the context of southern Sudan and through a *Do No Harm* lens, there are several significant issues that could compel an agency not to sign it. The preamble of the MOU includes a statement that all signatories commit themselves to operate in accordance with "SRRA objectives." As the humanitarian wing of a military movement, the SRRA has a range of objectives, both humanitarian and military. To agree to work under SRRA objectives is to become aligned with one of the many parties to a conflict; it is to agree to the partiality of aid.

Many of the *Do No Harm* lessons learned from around the world have demonstrated that one of the ways that aid can contribute negatively to conflict is through the use of NGO resources for military objectives. Within the MOU there are several references to the use of NGO resources by "local authorities." In the context of southern Sudan it is almost impossible to separate "local authorities" from the military. Article 4.7 notes that agencies may provide assistance to "SRRA staff" and that "it may also allow the same staff to use its communication and/or transportation facilities . . . for security issues related to the NGO." The article goes on to note that an agency "may also endeavour to make available its knowledge, experience and resources to the local counterpart, especially in an emergency or disaster situation." What constitutes a security issue or an emergency or a disaster is not defined and therefore subject to interpretation. Experience indicates that this ambiguity could also lead to abuse.

There are several references in the MOU to NGOs paying "fees for services" to the SRRA. Article 6.9 notes that "the principle of a payment of a reasonable fee for service has been agreed to between the parties." But neither the fees nor the services are outlined. Article 6.9b elaborates somewhat and makes note of "fees for the maintenance of a register of NGO vehicles [and] equipment such as radio communication sets, telephones, faxes and professional staff." As noted above, there is no reference to the amount that NGOs should pay to the SRRA for the service of maintaining a register of NGO equipment.

On numerous occasions in early 2000 WV Sudan operations were halted by local authorities who informed field staff that all vehicles needed to be registered at the rate of between US$500 to US$1000 per vehicle, depending on which location the vehicle was in. The amount that World Vision would have had to pay at the time amounts to over US$20,000. In August 2000 the SPLM issued a tax schedule for the New Sudan. Given the size of WV Sudan activities in March 2000, WV Sudan would have had to pay almost US$100,000 directly to the SRRA for various fees and services including work permits for expatriates, vehicle registration, driving licenses, and registration of radios and satellite phones. The question is not whether vehicle registration or airstrip maintenance is a service or whether NGOs should pay for such services. The question is: In the context of southern Sudan, where will this US$100,000 go? If past experience is anything to go by, we can be pretty sure that not much if any will actually find its way back to the community.

Article 10.1 states that "any person(s) employed as a counterpart staff by the NGO shall be paid pecuniary incentives as shall be determined by SRRA Head Office and the NGO." As with the fees for services, there is no indication which positions should be paid or how much. In a memo from the SRRA dated November 1999, a salary scale for Sudanese staff is outlined, noting that those with a university degree should receive US$2,000 a month. It is not clear in the MOU whether the salary scale outlined in the memo or another one will be the basis for the payment of Sudanese staff. The MOU also states in article 4.6 that hiring of Sudanese staff needs to be done in "close cooperation with the SRRA" and that "clearance for the employment of Sudanese staff can only be withheld by SRRA . . . for reasons adverse to public interest."

The problem here is not that the SRRA is suggesting an unrealistic salary scale, but rather that NGOs that agree to the above articles cannot guarantee who defines the "public interest." From our experience in Yambio, where there were the largest concentrations of WV Sudan local staff, we know the negative impact of hiring through the SRRA. Another LCPP concern would be the market effects of such a salary scale based on a war economy. The challenge for NGOs operating in southern Sudan is to think through the different ways that they can work with the SRRA to support its civilian functions rather than its military ones.

There are several references throughout the MOU to NGOs and their staff being held responsible to abide by "generally recognized laws" (articles 5.11, 6.4 and 6.9c) as separate from international humanitarian law. Though it is clearly documented what international humanitarian law is, there is no documented body of "generally recognised laws" in SPLM-administered areas. Does the term refer to Dinka traditional laws or Zande ones or a combination of the two? This ambiguity leaves agencies and their staff open to manipulation.

In late March 2000 the *Do No Harm* partner agencies (including CARE, Catholic Relief Services, International Federation of the Red Cross, Oxfam Quebec and Oxfam US; donors represented included Canadian International Development Agency, Danish Agency for Development Assistance and USAID) met in Cambridge, Massachusetts (USA), to discuss the MOU. After looking at the Do No Harm implications of signing or not signing the document, the group then looked at possible options for re-engagement with the movement. Two options were developed. The first was to sign the document as a demonstration of good faith but not to return to areas of operation until the document was negotiated and changed. The other option was to not sign but to continue to be involved in the discussion and lobby for amendments to the MOU. We had chosen the latter.

The backlash against World Vision was quick and harsh. WV Sudan was harshly criticised by the Christian Right in the United States, which stated quite vociferously that in the decision to withdraw WV Sudan was more interested in political neutrality than helping the suffering.[6] Many of the NGOs that signed the MOU have commented that World Vision's decision not to sign was prideful. World Vision has been described as arrogant and inflexible. Perceptions of World Vision's inflexibility have been likened to our stepping up on the humanitarian-principles soap box, only to find that there is no way to get down and still save face. Others have stated quite clearly that the MOU operationalised the status quo in southern Sudan and that not signing, while holding up the banner of neutrality and impartiality, was profoundly hypocritical.

In a similar vein, not signing was interpreted by the movement as a lack of commitment to the south and, more explicitly, to the cause of the south and the people of the south. Others have remarked that the MOU is only a piece of paper, a paper similar to others that World Vision has not had problems signing with more repressive and authoritarian regimes, "legitimate" or otherwise. Within the World Vision partnership, many argued that as a Christian agency, people must always come before principles; in reality, at least in the short term, principles don't save lives.

Those who support the WV Sudan decision are in the minority. Some of our European and Australian colleagues have lauded WV Sudan for making the decision, noting that signing would have compromised humanitarian principles and a commitment to humanity, that to sign would be a tacit approval of past aid abuses and would set the stage for other non-state entities to make similar demands on humanitarian agencies. Signing the MOU would represent political recognition and legitimacy of armed opposition movements. For others, it was believed that signing would not be in the interests of current and future beneficiaries because the document could reduce NGO access to beneficiaries. Some southern Sudanese, though not pleased with the overall situation, were anxious for agencies to move into some of the more remote and less accessible areas of southern Sudan and saw the expulsion of agencies from SPLM areas as an opportunity for this to happen.

TO SIGN OR NOT TO SIGN – DOES IT REALLY MATTER?

In many of the debates over why we chose not to sign, questions of legitimization arose. Would signing the document be tacit legitimization of a non-state entity, of an armed opposition group? In theory, WV Sudan did not have a problem with signing a MOU with the SRRA, the humanitarian wing of a military movement. We acknowledged that it would legitimise the SRRA's military objectives, but we also recognised that there are few other ways to access the population. In reality, a rebel movement today is a legitimate government tomorrow. And, in all honesty, who is World Vision to determine whether a government is legitimate or not? That should be the role of the Sudanese people. In fact, I would argue that a MOU is a good idea; that is, that it has the potential to be an instrument of accountability and better aid provision.

Within the document there are references to beginning project design in the field (article 3.1f) as a way of facilitating better co-ordination and more transparency among agencies. This would reduce duplication of services and lead to a broader range of services available throughout the south. Currently, there are "pockets of aid" because security concerns and issues of accessibility lead agencies to congregate in certain areas but not in others. The MOU sets out regular reporting guidelines (article 5.4) and inclusion of SRRA staff in project evaluations (article 6.1). Both would increase transparency.

The MOU also makes reference to the importance of hiring qualified southern Sudanese staff where possible (article 5.11). The lack of Sudanese project staff in decision-making positions in most international NGOs has been problematic for the Sudanese community, both in and out of Sudan. Most of the Sudanese staff with WV Sudan were based in the field as relief and commodity officers. There was only one Sudanese on the 19–member management team composed of Nairobi-based programme co-ordinators,[7] field-based project managers and Nairobi support (administration, finance and human resources). There is a widespread perception among the Sudanese community in Nairobi that WV Sudan was not interested in building the capacity of indigenous staff to manage programmes.

But even with all of the potential that a MOU could have in normalizing and regulating NGO operations in southern Sudan, the fact remains that the MOU that was presented for NGOs to sign was an incomplete document, reflective of a flawed negotiation process. The MOU was a symptom of a greater illness that plagued the relationship between the movement and the NGOs operating in SPLM-held areas and clearly meant different things to different parties. Therefore, signing or not signing was interpreted differently, making the possibility to renegotiate even more difficult. Much of the language in the August 1999 consolidated MOU text is ambiguous and interpretations varied.

Most southerners who were aware of the MOU, whether linked to the movement or not, saw the MOU as a symbol of southern independence and self-determination. NGOs who did not sign were perceived as not respecting the "laws of the land" and those that govern the land. There was a definite sense within the movement that the NGOs were operating without any rules or regulations and a general lack of transparency. Likewise, the NGOs saw that the movement was manipulating aid resources for its military objectives and personal gain. Given the general friction that in many ways defined the relationship between the movement and the NGOs, and was reinforced with poor negotiations and minimum respect, it is not surprising that the situation became as antagonistic as it did and that negotiations ended in an impassioned deadlock.

In the context of southern Sudan, in the harsh reality of aid diversion, the MOU is not just a piece of paper. As it stands, it is an instrument to regulate, control and possibly divert resources entering SPLM-administered areas of southern Sudan. It is an instrument to institutionalise and legitimise many of the abuses that routinely take place and are all too often ignored. Even with the guarantees that assets left on the ground would be safeguarded, was it any surprise when World Vision discovered that supplies (including food) left under SRRA control in late February disappeared and others were distributed to "non-targeted beneficiaries"? Keep in mind that the value of the resources in question was over US$1.2 million!

WHAT ABOUT THE HUMANITARIAN IMPERATIVE?

Even after looking at the LCPP implications in light of the operational environment in southern Sudan, the analysis is not complete. This is because the analysis is contextual, just one piece of the puzzle. Another sizeable piece of the puzzle can be found in the immense needs in southern Sudan. How do we weigh the *potential* negative impact on conflict with the *real* impact of not being able to provide needed services? How do we balance the humanitarian imperative to help the suffering and our mission statement of valuing people with the knowledge that in the end we might do more harm than good? How do we make the decision to pull out when we know that people might die because we do?

The sad reality is that the pragmatic argument, though relevant, does not exist in a vacuum where people have needs, aid agencies respond and people's needs are addressed. Anyone who has worked or lived in southern Sudan knows that the picture is not that simple or clear cut. Anyone who has had to negotiate a beneficiary list or manage a food distribution or tell a commander that no, he cannot have a drum of diesel, knows that there are no straightforward questions with easy answers. On the other hand, anyone that has been to southern Sudan knows that the needs there are like no-where else in sub-Saharan Africa. Before the MOU crisis, the results had always outweighed whatever problems or issues we had on the ground with the SRRA.

Through the years of working in southern Sudan, WV Sudan staff have struggled to ensure that beneficiary lists are accurate, that they have not been generated by the local authorities to increase the amount of aid entering their areas. Staff have had numerous conversations with the local authorities on why WV Sudan cannot set up or manage healthcare centres in garrison towns, why food cannot be given directly to local authorities, and why WV Sudan staff have to be present for all distributions. WV Sudan vehicles have been shot at when drivers refused to give rides to armed soldiers. Staff have been arrested and declared persona non grata by the SRRA when they refused to comply with SRRA requests for resources. One would be hard pressed to find any humanitarian agency in southern Sudan that has not experienced such encounters before, during and after the MOU stalemate. In our opinion, impact would be jeopardised if we signed the MOU and stayed.

In WV Sudan the *Do No Harm* framework was used as a tool to help us assess and reassess the dynamics of our relationship with local authorities and communities. The goal of the project has always been to develop ways to remain present with better systems of accountability. The catch phrase has always been that "do no harm" does not equal "do no aid," but rather, it is an attempt to "do better aid." WV Sudan's experiences in the implementation phase of the project and with the decision not to sign the MOU are reflections of this goal to "do better aid."

Through the years of working with the Sudanese people, WV Sudan has matured as an agency. Three years ago WV Sudan would have signed the MOU. No negotiations. No questions asked. No lengthy discussions on principles. The problem is not that WV Sudan matured or changed its modus operandi, but rather that it did so in isolation. No one thought that WV Sudan would pull out – not our fellow NGOs, not the movement, not the communities in which we worked. More illustrative is that many WV Sudan staff members were shocked by the decision. I distinctly remember one conversation in which a colleague from another NGO commented with some disparaging bewilderment that they would never have expected an agency such as World Vision to make a decision based on principles. That begs the question, Why not? Perceptions.

WV Sudan has been viewed by many as partisan to the south. There are embarrassing incidents where WV Sudan staff have thanked visiting donors for their support in "liberating the south" from northern Islamic aggression. Many such perceptions were shattered with WV Sudan's decision. The sad irony is that by not signing the MOU we have gained credibility with many of our donors and with our international NGO colleagues, yet we have lost considerable ground with many in the NGOs inside Sudan and with the southern Sudanese community, both in Nairobi and inside Sudan. We gained with donors because we articulated our position well. We lost with the communities because in our work with them and in the months leading up to the March 2000 withdrawal, we did not explain our rationale well. They believe the decision can be blamed on one person – the programme director at the time, who is French. And you do know that the French government is against the South, it is whispered.

We are told that the communities in southern Sudan want us to return without any conditions. In Nairobi, where the Sudanese intelligentsia is based, the feeling is less conciliatory. When the movement did its political calculus, it counted on WV Sudan's support and willingness to sign the MOU. WV Sudan has always had the stigma of being the "big, bad agency," the agency that does not hire Sudanese and increasingly as the agency that does not support the south. We are seen as the agency that, in the end, will do what we want because our size gives us that luxury and feeds our arrogance. Not signing the MOU has reinforced this, making WV Sudan

and most WV Sudan staff persona non grata in the eyes of the
Sudanese community in Nairobi.

WHO ARE WE AND WHERE DO WE GO FROM HERE?

In a 1997 article on the moral dilemmas faced by humanitarian
agencies, Hugo Slim argued that the more fundamental principles
held by an agency, the more moral dilemmas the agency will face.[8]
He defines a moral dilemma as a choice between two evils, where
one decision based on a fundamental principle impedes on another
fundamental principle. Slim continues by highlighting the fact that
what often falls under the category of moral dilemmas are not
always moral dilemmas; they are more often than not better desig-
nated as tough decisions. Decisions where not enough information
has been gathered; decisions between competing programme objectives; choice between two goods; or decisions that involve extreme violence are difficult decisions, not moral dilemmas.[9]

I think that what World Vision faced regarding the MOU was in
fact a moral dilemma. We had to choose between two evils. To not
sign meant that we were essentially abandoning thousands of beneficiaries – not future beneficiaries, but actual beneficiaries with
names and families and very marginal lives. To sign meant that we
would not only compromise our neutrality but we would also be
implicitly and explicitly condoning a system of aid abuses. In World
Vision there are core values and a mission statement to guide our
operations and decision-making processes. In our corporate arena
values statements such as "we are Christian" and "we value people"
permeate our personal lives and the work that we do. The guidelines for World Vision advocacy documents note that "WV seeks
to follow Christ's example by working with the poor and oppressed
in the pursuit of justice and human transformation."

Not only are we Christian, but our core values statement pro-
claims that we are also stewards, committed to be "faithful to the
purpose for which those resources are given and [to] manage them
in a manner that makes the maximum amount available to benefit
the poor. . . . We strive for consistency in what we say and what we
do." WV Sudan has several position papers and guidelines on issues such as the promotion of justice, working with the military
and the application of sanctions. More recently, we have also

adopted the Sphere guidelines, which outline minimum standards for disaster response, in addition to the IFRC/NGO Code of Conduct for Disaster Relief. WV Sudan has adopted another principle – do no harm.

Together, these basic moral positions have come together to form what could be interpreted as a very principled agency. But with all these principled positions, how do we know which is most important in any given situation? How do we set priorities? How do we internalise principles so that they are not subject to personnel changes? How do we operationalise the Code of Conduct for Disaster Relief and other humanitarian principles? I believe the answer is to face those moral dilemmas and make those difficult decisions that improve upon the quality of the aid delivered. World Vision can operationalise its core values and mission statement by moving beyond the rhetoric. It is not just a position that one takes on a specific issue; it is the *way* one works.

This challenge is further compounded because World Vision International is a corporate entity, of which WV Sudan is just one of the many World Visions around the world. WV Sudan is composed of individuals with their own sense of right and wrong, their own perception of who WV Sudan is, and how they, as individuals, should respond in different situations. I am Sudanese, from the south, and it pains me to see the south at war with itself, southerners killing southerners. For the two and a half years that I worked with World Vision in Sudan I was responsible for the implementation of *Do No Harm* principles into the planning, implementation and evaluation of WV Sudan programmes. During that time I struggled to balance the corporate with the personal, with knowing that even though I have a personal stake in the outcome of the war in Sudan, there are some things that a humanitarian agency should never be expected to do.

With the decision not to sign and to pull out, WV Sudan is forever changed. I would argue that it is changed for the better. Forced to make a critical decision, World Vision did so based on principles rather than on what it would mean to the agency financially. I do not know about others, but I can say that I am incredibly relieved by the direction that WV Sudan has chosen. The relief comes not from the decision itself but from the fact that even though I acknowledge and understand the root of many of the grievances against the NGOs, I never want to be an instrument of war, tacitly condoning the diversion of civilian resources for the war effort or the personal gain of a few people in key positions. I never want to work for an organisation or a programme that is not aware of the impact of its aid on the conflicts where it is working and is not intentionally striving for better programme quality in conflict situations.

Knowing that my personal position will be interpreted as a choice between the corporate and the community, my continued ties to World Vision will not be viewed kindly by the Sudanese community. To the community I am a "sell out." This is my dilemma. But I would still choose the principled decision that was made, a decision that in effect means leaving my people to continue their daily struggles without the benefit of humanitarian assistance, a decision that I know is interpreted by the Sudanese community as my being more loyal to World Vision than to southern Sudan.

I now find it awkward to visit with people in the Sudanese community in Nairobi where questions of the MOU still come up. Eyes turn to me as the discussion comes back to World Vision, eyebrows raise when they realise that I am still working with the agency. The question is the same as before the withdrawal, even the tense has not change: "Why don't you convince World Vision otherwise?" Even if I were to state my opinion as clearly as I can, no one would listen.

Months after the withdrawal, I still think about the decision that was made. Even though there is a strong need for assistance in other areas of southern Sudan and we will be able to address those needs, in our decision to leave SPLM areas we have left behind so many people, so many lives. Knowing that World Vision chose the better of two evils does not help me sleep better at night. Over the next few months the WV Sudan programme team will focus on researching and articulating precisely what our principles are. How capable we are of articulating and abiding by these principles will influence the when, how and where of our re-engagement with the movement and our possible return to SPLM areas.

This painful episode in WV Sudan's organisational development has shown first and foremost that WV Sudan needs to know specifically what our principles are and what our bottom line is when working in constrained contexts. We also need to ensure that the people we serve know what our principles are and under which conditions we can and cannot operate. Some lessons have emerged quite clearly – lessons for the World Vision partnership on the challenges of defining relationships with non-state entities, lessons about the optimal size of a relief programme in southern Sudan, lessons about what kind of orientation should take place before staff go to the field, lessons about how the Sudan programme can work with other World Vision offices to encourage a broader and deeper understanding of the Sudan conflict for those who are not embroiled in it on a daily basis.

As WV Sudan carries out assessments in Eastern and Mid West Upper Nile and possibly the Nuba Mountains, I realise that the probability of starting projects in those areas is high. WV Sudan has been given a unique opportunity to begin projects with a more keen understanding of ourselves as a Christian agency working in a constrained context and our relationships with the communities that are governed by non state entities. I can only hope and pray that the lessons learned over the past few years will inform WV Sudan's decision to operate in these new areas and will guide the ways in which WV Sudan works and operates in the complex situation that is southern Sudan.

NOTES

[1] Save the Children UK, CARE, Oxfam, Veterinaires Sans Frontières – Belgium, World Vision International, Carter Center, Médecins Sans Frontières – Holland, "Combined Statement on the Forced Relocation of NGOs from Southern Sudan" (Nairobi, 1 March 2000).

[2] These commanders were K. Kerubino, Joseph Odouh, William Nyong, Lam Akol and Riek Machar.

[3] MSF-Holland, one of the agencies that did not sign the MOU, withdrew its membership to OLS in May 2000, noting that membership in the consortium does "not outweigh the inherent compromise."

[4] This section is adapted from Abikök Riak, "The Sudan Experience with the Local Capacities for Peace Project," *Together* (October-December 1999). WV Canada and the Canadian International Development Agency have funded the implementation of LCPP in the Sudan programme.

[5] Mary Anderson, *Do No Harm: How Aid Can Support Peace – Or War* (Boulder, Colo.: Lynne Rienner Publishers, 1999); Mary Anderson, ed., *Options for Aid in Conflict: Lessons from Field Experience* (Cambridge: Collaborative for Development Action, 2000).

[6] See Mindy Belz, "Out of Africa," *World* 15/49 (16 December 2000).

⁷ Due to the logistical constraints of managing a large relief programme inside Sudan, many agency functions such as procurement, administration and human resources are handled in Nairobi, Kenya.

⁸ Hugo Slim, "Doing the Right Thing: Relief Agencies, Moral Dilemmas and Moral Responsibility in Political Emergencies and War," *Disasters* 21/3 (1997), 244–57.

⁹ Ibid., 249–50.

BIBLIOGRAPHY

Anderson, Mary. 1999. *Do No Harm: How Aid Can Support Peace or War.* Boulder, Colo.: Lynne Reinner Publishers.

Anderson, Mary, ed. 2000. "Options for Aid in Conflict: Lessons from Field Experience." Cambridge: Collaborative for Development Action.

African Rights. 1994. *Humanitarianism Unbound?* Discussion Paper #5. November.

Belz, Mindy. 2000. *World Magazine.*

Collins, Cindy. 1998. *Critiques on Humanitarianism and Humanitarian Action.* Discussion Paper prepared for OCHA at the Seminar on Lessons Learned on Humanitarian Coordination, Stockholm, 3-4 April.

Financial Times Limited. 1998. "Food for War." May 15.

Greenaway. Sean. 2000. "Post-modern Conflict and Humanitarian Action: Questioning the Paradigm." Posted on *Journal of Humanitarian Assistance* website on 9 January.

Jackson, Stephen, and Peter Walker. 1999. "Depolarising the 'Broadened' and 'Back-to-Basics' Relief Models." *Disasters* 23/2: 93-114.

Leader, Nicholas. 1999. "Humanitarian Principles in Practice: A Critical Review." A Relief and Rehabilitation Network (RRN) Discussion Paper. December.

Levine, Ian. 1997. "Promoting Humanitarian Principles: The Southern Sudan Experience." A Relief and Rehabilitation Network (RRN) Paper. May.

Macrae, Joanna. 1998. "Purity or Political Engagement?: Issues in Food and Health Security Interventions in Complex Political Emergencies." Posted on *Journal of Humanitarian Assistance* website on 7 March.

Médecins Sans Frontières – Holland. 2000. *MSF Holland Leaves Operation Lifeline Sudan.* Position Paper. Limited Circulation Only.

"North Korea: Conflict Management, Food Aid and Humanitarian Principles." 1999. A Relief and Rehabilitation Network (RRN) Discussion Paper.

Overseas Development Institute. 1998. *Principled Aid in an Unprincipled World: Relief, War and Humanitarian Principles.* Conference Report. ECHO/ODI Conference. 7 April.

Paul, Diane. 1999. "Protection in Practice: Field-Level Strategies for Protecting Civilians from Deliberate Harm." A Relief and Rehabilitation Network (RRN) Paper. July.

Prendergast, John. 1996. *Frontline Diplomacy: Humanitarian Aid and Conflict in Africa*. Boulder, Colo.: Lynne Reinner Publishers.

Riak, Abikök. 1999. "The Sudan Experience in the Local Capacities for Peace Project." *Together*. October–December.

Siegle, Joe. 1997. "Reflections on Lessons Learned from World Vision Eritrea, with Implications for Africa Region and the World Vision Partnership". Unpublished, internal WVS document. December.

Slim, Hugo. 1997. "Doing the Right Thing: Relief Agencies, Moral Dilemmas and Moral Responsibility in Political Emergencies and War." *Disasters* 21/3: 244-57.

———. 1997. "International Humanitarianism's Engagement with Civil War in the 1990s: A Glance at Evolving Practice and Theory." A Briefing Paper for ActionAid UK, 19 December 1997. Posted on *Journal of Humanitarian Assistance* website on 1 March 1998.

———. 1997. "Positioning Humanitarianism in War: Principles of Neutrality, Impartiality and Solidarity." Paper presented to the Aspects of Peacekeeping Conference, Royal Military Academy, Sandhurst, UK. 22-24 January.

———. 1998. "Sharing a Universal Ethic: Spreading the Principle of Humanity Beyond Humanitarianism." Paper presented at the ECHO/ODI Conference, Principled Aid in an Unprincipled World: Relief, War and Humanitarian Principles. 7 April.

Smock, David R. 1997. "Humanitarian Assistance and Conflict in Africa." Posted on the *Journal of Humanitarian Assistance* website on 4 July.

Weller, Mark. 1998. "The Relativity of Humanitarian Neutrality and Impartiality." Paper presented at the American Society of International Law, 1997 Annual Conference, Washington D.C. Posted on the *Journal of Humanitarian Assistance* website on 10 December.

Westwood, David. 1999. "Working in Constrained Contexts: Human Rights versus Humanitarianism; Bridging the Divide." Unpublished, internal World Vision UK document. October.

World Vision Partnership Offices. *Core Policy Documents*. Mission Statement, Core Values, Transformational Development.

World Vision. 1998. *Reconciliation Commission Report*. September.

6.

Do Values Count?

Accepting the Ethical Basis of Development

BRUCE BRADSHAW

The lack of development in Africa during the recent two decades has caused the United Nations to claim the 1980s and 1990s as the lost decades of development. The international development community, suffering from donor fatigue, has often blamed mosquitoes, money and missionaries as the major factors in this loss. Mosquitoes carry malaria, which continues to maintain its lead over HIV/AIDS as the leading cause of death in Africa, claiming about 20 per cent of that continent's infant population each year. Money continues to pour into Africa's impoverished nations, yet is unable to create sustainable change, and missionaries continue to esteem Africa as a major frontier of spiritual transformation.

Each of the three Ms provokes stimulating discussion on its role in the cultural erosion of Africa. The biggest threat, though, to the cultural survival of Africa – and to that of any other continent – is the belief that cultural change is value free or morally neutral. Development has always been based on the value premises of some culture. The Marshall Plan, a development effort to reconstruct the devastated economies of Europe after WWII, which initially served as the model for efforts to develop the economies of Latin America, Asia and Africa during the past several decades, owed its success to the worldview assumptions and values of Western culture,

---

Major parts of this chapter are from the author's recent book *Change Across Cultures: A Narrative Approach to Social Transformation* (Grand Rapids, Mich.: Baker Books, 2002).

particularly those of the Protestant Ethic: hard work, frugality, savings, self-discipline and the good use of time.

The Marshall Plan was successful because the worldview assumptions and value premises of Western Europe were quite similar to those of North America. Unfortunately, Western nations used the Marshall Plan and subsequent economic theories of development as models for their effort to develop their present and previous colonized nations of Africa, Asia and Latin America. Among these theories of development were Walt W. Rostow's belief that economic development is similar to the Western belief in physical evolution, that is, that an "inner logic" guides economies through an evolutionary process of development. The Harrod-Domar Growth Model assumes the value of savings and investment, postulating that economies grow when they invest a percentage of their Gross National Product in the construction of an infrastructure. Similarly, W. Arthur Lewis assumed that economies grow when idle people in rural areas migrate to the cities and invest their labour in local industries.

The values in each of these theories are so implicit that economists use them without realising they exist, giving the impression that development is a value-free expression of cultural change. The contemporary challenges to development, though, create the need for development practitioners to discern the values that are inherent in various cultural practices and to consider methods of affirming or transforming these values; they can no longer pretend that development is a value-free endeavour.

The epidemic of AIDS illustrates that need for values transformation to accompany behavioural changes. A few years ago I worked on a project that was that was designed to educate the residents of the Rakai District of Uganda on the causes of AIDS. The need for this training seemed obvious. About 80 per cent of the residents of Rakai either suffer from or have died from AIDS. The majority of the population between the ages of 15 and 45 have either died or are dying from AIDS. The elderly residents of Rakai, having lost their children, care for as many as thirty grandchildren. Every village contains child-headed households, and unaccompanied children, children whose grandparents and parents have died, probably from AIDS.

The people with whom I worked claimed that their project was funded by an agency that prohibited them from addressing the values and traditions of the culture; the project workers, who were Christians, could not address indigenous religious traditions, values or beliefs. The funding agency believed it was promoting value-free and morally neutral development by providing educational services concerning the spread of AIDS; it assumed the indigenous people would change their behaviour after they learned some information concerning the transmission of HIV. This assumption, which contributes to the fallacy of value-free change and morally neutral development, exacerbated the problem that the project was attempting to solve.

The funding agency, in restricting the health educators to teaching the village residents information about the means through which HIV is transmitted, assumed that ignorance about HIV was the source of the problem concerning the epidemic of AIDS in the village. The primary cause of AIDS in the culture, though, was a wedding rite that obligated women to consummate their marriages with their future husband's brothers and cousins.

This practice has several functions in the culture. It affirms a husband's commitment to practising hospitality among his brothers and cousins. It protects the husband from the embarrassing consequences of infertility; the woman will probably get pregnant regardless of the husband's sperm count. However, the practice also fosters the spread of AIDS in the community, and it has done so to the point where its harmful consequences are greater than any benefit it can claim. The development facilitators agreed that they needed to change some cultural practices and religious beliefs that fostered the transmission of HIV if they were going to have some influence on reducing AIDS-related illnesses and deaths in that village.

In accepting the terms of the original contract, the development agency assented to the myth value-free development and ascribed to functionalism, a branch of anthropology that affirms all cultural practices, believing they enhance the ability of people in a culture to survive. Functionalism has created a moral gap in development work by separating anthropology from ethics. The purpose of this chapter is to bridge that gap by analyzing the fallacy of cultural relativism, the major outcome of functionalism. The purpose of this analysis is to argue that the very nature of development work has made functionalism an obsolete concept. The world is changing, causing all cultures to change. The central ethical issue is not whether a culture should change but how to manage cultural change.

Cultural relativism has become obsolete because it postulated that cultures get corrupted when they change, suggesting that they should exist in isolation of one another. The very nature of development challenges the validity of this assumption, assuming that cultural boundaries are permeable and that all cultures benefit from sharing tangible and intangible artifacts. This chapter will examine the nature of cultural relativism and suggest that development, by nature, shifts the values of a culture, and it must have a source of these value shifts.

Development practitioners who are managing cultural change are influencing decisions that are ethical in nature, causing them to discern the sources of their ethics. These sources answer, for example, the question: Why do I believe that people should not engage in a sexual practice that is vulnerable to destroying them? The answer can be personal, organizational, cultural, religious or any number of other factors.

We must define the sources of our ethics. We can say that the practice is offensive to our personal preferences, our organizational decisions, our cultural traditions or our religious convictions. We might even say the practice is unreasonable. In any case, there is some motivation for us to work toward changing a cultural practice that we believe is threatening the welfare of a community. That motivation defines the sources of our values.

The chapter concludes by arguing that the sources of value shifts are religious in nature. We can argue that a practice that risks life offends our personal, organizational, or cultural convictions. However, this argument raises the question of authority. Is a preference from one person, organisation, or culture authoritative enough to change a practice in another culture? Cultural relativism is correct in offering a negative answer to this question. The problem is whether a religious tradition has this authority. This chapter argues that it does.

THE NATURE OF CULTURAL RELATIVISM

French philosopher Michel Foucault said, "Every interpretation of reality is an assertion of power;"[1] "we are subjected to the production of truth through power and we cannot exercise power except through the production of truth."[2] Power is the ability to have your interpretation of reality accepted as truth – to get your own way, regardless of any truth that your interpretation of reality might contain. This reliance on power to produce an accepted interpretation of reality makes truth vulnerable to becoming a product of power. The validity of the truth can remain questionable or even doubtful.

The malady of power producing truth, powerful people getting the reality counted, is all too common in the development industry. This issue is problematic, not only because it prevents people from recognising the multiple perceptions of reality that exist in our postmodern world, but because it is also the source of cultural relativism, the affirmation that what is right or wrong, good or bad, depends on one's culture, that there are no universal norms that apply to all peoples and all cultures.

Cultural relativism, the prevailing philosophy of too many development projects, is a half-truth. The truthful half is the recognition that all cultures have worth, and no single culture can be esteemed as the standard against which other cultures are compared or valued. The false half is the implication that, since no single culture is absolute, there are no absolutes.

The truthful half of cultural relativism, that all cultures have worth, was a valuable corrective to attitudes that early anthropologists took toward studying other cultures. E. B. Tylor's early anthropological writings on religion are typical of the belief that Western culture is the anthropological standard. While writing in the 1860s, Tylor made continuous references to non-European people as "lower races."[3] Similarly, the influential German theologian Ernest Troeltsch "believed that outside European civilization, true historical consciousness did not exist. The domains outside Europe lack historical self-consciousness and the critical knowledge of the past for which only the European *Geist* has experienced a need."[4] This belief influenced "the general European assumption that Africans did not have enough human consciousness to become citizens of a sovereign state."[5]

Cultural relativism made a positive contribution to anthropology by challenging the tendency of early European anthropologists to use European cultures as the standard to which non-European cultures are compared. This comparison influenced Europeans and other Westerners to view people from non-Western cultures as primitive, pre-logical and irrational. Georg Hegel, who was characteristic of these writers, saw Africa as a "wasteland filled with 'lawlessness,' 'fetishism' and 'cannibalism' – waiting for European solders and missionaries to conquer it and impose 'order' and 'morality.'"[6] He "depicted Africans as incapable of rational thought or ethical conduct,"[7] and believed "nothing consonant with humanity is to be found in [their] character."[8]

Cultural relativists challenged the idea that any single culture should be used as the standard to which other cultures are compared and valued. Ruth Benedict, who studied in the tradition of Franz Boaz, was one of the major proponents of cultural relativism. She proposed that anthropological study "requires that there be no preferential weighting of one or another of the items in the series it selects for its consideration." She added that anthropologists must "arrive at that degree of sophistication where we no longer set our belief over against our neighbor's superstition."[9]

Benedict's anthropological principle seems elementary today. As Elvin Hatch writes, "[It] denies the social, moral, and intellectual preeminence of Western society: it asserts that [Western] values, beliefs and institutions cannot be shown to be better, and that the principle which underlies our position vis-a-vis other societies is the principle of equality."[10] Narrative ethicists are not against the validity of those concepts. Western culture is certainly not superior to other cultures; all cultures have values that are morally positive and negative.

The second half of the concept of cultural relativism – the false side of the half-truth – becomes problematic for development practitioners. It postulates that cultures are "stable and self-correcting,"[11] affirming that "anything one group of people is inclined toward doing is worthy of respect by another [group of people]."[12] Functionalism "can make almost anything right, and prevents condemnation of anything."[13]

Functionalism moves toward making cultures morally absolute with its assumption that "human affairs are explained . . . by the perfectly natural process of cultural evolution."[14] Donald T. Campbell, a past president of the American Psychological Association, illustrated this relationship by comparing natural evolution and cultural evolution:

When an evolutionary biologist encounters some ludicrous and puzzling form of animal life, he approaches it with a kind of awe, certain that behind the bizarre form lies a functional wisdom that he has yet to understand. I believe the case for socio-cultural evolution is strong enough so that psychologists and other social scientists when considering an apparently bizarre incomprehensible feature of their social tradition, or that of another culture, should approach it with a similar awe, expecting that when eventually understood, when our theories have caught up with it, that seemingly bizarre superstition will turn out to make adaptive sense.[15]

Marvin Harris, in a variety of popular anthropological writings, sought to solve the riddles of culture through functionalism. His popular anthropological writings offer solutions to many cultural riddles by analyzing the roles of particular cultural practices in balancing ecological factors. He gives a rather pithy explanation of why Christians eat pork, but Muslims and Jews don't: pigs are hazardous to a fragile ecosystem because they don't graze. For this reason, apparently, the Levitical law, which Muslims and Jews observe, forbade raising and eating pigs. Christians don't observe this aspect of the Levitical law, evidently because they lived in urban environments and thus were less dependent on the pastoral ecosystem.

Harris's theory on the dietary restrictions of the Levitical law seem to have some value. However, his efforts to justify warfare as an "ecologically adaptive lifestyle among primitive peoples"[16] fail to recognise the value and dignity of human life. Functionalists have also attempted to garner virtue out of other practices that insult the dignity of human life, such as female genital mutilation (FGM). Daniel Gordon, who wrote about FGM to challenge the validity of cultural relativism, noted, from the work of Janice Boddy, that FGM has been defended because

an accumulation of demons *(djinn)* is feared at all orifices, and many remedies are based on the assumption that illness is caused by things opening and coming apart. The enclosed womb protects a woman's truest possession, her fertility, as well as the future lineage of her husband. In this way . . . infibulation is an assertive and symbolic act, controlled by women, in which the womb becomes a social space – enclosed, guarded, and impervious.[17]

This argument is weak because the functions that Boddy cites can be fulfilled without cutting the vagina.

The epitome of these ideas is the apocryphal story about the anthropologist who said missionaries should not feed starving people because doing so will disrupt the cycle of nature – dead bodies participate in this cycle by fertilizing trees.

Functionalism, which is falling out of fashion in much anthropological thinking, is a misguided response to a positive belief. It affirms that all people are worthy of respect regardless of their culture. However, it does not make a distinction between the inherent worth of people and the ability of people to create some destructive cultural practices. It fails to distinguish the value of people from the values of their cultures, and of their particular cultural practices. In this failure it makes truth relative to culture, and it creates a legion of ethical problems for development practitioners who are involved in the management of cultural change. How do health educators, for example, discern the basis for educating people to transform a practice that is making them vulnerable to AIDS?

THE MYTH OF TRADITIONAL HARMONY

The myth of traditional harmony, (formerly known as the myth of primitive harmony) is a belief that people who live in traditional cultures have harmonious lives because their values, beliefs, customs and behaviours foster their individual welfare and ensure their corporate survival. The essence of this belief is the assumption that people do not engage in behaviour that can jeopardize their individual or communal welfare; it also implies that people will change any particular behaviour if they learn that the behaviour is hazardous to their welfare. This myth is the source of the belief that truth is relative to cultures; it assumes that beliefs are true and behaviour is good if the people in a particular culture believe the beliefs and behaviours are true and good.

The myth of traditional harmony emerges from a symbolic reality where rationalism is a supreme value. People who live in traditional cultures would not affirm it; they are too busy coping to survive in cultures that contain many practices that do not foster their social or individual welfare. However, the myth does make sense to people who can extract particular cultural practices from human cultures and analyse their value in de-contextualised environments, such as classrooms.

The myth of traditional harmony has been a major obstacle to development work. Its central assumptions are that traditional people will accept change only when it is imposed on them, and that they will not benefit from that change. It postulates that changes can only destroy a culture, and it depicts missionaries and other agents of cultural change as "not only illegitimate, but morally offensive."[18]

The myth of traditional harmony has some validity. Functionalism, the foundation of the myth, opposes evaluating the behaviour in one culture based on the standards of another culture. Functionalism also challenges people who are unfamiliar with a culture to give careful consideration to how particular cultural practices contribute to the integrity of that culture. Most cultural practices make sense to outsiders if the outsiders learn the functions of these practices within the context of the culture. Levirate marriage, for example, the practice of a widow marrying the brother of a deceased spouse, makes sense in cultures that do not offer life insurance and pension plans.

Despite many reasons to support the myth of primitive harmony, this myth does not account for many important factors that generate the need to manage cultural change by transforming many cultural practices. The central value of functionalism is efficiency. As we saw earlier, Donald T. Campbell compared functionalism with evolutionary biology. This comparison, which was based on the assumption that nature works efficiently, extends this natural sense of efficiency to human cultures. Functionalism assumes that human cultures, like nature, abhor vacuums, and that they fill space efficiently.

The are at least three reasons why the efficiency of nature does not extend into human cultures. First, cultural customs outlive their usefulness, but people do not develop intentional or rational processes to change them. Some customs might fade as cultures change, but traditions perpetuate many obsolete customs. The presence of HIV, for example, means the practice of consummating a marriage through multiple spouses facilitates the destruction of a culture, making the practice culturally maladaptive regardless of what functional value it might once have had.

The second challenge to the validity of the myth of traditional harmony is the assumption that traditional cultures are immune to corruption. This assumption is simply not valid. All cultures reflect the fallen state of humankind; they are characterised by practices that embody humankind's propensity toward greed, selfishness, dishonesty, lust, promiscuity, envy, covetousness, pride and other expressions of sin.

People do not always make deliberate efforts to change behaviours that embody destructive traits. In fact, they might support behaviours that benefit but are communally destructive. A major factor in the spread of AIDS, for example, is the powerlessness of women to insist that men wear condoms. "'The men don't like them.' And the women? 'They have so many other problems to think of, why should they think about something that kills you in 10 years?'"[19]

Reification is the third challenge to the validity of functionalism. "Reification implies that man is capable of forgetting his own authorship of the human world, and further, that this dialectic between man, the producer, and his products is lost to consciousness."[20] It implies that people čan create a reality and then lose control of it. It occurs when people are no longer nurtured by social institutions but subordinated to them.[21]

Reification means the social institutions, cultural practices, and other social creations and perceptions become bigger than the people who created them, and the people are powerless to do anything except submit to them. The people practice behaviours that are detrimental to their welfare simply because they do not believe they have the power to change them. The people lose their freedom and their moral agency – to their own creations.

People in every culture need liberation from traditions that are jeopardizing their welfare. The tragedy is that they are allowing their traditions to be reified. For example, when the health educators asked village elders about stopping the practice of consummating a marriage through multiple sexual partners, the village elders said they could not stop the practice, that it is part of their culture. Their tradition is taking control of them, and it is killing them. Their culture will not end when this practice is stopped; it will end when HIV puts an end to their cultural narrative.

THE MYTH OF VALUE-FREE DEVELOPMENT

The myth of value-free development is an offspring of the myth of traditional harmony. It implies that religious beliefs, cultural traditions and community values should not be changed, particularly by innovations that are foreign to a culture. In recent years, though, the power of the myth has been eroding; values have become more fashionable in the administration of development aid. Development and donor agencies have become aware of the need to recognise the values they attach to their work. These values can include, among thousands of others, human rights, world peace, economic justice and political reform.

The role of values in development work across cultures creates the need for development practitioners to define and defend the values that are inherent in their ministries. The health educators dealing with HIV believed they were introducing value-free innovations into the cultures because they believed "scientific facts" comprised the basis of their innovation. However, they were simply attempting to universalize values that they did not define or defend.

The health educators taught the people who lived in the community about virus transmission, but their respect for the myth of traditional harmony prevented them from addressing the methods through which the people consummated their marriages. Methods of marriage consummation, in their view, fell into the realm of religious beliefs, cultural traditions or community values.

CRACKS IN THE FOUNDATION OF FUNCTIONALISM

The myth of traditional harmony does not imply that development can be value free; instead, it specifies that any development innovations have profound implications for managing cultural change. It also challenges cross-cultural ethicists to take a second look at the validity of functionalism. A superficial glance at any culture in the world casts doubt on the validity of this belief and on that of the myths that are associated with it. People in every culture of the world are suffering and dying from cultural practices that have either lost their validity or have never had any.

The realisation that cultural practices do not necessarily foster the welfare of a community has created the need for cross-cultural ethicists to define the basis of managing cultural change. This task is formidable, primarily because it has so many expressions. Robert B. Edgerton, the author of *Sick Societies*, a book dedicated to challenging the myth of primitive harmony, implies that cultural change must have a scientific basis.[22] Science, evidently, is a central element in his cultural narrative. However, it might not be the most effective basis for cultural change.

Elvin Hatch also was concerned about developing a basis for cultural change. He concluded that cultural relativism, the philosophical foundation of functionalism, "carries the obligation that one cannot be indifferent toward other ways of life; [this indifference] obligates us to approve what others do"; it puts people in the "morally awkward position of approving "starvation, the rape of abducted women, [and] the massacre of whole villages."[23]

Hatch attempts to solve the problem of functionalism by recognising that tolerance, the central tenet of functionalism, is not a commitment to neutrality; it is "a moral commitment to the status quo."[24] His recognition that anthropology entails some moral commitments is encouraging; it recognises the need to define some moral foundation for cross-cultural ethical inquiry. However, Hatch's solution to creating this foundation is weak. He takes a social-political approach to change, stating that "it is clear that what is at issue is freedom . . . freedom from the deliberate coercion of others."[25]

Freedom occupies a central position in the narratives of Western cultures; it is the foundation of the vitality of democratic societies. Freedom is also beneficial to the welfare of humankind. Freedom without coercion makes freedom even more appealing. The welfare of people who live in cultures that value religious, political and economic freedom is generally higher than that in cultures where freedom is limited. However, freedom without coercion does not serve as an adequate basis for establishing a viable basis for cross-cultural ethics.

The problem with making freedom without coercion the ethical basis of managing cultural change is that freedom comes with a responsibility to protect it. The freedom of speech, for example, assumes responsibility for speaking without libel. This responsibility might be protected by some form of coercion. To claim freedom without coercion as a valid cross-cultural ethic is only a half-step away from functionalism. It recognises the invalidity of functionalism, but it does not transform the assumptions of functionalism. It continues to assume that people are free and will do what is good for them and for other people in their culture of their own volition.[26]

Freedom, like many other values, is commendable in any culture. However, isolating it as a supreme cross-cultural ethic is an effort to salvage functionalism by elevating one element of functionalism over the others. It makes one value absolute and other values relative to it. Neither freedom nor any other element of functionalism can serve as an absolute basis for cross-cultural ethics.

A valid basis for cross-cultural ethics requires an alternative to functionalism that incorporates some of the elements of functionalism but does not make absolute any of these elements. The thesis of this chapter is that redemption is the only absolute value that can serve as a cross-cultural ethic. Redemption is defined unapologetically as assuming that the universe has a moral slant and that the development efforts of people within the Christian tradition are done with the express purpose of facilitating the ability of the elements of creation to fulfil the purposes for which they were created. Redemption incorporates many of the elements and values of functionalism, but it does not make them absolute. It is best realised through the conviction of St. Ireneaus, the third-century theologian who observed, "The glory of God is a human being, fully alive."

When I discussed the struggle to establish an adequate basis for cross-cultural ethics with a friend who is an anthropologist, she said there is no single basis for cross-cultural ethical reflection. She is no functionalist, and she would agree that functionalism is losing its appeal in a multi-cultural post-modern world where there are diverse multiple realities but a more uniform global meta-culture that is losing its tolerance for cultural practices that are causing individuals and societies to become dysfunctional. In asserting that there are multiple bases for the task of establishing a basis for cross-cultural ethics, she listed economics, politics, gender and ethnicity, among others. She also mentioned that someone could even base an ethics of cultural change on the weather.

I asked her what she thought about redemption as the basis of cross-cultural ethics. She claimed that it was inadequate.

I asked why.

She said, "Because it cannot be defined or evaluated."

I said, "Redemption is the result of God's reconciling work in creation; it empowers the elements of creation to fulfil the purposes for which they were created. It includes economics, health, sanitation, education, agriculture and a host of other enterprises as they contribute to enhancing the welfare of human life. None of them is adequate by itself, but their value is determined by how they contribute to restoring the ability of creation to support life. Redemption points toward, and results in, *shalom*. It can be evaluated and possibly measured by defining the increase that a community experiences in the ingredients of redemption.

A functionalist can argue that the death of a child contributes to the welfare of a community by making more economic resources available to support the other people in the community. Christians who support redemption as the basis of cultural change will not support such an argument. Economics is the basis of that decision, and economics might not be the most redemptive factor in that social situation. Efficiency is the central value of economics; life is the central value of redemption. Economic factors can be given consideration in redemptive decisions. However, to make economic efficiency the basis of ethical decisions becomes idolatrous. Redemptive solutions seek to manage economic resources to enhance the lives of all people.

She argued, "Redemption is a religious construct that cannot be verified. You can't prove it exists; you cannot measure it or validate it. You only know redemption by what you call redemption. If you call something redemption, you interpret what you see as redemptive, believing you are proving that it exists because you named it."

She continued, "You are caught in a vicious cycle, because you can't find any evidence for your concept! Redemption is too subjective. You can find objective evidence for economics, politics and the weather, but you can't research redemption. The construct has no more validity than the word you are using to name it. The word is not the object." Language, she asserted, does not produce reality.

FROM FUNCTIONALISM TO REDEMPTION

This discussion did not influence me to abandon the idea of advocating redemption as the basis for ethics. Rather, it challenged me to define redemption and substantiate it. Redemption is a broad concept with two factors that make it a valid ethic for managing cultural change. It is universally valid and culturally specific. It rests on the authority of a universal religious tradition, and it can be applied to particular cultures to affirm positive values and transform negative ones. It can affirm the practice of not eating pork in many Islamic/Arabic cultures, noting that pigs are inefficient to raise because they have a destructive influence on a desert ecosystem. It can also inspire a social transformation that will prevent unhealthy rites to consummate a marriage.

The myth of traditional harmony causes Westerners to wince at the idea of resorting to any religious tradition as the moral authority of cultural change. As mentioned earlier, this myth depicts any foreign religious or cultural influence as detrimental to the culture; it eliminates redemption, a central value of Christianity, as a viable ethic for managing change. The alternative ethic to any religious construct, though, is cultural or individual preferences. Cultural change, and any expression of it, is neither ethically nor morally neutral or value free. All cultural change is motivated by values. These values can be religious, cultural or personal.

The notion that development, or any other means of cultural change, can be value free is a fallacious implication of functionalism. It creates cultural change that becomes a veneer. In the example of multiple spouses, health educators can distribute condoms and information on virus transmission. However, the information will not effectively transform the culture unless it transforms the customs that facilitate HIV transmission. Unless the health educators speak to the cultural traditions, their work will become only a cultural veneer. It will not have any sustainable influence on the culture because veneers become unglued.

The demise of functionalism and its accompanying myths – those of traditional harmony and morally neutral development – does not give health educators the privilege of choosing whether they want to address the cultural traditions that transmit HIV. They must address these traditions if they want to manage sustainable change in the culture, and they must choose the ethical basis of their efforts. Why do they believe one basis of change is ethically preferable to another? For example, why do they believe a personal or cultural preference is preferable to a religious preference? (They could argue that they are giving people the choices, and letting the people decide for themselves. This argument has some validity. However, the fact that health educators are participating in the decision by identifying choice is not morally neutral or value free. Their choice to participate in the project has moral implications.)

I used this case study in a workshop with a group of health educators who concluded that they preferred to distribute condoms rather than influence the villagers to change their sexual customs. When I asked them to define the basic assumptions of this decision, they agreed that they were content to accept their personal and cultural preferences as the moral authority of their decision. They believed this decision was a morally superior alternative to making any efforts to change this cultural tradition by resorting to a religion, such as Christianity. Individual liberty was a greater value in their narratives.

The community identified hospitality and gender relationships as the central values that perpetuate the practice. An adequate ethic of change, then, has to address both these issues. The men in the community defend the custom as an essential characteristic of their culture because it expresses hospitality. However, the women would like to change the custom, but they are powerless to do so. This community will begin to realise some sense of redemption when women empower themselves to participate in a conversation to address changing this practice.

The basis of this conversation is an approach called Appreciative Inquiry, an approach to social change that empowers people to define and preserve the values that any cultural practice embodies. One basic assumption of Appreciative Inquiry is that behaviours and customs embody values. These values should be preserved even when the behaviour and customs change. The first step in Appreciative Inquiry is diagnosing the nature of the problem. The central diagnostic questions are: What is the behaviour? Why does it persist in the community? What values are sustaining it? The second step is identifying the stakeholders in the practice. Who is benefitting from the practice? What benefits are they gaining? What will they, and other people in the community, lose if the practice ends? The third step in Appreciative Inquiry is defining the beliefs, values and attitudes that influence the practice and considering how changing the custom will affect these issues.

The three steps in this condensed form of Appreciative Inquiry are sequential; one step leads to the other. The diagnostic questions have many answers. In the transmission of HIV, for example, the answers can also include gender relationships and hospitality. These answers identify the stakeholders of the practice, and they define the values that influence the stakeholders to sustain the practice.

If hospitality and gender relationships are the central values that sustain this practice, an ethic of cultural change has to address both of these issues in a manner that is acceptable to all stakeholders. It must express the male concerns for hospitality and the female concerns for equality – or at least lack of subjugation. One redemptive possibility is having the community celebrate marriages by eating together. Sharing meals is steeped in the narrative of Christian tradition, and it is a universal expression of hospitality. The anonymous letter to Diogenes, a significant piece of ancient Christian literature, mentioned that Christians "have their meals in common, but not their wives."[27] The value of hospitality can be retained and redeem the practice of consummating marriage through multiple partners.

NOTES

[1] Stanley J. Grenz, *A Primer on Postmodernism* (Grand Rapids, Mich.: Eerdmans, 1996), 6.

[2] Michel Foucault, "Two Lectures," *Power/Knowledge: Selected Interviews and Other Writings, 1972–1977,* ed. Colin Gordon (New York: Pantheon Books, 1980), 93.

[3] Sir Edward Burnett Tylor, *Religion in Primitive Culture* (New York: Harper and Brothers Publishers, 1958 [1871]), 12.

[4] Irvin, 25.

[5] Ernest Troeltsch, quoted in Battle, 29.

[6] Georg Hegel, quoted in *Postcolonial African Philosophy: A Critical Reader,* ed. Emmanuel Chukwadi Eze (Cambridge, Mass.: Blackwell Publishers, 1997), 8.

[7] Eze, *Postcolonial African Philosophy,* 8.

[8] Georg Wilhelm Friedrich Hegel, *Lectures on the Philosophy of World History,* trans. N. B. Nisbet (Cambridge: Cambridge University Press, 1980), 177.

[9] Ruth Benedict, *Patterns of Culture* (Boston, Mass.: The Riverside Press, 1934), 3.

[10] Elvin Hatch, *Culture and Morality: The Relativity of Values in Anthropology* (New York: Columbia University Press, 1983), 32.

[11] J. M. Blaut, *The Colonizers Model of the World:Geographical Diffusionism and Eurocentric History* (New York: The Guilford Press, 1993), 27.

[12] Clifford Geertz, *The Interpretation of Cultures: Selected Essays* (New York: Basic Books, 1973), 44. Geertz was referring to Ruth Benedict's book *Patterns of Culture*.

[13] Robert B. Edgerton, *Sick Societies: Challenging the Myth of Primitive Harmony* (New York: The Free Press, 1992), 25.

[14] Hatch, *Culture and Morality*, 14.

[15] Donald T. Campbell, "On the Conflicts Between Biological and Social Evolution and Between Psychology and Moral Tradition," *American Psychologist* (December 1975): 1121.

[16] Marvin Harris, *Cows, Pigs, Wars and Witches: The Riddles of Culture* (New York: Vantage Books, 1974), 57.

[17] Janice Boddy, quoted in Daniel Gordon, "Female Circumsion in Egypt and Sudan: A Controversial Rite of Passage," in *Magic, Witchcraft and Religion: An Anthropological Study of the Supernatural*, 4th ed., ed. Arthur Lehmann and James E. Myers (Mountain View, Calif.: Mayfield Publishing Company, 1997), 51. This article was originally published in *Medical Anthropology Quarterly* 5/1 (March 1991): 3–14.

[18] Wolfhart Pannenberg, "How to Think About Secularism," *First Things* 64 (June/July 1996): 27–32.

[19] David S. Landes, *The Wealth and Poverty of Nations: Why Some Are So Rich and Some Are So Poor* (New York: W. W. Norton and Co., 1999), 501. The Landes quotations herein are taken from Howard W. French, "Migrant Workers Take AIDS Risk Home to Niger," *NY Times* (8 February 1996), A-3.

[20] Peter L. Berger, and Thomas Luckmann, *The Social Construction of Reality: A Treatise on the Sociology of Knowledge* (New York: Anchor Books, 1966), 89.

[21] Bruce G. Brander, *Staring into Chaos: Explorations in the Decline of Western Civilization* (Dallas, Tex.: Spence Publishing Company, 1998), 75.

[22] Robert B. Edgerton, *Sick Societies: Challenging the Myth of Primitive Harmony* (New York: The Free Press, 1992), 2.

[23] Elvin Hatch, *Culture and Morality: The Relativity of Values in Anthropology* (New York: Columbia University Press, 1983), 92, 93.

[24] Ibid., 94.

[25] Ibid., 96.

[26] Since people do not always fulfil their responsibilities to act for their own good or for the good of other people, nonviolent coercion is a morally

acceptable means of preventing some people from abusing power and protecting other people from such abuse. Coercion is not necessarily un-ethical or immoral. It is a use of power that can serve the good of society by influencing people to do what they should do but might not want to do. Advocacy organisations throughout the world expend considerable efforts through nonviolent coercion to limit the influence of corruption and other abuses of power.

[27] "The Letter to Diognetus," trans. J. B. Lightfoot (ca. 200). This is available in multiple sources as well as on the Web.

7.

Coping with Chaos
in the New Millennium

DON BRANDT

Former US president George Bush may best be remembered for paint-ing a verbal picture of a world that would never be. The "new world order" designed to succeed the Cold War was stillborn. Or perhaps it was consumed by the Persian Gulf War of 1991. Either way, disor-der prevailed over the utopian dreams of a civil and logical world chaired by the United States and mediated by the Paris Club.[1]

Perhaps we should be relieved that Bush's new brand of colo-nialism failed to survive. Yet, we are left with a world that looks very similar to the one we have experienced since the early 1990s. Further, the factors that create instability, civil disruption and vio-lence will likely increase, at least in the short term. While the total number of acts of internal violence may have declined recently, there is no ground for confidence that this will become a trend. We only have to look at the Balkans and parts of Africa to see how readily blood and refugees flow.

This is the world setting that NGOs face – a violent and uncivil world where UN conventions are ignored and where NGOs are supposed to operate as caring, neutral and impartial parties. NGOs will become increasingly responsible for both poverty eradication and disaster mitigation (relief) programmes. These operations will accelerate the size and influence of many NGOs. In reaction, big NGOs, particularly, will face tough and sceptical critics. Some of the criticism will be healthy; some will be more spurious than use-ful.[2]

The purpose of this chapter is rather ambitious. I wish to dem-onstrate that the world of today *is* the world of tomorrow; that is, we should expect a steady dose of violence that leads to social disruption, if not civil destruction, in many countries. Concurrently, we may also expect natural disasters. Hurricane Mitch, earthquakes in Turkey and Taiwan, and the cyclone that devastated Orissa, India, may have been exceptional in their magnitude but not their occurrence. NGOs are expected to be there to help. Just how NGOs help will be increasingly scrutinised.

CONTINUATION OF VIOLENCE

I see no reason to expect a diminution of internal violence in the coming decade. "Ingredients" for a violent cocktail are all there in abundance: unrepresentative and repressive governments; prejudice and communal hatred; decreasing respect for authority; population growth and lack of jobs; environmental degradation and decreasing safe water supplies; and near-ubiquitous trafficking in drugs and small arms. Most of these factors are interrelated, of course. Equally obvious, some of these conditions have existed for centuries and have only recently given rise to overt action. Perhaps what has changed so dramatically today is the means to undertake civil turmoil, whether reasons stem from freeing the bonds of ethnic repression or kidnapping for blatant economic gain. Some people may feel that age-old injustices are being corrected in a type of redemptive violence.

Rogue governments, disgruntled groups and deranged individuals have one thing in common. They can all make devices that cause incalculable human misery. We may expect more terrorist attacks for the simple reason that almost anyone can make a bomb. All it takes is synthetic fertiliser and a couple of other readily purchased chemicals. These "low tech" explosives may not be suitable to transport across international borders, but their effectiveness against domestic targets can be devastating. Unforgettable are the horrific scenes of the World Trade Towers in New York, the US Federal building in Oklahoma City and the US Embassy in Nairobi.

Even more worrisome are possible terrorist attacks using nuclear, chemical, or biological weapons. "Mini-nukes" or "nukes in a suitcase" are operational. Some security specialists fear that such weapons made in Russia are already in the hands of potential terrorist groups. Scarier still are the possibilities of a few dedicated or demented souls using chemical or biological products to make a statement by killing thousands of people. While it takes some sophistication to make sarin or anthrax, hundreds of laboratories in scores of countries can do the job. Transporting these deadly weapons across international borders poses no problem. Drug cartels already use routes that are 90 per cent effective.

We live in a time when it is increasingly difficult to differentiate between political and criminal terrorists. Do Somali warlords have competing political agendas, or are they clan-based thugs out for spoils and power? Do kidnappers in the Philippines want to make a political statement, or are they criminal entrepreneurs? Anyone who reads a newspaper can cite cases from many other countries. The point is that civilians, including humanitarian workers, are increasingly threatened by violent and lawless bands of unhappy people. We should expect that more NGO staff will be harassed, abducted and tormented. Some will be killed by groups of criminal or political terrorists.

Working in violent and insecure environments forced World Vision (WV) to take a more active position towards staff security. Since 1995 WV has employed a director of corporate security who works with staff on safety and vulnerability issues, both on the job and at home. Several training sessions were held, including ones that simulated road blocks by "rebels" and demands for vehicles and other assets.

To reinforce its concern for security, WV produced a 150–page, pocket-size manual that deals with staff security issues. Written with the help of expert consultants, the book covers virtually every condition that field staff face.

Civil wars generally are not fought by Renamo and RUF types only out for economic gain. Most rebel groups want to right perceived injustices, but that also includes obtaining a greater share of the economic pie. Examples include both factions of the Rassemblement congolais pour la democratie (RCD) in the Democratic Republic of Congo, SPLA in Sudan, Tamil Tigers (LTTE) in

Sri Lanka, Abu Sayyif in the Philippines, dissidents scattered across Indonesia, and even Peru's Shining Path guerrillas.

Justifications for civil disobedience and violence are found in complex and volatile blends of socio-economic and political discrimination. Complexity is accentuated by the communal character of most protracted conflicts as antagonists are marked by ethnic or religious differences. That these differences are often manipulated by unscrupulous factional leaders may be readily witnessed in the Balkans and Central Africa.

Civilians are the foremost tragedy of civil wars. Working with huge numbers of refugees and internally displaced peoples will continue to be a major task of international NGOs. The UN High Commissioner for Refugees estimated that of the 50 million displaced people in 1997, probably 35 million were internally displaced persons.[3] This makes terrible sense, because most wars are internal. Host countries faced with "compassion fatigue" find ways to limit refugees, or, against the UN Conventions, to send displaced people back to their home countries against their will.

Not that the threat of international warfare has disappeared. In fact, as wars in the Persian Gulf, Balkans, Horn of Africa, and Central Africa remind us, cross-border conflicts have not gone away. Other threats to world and regional peace are easily found in India and Pakistan, Israel and Palestine, the Korean Peninsula, and even Namibia and Botswana in the Caprivi Strip.

Much of the increase in global violence is attributed to the widespread and generally illegal sale of small arms or light weapons. Probably 90 per cent of current war casualties are civilians, and almost all those deaths and injuries are caused by 500 million to 1 billion AK-47s, Uzis, M-16s, and their ilk.[4] The world is bathed in small arms that are cheap to make, easy to transport, extremely lethal at short range, and simple to use, so simple that a child of 10 can use and maintain an AK-47 without difficulty. Thus we see one of the most horrendous tragedies of the 1990s: child soldiers used as infantry by both governments and rebels.

Financing light weapons that provide the means for so much civil violence is frequently accomplished through drug sales. Drug trafficking will remain one of the world's largest businesses. Currently valued at US$400 billion annually, illegal drugs account for at least 8 per cent of all international trade. This makes the export of drugs equal to textiles and greater than any other manufactured commodity except automobiles. Estimates suggest that 140 million people use marijuana and about 100 million sniff, snort, swallow, or inject heroin, cocaine, or synthetic drugs.

CHILDREN AS VICTIMS

Battles using small arms are often fought by children. Why are children recruited by rebel or government armies? This question is easily answered: children are cheap and obedient. So cheap are child soldiers that they often work just for food. Not all children serve as gun-carrying combatants. Many children work as cooks, porters, spies, lookouts and messengers. Others are forced to clear land mines by walking across fields or along paths. The child who steps on a mine is killed or seriously wounded, of course, but a child is far more expendable than older, experienced soldiers.

Given the barbaric life of the child soldier, why are so many children serving in wars? Some children join to avenge the death of parents, siblings, or other relatives. Others hope for excitement and adventure. More enlist to escape hunger and poverty. They may hope for plunder but usually must be satisfied with an insufficient amount of food served on an irregular basis. Poverty also encourages desperate parents to send their sons into battle. These cases of more-or-less voluntary induction of children are considered by many experts as an illicit form of child labour. National and international laws concur. Using children as combatants is illegal in most countries and is a violation of the UN Convention on the Rights of the Child, Article 77 of Additional Protocol I and Article 4 of Additional Protocol II to the 1949 Geneva Conventions, and Article II of the African Charter on the Rights and Welfare of the Child (adopted but not yet in force).

Probably most children don't volunteer but are forced to become soldiers. This is certainly the case in Uganda, where the ruthless Lord's Resistance Army (LRA) recruits by kidnapping children and then beating them into compliance. Another example is Myanmar (Burma), where the army cordons off schools and press-gangs students as young as 10. These are not isolated cases. Rogue armies, rebel groups and right-wing militias all see children as a valuable military asset.

DEMOGRAPHY – IT'S IN THE NUMBERS

Population growth in much of the world will contribute to resource and job scarcity in the future, as it has in the past.[5] This means there is good reason to believe that the numbers of poor and disillusioned people will increase. The difference in demographics between the South and North shows that while the developed world and China are greying, much of the rest of the world is incredibly young. One-third of the world's population is under the age of 15, and 85 per cent of these young people live in the Third World. In Angola, Ethiopia and Niger today, almost half the population is under 15. In a world often inhospitable to uneducated young people, large numbers of them live on the streets, are used to staff underage armies, or are exploited for their labour, sex, or body parts.

This demographic reality cannot be escaped. Many of the world's poor will be in their teens and twenties, when the propensity for violence is at its highest. The march towards global capitalism may create jobs in the long term, but short-range prospects for many people look grim. In many societies jobs simply cannot be generated fast enough to absorb the employable population. Compounding this problem is the reality that jobs increasingly demand a better educated and technologically proficient work force.

At the same time that many of these young people are struggling to find a future, a global youth culture is emerging made up of adolescents in the North and a growing number of counterparts in the South. Watching the same TV, reading the same magazines, these young people are singing the same songs, eating the same food, and wearing the same clothes. This "Westernisation" is seen as a major cultural threat in the Third World. Yet this may be modernisation, not "Westernisation."

A new generation or cohort group is coming of age, and for the first time, it may be global. This generation in its teens and early twenties (called millennial kids, busters, and other uncharitable names) may be a worldwide group with greater world-changing impact than the post–World War II generation called the Baby Boomers in the North. Whilst there are fewer young people in each country than the generation that preceded them, there are still a huge number of teenagers and twenty-something folk in the world. With MTV and the Internet, they are getting connected.

As knowledge becomes the primary means of creating wealth, those who are educated and who know how to learn will enjoy a permanent competitive advantage. Those who cannot learn or who have not learned the right skills will find themselves on the margin, possibly for their lifetime, of a world which is learning faster and faster. This trend is exacerbated by the fact that those who can use technology now have a permanent and perhaps even increasing advantage over those who cannot make use of technology.

FOREIGN INVESTMENT AND INEQUITABLE GROWTH

So for the individual, so for the nation. Those countries where a primary education is a luxury will become even more disadvantaged in global markets. Indeed, these countries may be ignored by foreign direct investment except for mineral exploitation. Much of sub-Saharan Africa already fits this description. Emphasis on foreign direct investment has come at the expense of official development assistance, which fell 40 per cent between 1991 and 1996. At the same time, food aid deliveries were cut in half.

Most sub-Saharan African nations that make up 33 of the 47 least developed countries received almost no foreign direct investment; only three low-income sub-Saharan African countries received appreciable amounts during the past 25 years: Angola, Ghana and Nigeria. Much of the dearth of foreign direct investment in sub-Saharan Africa is attributed to lack of domestic markets and manufacturing export potential. A list of factors that encourage private investment reveals deficits in most sub-Saharan African countries towards which foreign direct investment flows. Transnational corporations may be willing to locate in small countries with access to regional markets. Unfortunately, regional trade associations are weak or dysfunctional in sub-Saharan Africa. We also need to be mindful that all businesses, but particularly those operating on regional and national scales, seek political stability – a condition in short supply in Africa today.

All is not bleak for transnational corporations and other investment in Africa. International private capital flows there are small but not insignificant. The region received US$11.7 billion in 1996, 4.5 times the amount recorded in 1990. Further, foreign direct investment accounts for a surprising 45 per cent of all capital flows to sub-Saharan Africa. (The other 55 per cent is from governments and public institutions.) Africa boosters may recognise that transnational corporations will not be attracted to most countries due to limited market potential. Nevertheless, transnational corporations see potential in sub-Saharan Africa for export-oriented industries. Most authorities agree that if sub-Saharan African countries are to grow, they must focus on exports rather than import-substitution.

Experts today question the sustainability of economic growth that is not equitable. This means that governments must amend market forces and allow public investments in education, health, welfare and nation-building infrastructure. Without some degree of equitable growth, class and ethnic resentment will build into civil violence. Rebel activity is one example. A recent phenomenon is general violence that takes the form of kidnapping for economic gain, car jacking, and home robberies not by individuals but by gangs. These criminal activities are major threats to NGO staffs as well as the people they serve.

The disparity between rich and poor will widen both within countries and among nations. Large numbers of people will find themselves marginalised from the global economy, even if they make modest progress in their own development. Many fear this will be the case for Africa, but millions in parts of Latin America and Asia may also find themselves on the periphery of new global markets. The trend towards a widening gap between rich and poor will provide momentum to two trends: increasing low-level conflict and the movement of people within and between nations. Urbanisation will continue unabated, while refugee movements and illegal immigration will increase.

ENVIRONMENTAL STRESS

Accelerating environmental problems are aggravating the lack of jobs. Poverty in many countries contributes to land degradation, including desertification and salinisation. Stripping of tropical forests has reached scandalous proportions in countries such as Cambodia, Indonesia and Brazil. Not only have valuable forests been indiscriminately cut, but also the rights of indigenous people have been brazenly ignored. This injustice has fuelled rebel activity in

West Kalimantan and Irian Jaya in Indonesia and among ethnic groups in Myanmar.

The environment is evidencing limits in terms of what abuses can be absorbed. On a per capita basis, consumption by the few in the North results in far more environmental damage than that generated by the many in the South. The remnant waste of nuclear arms reminds us that we are better at building things than at disposing of them safely. Nuclear accidents in unsafe power plants, such as Chernobl, are likely to recur unless these antiquated facilities are demolished. Fast-growing economies in newly developing parts of the world are ignoring the environmental cost accompanying this growth. In the face of growing global population, the availability of land for cultivation, fresh water, and even fish in the sea is diminishing measurably.

Few scientists still doubt the harmful "greenhouse effect" caused by carbon dioxide emissions from burning fossil fuels or the damaging ozone holes over Antarctica and Siberia. Already the short-term results of global warming include more violent storms and rapid swings from wet to dry years. Medium- and long-term consequences will probably include more negative than positive effects. Despite the possible extension of agricultural lands in Canada and Russia, dryer conditions will prevail in many sub-humid and semi-arid regions, including sub-Saharan Africa. Warmer winters mean less snow pack in mountains for summer crop irrigation on plains and valleys. Meanwhile, rising sea levels will create hardships for coastal populations.[6]

Emissions of chlorofluorocarbon compounds (CFCs) that caused the gaping ozone holes have dramatically declined since 1987 and passage of the Montreal Protocols. That's the good news. The bad news is that the atmosphere will need 40–50 years to rebuild the ozone shield. This means that for the next 20 years we'll be especially vulnerable to cancer-causing ultraviolet radiation. During these decades we may also expect diminished yields of certain crops and damage to aquatic life.

Another pressing environmental concern is biodiversity. Long-term human well-being depends on a large gene pool of foods, especially cereals. How can we safeguard a wide variety of species when fewer and fewer plants account for most of our cereals? Probably not through seed banks set up for short-term commercial gains that do not preserve sufficient germ plasma. While encouraging increased productivity in most fields, we may wish to keep other, less productive areas for diversity.

Such an *ex situ* programme may also benefit tribal or indigenous peoples who occupy many of the least densely populated areas. Indigenous people are losing the battle to pharmaceutical companies for rights over native drugs. International programmes to protect indigenous cultures can, as an added benefit, maintain a large gene pool of plant and animal species.

Population growth is high in regions least able to sustain more people. Poverty leads to environmental degradation (deforestation, soil erosion and misuse of chemical additives) that, in turn, creates greater poverty. Diseases once thought eradicated are now re-emerging and becoming resistant to the considerable power of modern medicine. In many countries fresh water is scarce. Water use will climb with population growth, industrial development and irrigation schemes. Already, 30 countries are water-stressed today, and 20 nations are water-scarce. This latter number will rise to 35 by the year 2020. The Middle East is the most likely site of "water wars," but we can expect conflicts in Africa, Asia and Central America as well. "Virtual water" (imported grains) has reduced some water deficits since the 1970s. The number of environmental refugees and internally displaced persons (estimated by some to be as high as 25 million) going to cities and across borders will continue to increase.

Environmental conditions may generate movements of people, as in the 1970s and 1980s. Then, we spoke of environmental refugees numbering in the millions. The same set of circumstances can create masses of displaced people today. Witness southern Sudan and Somalia in 1998 and 1999. Granted, the underlying causes of environmental refugees is really not "natural." Yet these movements clearly indicate how poor many of the world's people are, how few assets they have, and how closely they live with hunger.

For years WV worked in chronic food deficit areas of Ethiopia. Even small bouts of dry weather could reduce grain yields enough to cause widespread hunger and the need for food aid. Wishing to move away from what was perceived as a "BandAid" approach to development, WV Ethiopia staff began to ask serious questions related to the causes of food insecurity.

Their answers seem obvious today, but they were not a few
years ago. The basic problem was a lack of assets that prevented
farmers from coping with reduced grain and livestock produc-
tion. The answer was to build assets at community and house-
hold levels. Most resources to repair or build infrastructure, in-
cluding irrigation ditches, terraces, check dams, micro-basins, and
market roads came from targeted food-for-work projects. Some
food-for-work resources were used in innovative ways by com-
munities as loans to help families fund micro and small enter-
prises.

DISEASES, NEW AND OLD

As environmental problems mount, so too do concerns about disease. Poverty is the main barrier to eradicating most communicable diseases. Unfortunately, poverty alleviation has proven difficult. Other factors that may trigger new pathogens or re-emergence
of old diseases are associated with a growing pool of unexposed or
vulnerable people through population growth, urbanisation, travel
and ageing.

While we should expect to see more new diseases, such as Ebola,
old diseases are making a comeback. Almost 9 million people were
victims of tuberculosis in 1994, and 300 million people suffer from
infectious diseases that were responsible for 32 per cent of all deaths
in 1993. The AIDS epidemic may be shrinking in the North, but it
is still growing rapidly in the South. Worldwide, over 40 million
people have HIV/AIDS, a number expected to grow to 50 million
by 2010. In 2001, 3 million people died from AIDS; 590,000 were
children less than 15 (19 per cent of cases).[7]

Non-communicable or chronic diseases will increase from killing 28.14 million people in 1990 to 49.65 million in 2010. The
reason for the rapid increase in heart attacks, strokes, cancers, dia-
betes, and other non-infectious diseases is related to age. While the
percentage of older people is increasing in the North, it is the South
where the largest number of people over 60 are found. In 1995,
330 million of the world's 540 million people over 60 (61 per cent)
lived in less developed countries. Stated another way, the percentage of people over 60 will increase from 9.5 per cent in 1995 to 20
per cent by 2050. Most of those gains will be in the South.[8]

Will adequate medical care for these large numbers of ageing people be provided? The answer in most of the world is no. Poor countries already face difficulties providing relatively cheap vaccinations to prevent infectious diseases. Much more costly medical care for chronic diseases will be impossible to provide except for a small number of the wealthier citizens.

Another worrisome problem is the increase of mental illness. Very little public help is available to patients with mental diseases in most less developed countries. Yet, it is in these rapidly changing societies that depression, anxiety, schizophrenia, dementia and other mental diseases are increasing fastest. Approximately 24.4 million people in low-income countries will suffer from various mental diseases by the turn of the century. While incidences of different mental disorders vary by culture, common causes of mental illness are nearly universal: ageing (dementia), rapid urbanisation, and disruption of social patterns.[9]

Will the mentally ill receive sufficient care? If the present is any indication of the future, no. As with chronic physical illness, adequate treatment for mental diseases is expensive. Most countries don't have the resources to provide sufficient care. The result will be a large-scale replication of the US scenario – large numbers of mentally ill people homeless and on city streets.

FOOD IMBALANCE

Discussions of population, environment and disease are incomplete without consideration of food supplies. Evidence warrants some optimism. Today's people eat more, and eat better, than ever before. Some signs of a "green revolution" in sub-Saharan Africa include new disease-resistant species of maize, sorghum, millet, cassava, cow peas and other plants important to the lives of millions of people. In laboratories genetic research is developing plants and animals that generally are disease-free producers of grain, fibre, meat and animal products.

Yet grounds for pessimism abound. By 2020 child malnutrition may drop from 33 to 25 per cent, but the number of affected children will exceed 150 million. Most of those children will be in sub-Saharan Africa or South Asia.[10] In sub-Saharan Africa today, 45 per cent of children are malnourished. In South Asia the rate is 40 per cent. Due to inclement weather and civil strife, among other reasons, the world's food stocks are at an all-time low, as is food aid. The world needs to produce 26 million more tons of grain each year to keep up with population growth. This is happening, but grain production per capita has barely kept pace with population growth since 1980. In sub-Saharan Africa, it has not.

In a future of further population growth (1.4 per cent per year), genetic engineering may be the best way to achieve increases in food production, subject to environmental and bio-diversity concerns. Not much land is available for substantial increases of grain production without irrigation, and since 1979, population increase has exceeded growth of irrigated land. The 70 per cent of the world's fresh water that is currently used for agriculture will surely decline with the growing water demand of urban populations.

Genetically modified organisms (GMOs), though, are fraught with difficulties. Fears of "franken foods," weed killer–proof traits, and terminator genes have caused mass rejection of GMO technology, especially in Europe. More consumers in the United States are joining protests against genetically engineered foods. In Africa, WV agronomists condemned potential terminator-gene seed stock. WV recommended that GMO seeds in general be eschewed for the time being for environmental, cultural and cost-related reasons.[11]

In any case, providing greater household food security is one of the most important tasks of many NGOs. For example, working with small farmers in the South, NGOs help select and produce seeds appropriate to the local environment and culture. In the North, perhaps it is time for international NGOs to advocate a "Mediterranean" high-grain, low-meat diet for their donors. Such a diet assures healthier lives and less conversion of grains to meat.

The stated mission of WV agronomists in Africa is to seek farmers' best options. This approach led WV to disseminate adapted technologies to many farmers who otherwise fail to benefit from investments in agricultural research. WV operates in direct collaboration with the Consultative Group on International Agricultural Research (CGIAR) and national agricultural research systems (NARSs). WV introduced several new crops and numerous new varieties of commonly grown crops that are superior producers, grow well on poor soils, and carry biological resistance to important pests and diseases. Examples include the identification and distribution of early maturing, virus-resistant varieties of maize in Mozambique and Sudan; the introduction of some 216 varieties of cassava in Angola; and the introduction of early maturing cowpeas in Senegal.

UNCERTAINTY AND DEMAGOGUES

Given so many global concerns in a world at a loss for answers, claims of certainty are appealing. In a world eager to recover the spiritual and the religious, unambiguous religious claims are attractive. Fundamentalist movements of many types are growing in power and authority everywhere. Hindu fundamentalists are aggressively calling India back to its religious and cultural roots, accusing Christians and the secular West of destroying Indian culture. Fundamentalist Buddhist movements are emerging in Taiwan and Sri Lanka. Some advocates of capitalism as the ultimate answer to history's ills sound at times like religious fanatics. This is especially true when they are allied with the Christian fundamentalists in the North.

The rise of Islamic fundamentalism is well documented. This movement is a reaction to (1) Western colonialism, interpreted as another crusade on the part of Christendom, (2) the inadequacy of secular governments in Muslim countries, which are not doing well in terms of enfranchising and caring for their people, and (3) in the Middle East, to Jewish fundamentalism in Israel and Christian fundamentalism in the West. Where nation-building has been badly done, as in the Middle East and Central Asia, national identities are artificial and lack compelling force. In such places Islam offers a powerful alternative as a social or national organising force.

The fact that "Western" and "Christian" are linked in the minds of Muslim fundamentalists means that any Christian organisation with a social agenda will be suspect. Because many Muslims associate growth of the Christian church in this century with Christian mission concerned for the poor, the Islamic NGO movement has emerged as both a competitor and a threat to the Christian NGO movement. While many Islamic NGOs operate aboveboard and share genuine concern for the plight of the poor, a subversive element within the Islamic NGO movement intend to damage and replace Christian NGOs. Christian NGOs have been at risk in Bangladesh, and World Vision has experienced serious problems in India, Kenya, Mauritania and Senegal.

SCRUTINY OF NGOS

The world will desperately need care-givers in the next decade and beyond. The question to ponder is how well a special "tribe" of those care-givers, called international NGOs, will respond. These large NGOs, in the news supplying relief goods and operating feeding stations in third-world countries, employ most of their people and spend most of their money in development or poverty eradication activities.

Traditionally, the relief and development arms of NGOs operated on separate tracts. Relief met temporary needs created by natural disasters. After the worst trauma of the disaster was over, rehabilitation leading towards development could begin. The need for relief was seen as an aberration, like an injury to a healthy person. After emergency "treatment," the patient could be released back to the development practitioner.

The world of complex humanitarian emergencies (CHEs) presents us with a different "patient." The relief-to-development continuum no longer applies. Relief can be development, and development relief. Where one begins and the other stops is often ambiguous in the messy world of CHEs. Also, the "patient" may not be expected to return to "healthy" status for decades, even without further civil disruption or violence. WV's relief staff pioneered new approaches termed *developmental relief*. Conterminous with providing immediate foodstuff and other items to save lives, seeds and tools, for example, provide means to grow new crops in the next season.

Those seeds are frequently first grown in test plots in the local area and through seed multiplication programmes. They are then distributed to farmers affected by civil disturbances. Results in parts of Africa have been mini–green revolutions with disease-resistant and higher-yielding cassava, chick peas, plantains, maize and other food crops. Besides agricultural renewal, other developmental relief activities include creating marketing coops and enterprise development loans.

Regarding development, relief activities may be needed where none were previously required. If we assume a world where civil violence and wars are common, then we must also assume that an NGO's development efforts will not only be interrupted but may also be negated. The challenge is to infuse relief-like activities into development projects. Most staff with development training have little experience in relief operations. We have seen that managers of some field offices don't know how to think in relief terms. Yet this is what will be demanded of international NGOs: simultaneously to provide developmental relief and operate relief activities in development.

NGOs often must attempt both development and relief simultaneously because both are necessary. Stakeholders and critics demand both. Voices from donors and academicians have long criticised the "BandAid" approach of relief organisations, in which food and medicine are given as palliative treatments but underlying causes of poverty and injustice are not addressed. Nor is traditional relief sustainable, if what is provided this year won't feed people during the next emergency.

Relief operations are not the only activities that require greater accountability from NGOs. Donors, whether governments, individuals, or foundations, are all clamouring that NGOs' claims must be shown to work. Simply put, do NGOs "walk their talk?" Are most development projects sustainable? Do beneficiaries truly participate in project design, implementation and evaluation? Is poverty alleviation as quick and cheap as the NGO advertisements imply? The answer to these questions much of the time is a qualified no.[12]

In the past, NGOs didn't worry too much about accountability of their work. Donors seemed to assume that good bookkeeping made good projects. Today stakeholders demand quality products with measurable results. Major donors are concerned that the people most affected by NGO operations, the beneficiaries, generally have little control over the development process. If NGOs have difficulty releasing control or ownership of a project, how can development can be sustainable?

To better guarantee sustainability, major donors are insisting that NGOs strengthen civil society. For some donors this means that Northern NGOs must partner with Southern or third-world NGOs and community-based organisations. The thinking is that indigenous and national NGOs are necessary pieces of civil society, are closer to the people, and therefore know which development processes (programmes and projects) work best. This may be true. The trouble is, studies indicate that local NGOs tend to put less stock in beneficiary participation than do Northern NGOs. Still, civil society and indigenous capacity are worth building, and Northern government donors believe these are best accomplished by creating and encouraging local NGOs.

This partnering with Southern NGOs indicates a future where Northern NGOs will be caught between the proverbial rock and a hard place. This tension will reduce complacency. Anxiety levels, however, will sharply rise. Northern NGOs wishing to increase their effectiveness and/or market share are increasingly flirting with the giants: transnational corporations and the World Bank and its regional daughters. Both these groups are perceived to have deep pockets. NGOs hope to expand their work through working with these donor partners.

The trouble is that both transnational corporations and the World Bank have engaged in anti-developmental activities in the past. This is one reason that transnational corporations such as Nike and Unocal are looking for "white knights" in the NGO community. The reputations of oil, metallic mineral, food, drug and forest-product companies are equally tarnished. The World Bank now seems to have found its development focus, an identity lost for two decades while it played the debt restructuring game with the International Monetary Fund.

NGOs need to face the definite possibility that they may be coopted by big money. In real cash terms, NGOs are tiny by transnational corporation standards. The tendency will be to use development organisations as window dressing or eye wash. How well can NGOs speak the truth if part of their payroll and prestige is on the line? How difficult will it become to advocate a stronger boycott on Nestlé products, for example, if an NGO is using Nestlé money to fund maternal and child-care programmes!

Truth-telling will be especially critical as other donors insist that Northern NGOs become better advocates for the people they help, namely, the poor and marginalised. Already large Northern NGOs such as Oxfam claim a dual "development and advocacy" focus. WV, too, has seriously taken on responsibility for advocating on behalf of causes that benefit the people the organisation serves.

Most advocacy work is straightforward, even non-controversial. An example is the perennial pleading for more foreign aid from Northern governments. Other advocacy efforts are delicate and difficult tasks for operational NGOs, especially where staff safety is of paramount importance.

Advocacy is one activity that points towards more knowledge-based NGOs. WV is developing virtual teams using computer technology, including Lotus Notes and the Internet. Perhaps nowhere are new skills more needed than in disaster mitigation (relief) operations. Relief's one-time "cowboy" culture is being replaced by a "do no harm" and "think before you act" mentality. Negotiation and peace-building/conflict avoidance skills are encouraged. Staff security and stress management are recognised obligations of senior management.

TO SUM UP

Lessons being learned by NGOs today will be instructive for operations tomorrow. Working amidst violence will become normative, if it isn't already. Rebel groups and terrorists have ready access to arms, once a prerogative only enjoyed by governments and well-financed mobsters. More perpetrators will be child soldiers, who also have the dubious distinction of being victims of adult recruitment and abuse. Safety of NGO staff will become more complicated as kidnapping and other criminal activities increase.

Concerning violence, NGOs will be working in situations of generally worsening environmental problems, at least in the short term. Control of renewable resources, as well as minerals and fossil fuels, will provoke hostilities among groups of people and nation-states. Access to sufficient supplies of clean water may incite ethnic violence and war.

While strides have been made to control many communicable diseases such as polio and smallpox, malaria remains endemic. HIV/AIDS is out of control in much of East and South Africa. Chronic and mental diseases, once wrongly thought to be monopolised by the North, are beginning to receive attention in the South.

Disease is closely linked to hunger, especially in the young. More people are eating better today than ever before. Probably more will eat better tomorrow. Yet 25 per cent of the world's children will likely be malnourished in 2020. Most of these children will be in the sub-Saharan Africa and South Asia, the globe's poorest regions.

Poverty abatement in these regions will be slow to come. Progress is being made in Africa, but population growth still exceeds food productivity. NGOs have joined forces with agricultural research institutes to develop and test seeds that are higher producers and more disease-free than current varieties. Tested by farmers for suitability to indigenous conditions, these superior seeds are locally produced and disseminated.

Usually, agricultural improvements are considered development activities by NGOs and donors. Some of WV's seed multiplication and distribution is actually associated with relief programmes. During emergencies, including civil violence, a developmental relief programme emphasising dissemination of seeds has proven to be a successful way to quickly move rural families off food aid quickly.

While NGOs try to cope in a world that seems increasingly violent and chaotic, NGOs themselves will be more closely scrutinised. Northern NGOs, especially, will be pressured to change. Government donors are already insisting that much of the operational work be delegated to Southern NGO partners and community-based organisations. These donors and academic critics want Northern NGOs to be better advocates for the poor and more outspoken against human rights abuses. Private and public donors are also demanding more accountability. NGOs will need to prove they think before they act when providing emergency relief. NGOs also must back up their claims to be cost-effective alternatives to governmental agencies as poverty-eradication organisations. NGOs will need to adapt and change yet keep their focus or vision. Yes, the millennium promises bounties of both opportunities and challenges for NGOs. This can make for exciting places to work!

NOTES

[1] Members of the Paris Club or G8 are Canada, France, Germany, Italy, Japan, Russia, the UK and the United States.

[2] Examples of the former are Alan Fowler, *Striking a Balance: A Guide to Enhancing the Effectiveness of Non-governmental Organizations in International Development* (London: Earthscan, 1997); Michael Edwards and David Hulme, eds., *Beyond the Magic Bullet: NGO Performance*

and Accountability in the Post–Cold War World (West Hartford, Conn.: Kumarian Press/Save the Children, 1996). An example of the latter is Michael Maren, *The Road to Hell: The Ravaging Effects of Foreign Aid and International Charity* (New York: The Free Press, 1997).

[3] UNHCR, *The State of the World's Refugees: 1997–98* (Oxford and New York: Oxford University Press, 1997).

[4] There is no "official" definition of small arms. One definition simply says that light weapons are those that can be carried by a combatant or light vehicle over back country roads. A more detailed definition used by the British American Security Information Council includes pistols, revolvers, rifles, automatic rifles, hand grenades, machine guns, light mortars, light anti-tank missiles, light anti-aircraft missiles, and land mines. Advocates trying to curb the free-wheeling small arms trade may be able to capture some of the moral indignation against land mines that led to the convention to ban those abominable weapons. For a fuller treatment, see chapter 9 herein.

[5] Recently, WorldWatch discussed the slowing of world population growth. Although that trend was noticed more than two decades ago, the degree of reduction may have accelerated. The median UN projection is an 8.9 rather than a 9.4 billion world in 2050. (WorldWatch, "Our Demographically Divided World," news release [10 April 1999].) Yet, if we count people, that's a 3 billion increase (51 per cent) in 50 years, with over three-fourths of those people born in the developing countries. Providing adequate jobs, food, shelter, medical care, clean water, sanitation and other basic necessities will take Herculean efforts.

[6] For example, see Thomas R. Karl, Neville Nicholls and Jonathan Gregory, "The Coming Climate," *Scientific American* (May 1987), 79–83.

[7] UNAIDS, *Report on the Global HIV/AIDS Epidemic* (June 2000), 6; idem, "AIDS Epidemic Update" (December 2001). A handy source for communicable diseases is S. Jay Olshansky et al., "Infectious Diseases – New and Ancient Threats to World Health," *Population Bulletin* (Population Reference Bureau) 52/2 (July 1997). One of the dozens of articles on the rapid rise of HIV/AIDS in the Third World was produced by the Africa Policy Information Center (APIC), "Africa: New HIV/AIDS Report" (14 July 1998). Another excellent source is the World Bank, Africa Region, *Intensifying Action Against HIV/AIDS in Africa: Responding to a Development Crisis* (June 1999).

[8] As an example, see Anne Plat McGinn, "Preventing Chronic Disease in Developing Countries," in *State of the World: 1997*, ed. Lester R. Brown et al. (New York: W. W. Norton, 1997), 60–77; and UNAIDS, "AIDS Epidemic Update" (December 2001), 1.

[9] For example, see Arthur Kleinman and Alex Cohen, "Psychiatry's Global Challenge, " *Scientific American* (March 1997), 86–89.

[10] International Food Policy Research Institute, "The World Food Situation: Recent Developments, Emerging Issues and Long-term Prospects" (Washington, D.C.: IFPRI, 1997).

[11] WV agronomists would like to see much more testing of insecticide gene and weed killer–proof plants. Monsanto's decision temporarily to halt the development of terminator seeds was greeted with applause throughout the globe.

[12] See Fowler, *Striking a Balance.*

8.

Caught by Conflict

The Rights of Children in Times of War

KATHY VANDERGRIFT

Let us take this opportunity to recapture our instinct to nourish and protect children. Let us transform our moral outrage into concrete action. Our children have a right to peace. Peace is every child's right.

—Graça Machel,
"The Impact of Armed Conflict on Children"

When the community becomes a battlefield, children bear the brunt. Children are increasingly deliberate targets as well as unintended victims in more than 30 armed conflicts around the world. Between 1985 and 1995:

- 2 million children have been killed;
- 6 million were left seriously injured or permanently disabled;
- 12 million were left homeless;
- 1 million were orphaned or separated from their parents;
- 10 million suffered from serious trauma as a result of war; and
- 300,000 served as child soldiers.[1]

Protection of children from armed conflict is essential. Along with other humanitarian organisations, World Vision (WV) addresses

This chapter is a shortened version of Melanie Gow, Kathy Vandergrift and Randini Wanduragala, *The Right to Peace: Children and Armed Conflict,* working paper no. 2 (Monrovia, Calif.: World Vision International, March 2000).

this concern through four avenues: humanitarian assistance to children during and after conflict; child-focussed community development work, which helps to reduce some causes of war; peace-building and reconciliation activities in conflict-prone and post-conflict situations; and advocacy to improve public policies and practices which affect children.

The UN Convention on the Rights of the Child (CRC) provides a positive framework for action on this issue. It combines a recognition of the responsibility of adults to protect children and adolescents with the right and responsibility of young people to participate in their own development.[2] Within that framework, implementation of the recommendations of the Graça Machel report entitled "Impacts of War on Children" is a high priority. Additional steps are needed to strengthen compliance and public accountability for respecting the rights of children.[3]

Children are not merely victims of war; they, along with their families and communities, can be active participants in the prevention of conflict and the development or rebuilding of their countries. A comprehensive strategy will acknowledge the role of various actors to:

- prevent the involvement of children in armed conflict;
- protect children from the impact of armed conflict when it occurs;
- practice child-focussed post-conflict reconciliation and reconstruction; and
- promote the active participation of children and their families at every step.

WHY FOCUS ON CHILDREN IN CONFLICT SITUATIONS?

While children are part of the larger civilian population affected by war, they warrant a special focus for the following reasons: First, children are affected differently because of their vulnerability and the fact that they are still in formative stages of personal growth. What happens during childhood shapes one's understanding about the world, human society, and future roles in it. Everyone under 18 is considered a child under the Convention on the Rights of the Child, but the impact of armed conflict differs by age, gender and stage of development. These factors have to be considered in effective strategies to protect and restore the well-being of children and to allow them to participate in their own development.

Second, children who grow up living in violence are more likely to turn to violence themselves as a method of solving problems. Investing in the prevention of violence for children is an investment in human security for everyone.

Third, children represent the majority of civilians affected by armed conflict and the number of affected children is growing. And fourth, caring for children is one of the most basic foundations of society. Focussing on protection for children can be a powerful way to break down barriers between peoples, restore community values and contribute to peace-building.

Protecting children is a basic value in most cultures and religions. Christian organisations, such as WV, draw inspiration from the priority Jesus gave to the place of children within the community. Throughout his ministry Jesus demonstrated respect and love for children. Exercising responsibility for the next generation is a occurring theme throughout the Scriptures. Similar themes recur in other religious texts and ethical codes of conduct.

Respect and protection for children is a responsibility to be shared by parents, local communities, governments and the international community. Local communities participate in the provision of assistance to children in need and in child-focussed community development, which helps to reduce the causes of conflict. At a national and international level, NGOs join forces to advocate public policies and practices which respect the right of children to grow up free from the negative impacts of armed conflict.

POLICY CONTEXT FOR CHILDREN AND ARMED CONFLICT

A comprehensive policy framework to address this issue will build on the Convention on the Rights of the Child and the recommendations of the Graça Machel study mentioned above.

CRC as a framework for action

War violates every right of a child – the right to life, the right to be with family and community, the right to health, the right to the development of the personality and the right to be nurtured and protected.

—Graça Machel

The CRC provides an important framework for developing effective strategies. It covers all aspects of a child's life, each of which is also affected by armed conflict. Attention to all aspects is essential. This needs emphasis because of a current temptation among donor agencies in the field of international development to divert funds from basic needs into special, short-term initiatives with a high public profile. Based on 50 years of field experience, WV puts a high priority on an integrated, community-based approach as the most effective and the best investment for limited funds.

It is not a coincidence that most conflicts involving children are occurring in countries where families and communities do not have adequate resources to provide for their children. We know that the children most susceptible to recruitment into the military are children at risk under normal circumstances, such as street children, unaccompanied children, child prostitutes, child labourers, poor children and children deprived of education. Significant progress in implementing the CRC would address the root causes of many of the conflicts that threaten children today.

The resolutions on children and armed conflict passed by the Security Council, along with other declarations by governments and UN agencies, are important political commitments. The challenge is to turn these commitments into action that makes a genuine difference for children.

Developed countries frequently make official statements about the importance of children, but at the same time they continue to reduce the resources available for basic community development in poor countries. In addition, their representatives in international agencies, such as the International Monetary Fund (IMF), adopt policies that force fragile countries to divert resources from health and education budgets to meeting debt payments. If developed countries are serious about stopping the involvement of children in armed conflict, they will invest more in basic development for children, such as health and education. They will also examine the impact of their fiscal and trade policies on children at risk for involvement in armed conflict and children already affected by armed conflict.

The Graça Machel study

In 1993, Graça Machel, former minister for education in Mozambique and until recently South Africa's first lady, was appointed by the UN

secretary general to undertake a study of the impact of armed conflict on children. The study took two years of intensive research.
The report, "The Impact of Armed Conflict on Children," was submitted to the General Assembly of the United Nations in 1996. The
findings were devastating. They highlighted the urgent need for
particular protection of those under 18 from armed conflict. The
study concluded with a series of recommendations which continue
to form the backbone for a comprehensive international action plan
for war-affected children.

At the first International Conference on War-affected Children,
held in September 2000, Graça Machel presented a progress report. There has been some progress in programmes, international
legislation and advocacy for children. At the same time, the complexity, longevity, and level of violence involved in contemporary
conflicts means that the reality for children in situations of armed
conflict has not improved substantially since 1996; in many situations it has become worse.

> *Our promises to children remain unfulfilled. This review is a sec
> ond urgent call to action. It is a desperate plea for the compas
> sion, the commitment, and the tenacity needed to protect chil
> dren from the atrocities of war.*
>
> Graça Machel, *The Machel Review, 1996–2000*

Implementation of the CRC

The CRC is the first international legal instrument to incorporate
both human rights law and humanitarian law. The wider CRC provisions are equally applicable in times of armed conflict, since the
convention does not allow for derogation in times of war. This
position is supported by the Committee on the Rights of the Child.[4]
As stated by Thomas Hammarberg, "There is no derogation clause
in this Convention, it applies in its entirety also in times of war or
emergency. The child has a right to a family environment, to go to
school, to play, to get healthcare and adequate nutrition—also during the armed conflict . . . that the right to life, survival and development be protected."[5]

The difficulties of monitoring and implementing the CRC are
widely recognised and mean that a legal response alone is insuffi-

cient. The enforcement provisions are weaker than those provided in other international human rights treaties. Countries report once every five years, and a committee established by the United Nations reviews the report and makes recommendations for improvements.

As well as using the CRC as a framework for programmes, WV suggests that it is time to consider additional mechanisms to improve accountability for compliance, especially in cases of serious, massive violations, such as those that occur during armed conflict. In addition to stronger accountability mechanisms under the CRC, it is time to take the violations of the rights of children more seriously under other international laws as well, especially those who have stronger enforcement mechanisms.

First, it is helpful to consider the range of basic rights and responsibilities which are impacted by armed conflict. This analysis provides the basis for the strategy which follows.

SPECIFIC RIGHTS AND RESPONSIBILITIES

The right to life, survival and development (Article 6)

The most fundamental challenge for any . . . system which wishes to mitigate the suffering of children in war is to ensure their very survival.

—Carolyn Hamilton and Tabatha Abu El-Haj

Article 6 of the CRC states: "Every child has the inherent right to life. States parties shall ensure to the maximum extent possible the survival and development of the child." UNICEF states, however, that the proportion of child deaths during armed conflict has been rising steadily since the end of the Second World War.[6]

The use of humanitarian cease fires can help protect the survival of children. Agreements have been reached during conflicts to allow for the delivery of humanitarian assistance and healthcare, the immunisation of children, safe passage and the identification of safe zones. Greater use of such initiatives was advocated by the secretary general of the United Nations in "Report on the Protection of

Civilians in Armed Conflict," presented to the Security Council in September 1999. Now the challenge is to incorporate and implement these tools in the strategies adopted for specific conflicts by all agents in the international community.

Violations of agreements to allow access to vulnerable populations for humanitarian assistance and to exempt schools and hospitals from attack must be taken more seriously. In the case of Sudan, for example, violations of this nature have been documented and reported by both human rights and humanitarian agencies, but little serious action has been taken.

The use of landmines has also contributed to an increase in the number of children affected directly and indirectly by armed conflict. The indiscriminate nature of landmines has led to particularly high numbers of childhood deaths and amputations. Children injured when they are gathering wood, walking to school, or playing make up to 30 per cent of landmine injuries in Cambodia and Laos.[7] According to UNICEF landmines cause 800 deaths or serious injuries every month and children in 68 countries live with more than 100 million landmines.

Progress has been made to ban the use of the landmines through an international treaty adopted two years ago. Much remains to be done to implement it.

The right to food, health and the basic necessities of life (Articles 24 and 27)

It is a sad fact that infants and young children are often the earliest victims of . . . diseases and malnutrition which accompany population displacement and refugee outflows.

—Sadako Ogata, UN High Commissioner for Refugees

Direct physical trauma causes 5 per cent of the child deaths overall; 95 per cent result from starvation or illness, mostly preventable with reasonable access to basic services. (In specific attacks the percentage of children killed directly may be higher.) One factor is the increasing manipulation of food supplies and assistance as weapons of war. Medical centres and community health services may be destroyed. And there is an imminent risk of contaminated water.

Immediately after the recent Kosovo conflict, a preliminary rapid nutritional assessment conducted by WV indicated that 15 per cent of children were severely or moderately malnourished. Children two years old and under were found to be particularly at risk because of lack of weaning foods and proper sterilisation facilities, disruption of breastfeeding due to long marches, poor maternal nutrition, stress and fatigue.[8]

The right to a stable family environment (Articles 7–9, 16, 20 and 22)

Those who belong to caring and supportive families withstand severe psychological stress better than others. Stable, affectionate relationships between children and their closest care-givers are a protective factor against psychological disturbance.

—International Save the Children Alliance

Article 7 of the CRC states that every child "shall have the right from birth to a name, the right to acquire a nationality, and, as far as possible, the right to know and be cared for by his or her parents." Article 16 provides that "no child shall be subjected to arbitrary or unlawful interference with his or her privacy, family, home," Articles 8, 9, 20 and 22 require states parties to "provide assistance and protection to re-establish a child's identity and reunite the child with the family."

In a recent report UN Secretary General Kofi Annan stated that 30 million people are now in refugee and displaced-persons camps, and half of them are children. Children and adolescents are often overlooked during massive population shifts that accompany armed conflict. Survey studies have pointed out that some unaccompanied children wait years for family reunification.

Birth registration, prevention of separation whenever possible and early family reunification are basic elements of a child-focussed strategy. An international conference on children and armed conflict, held in Oslo in 1998, developed detailed recommendations for improving the co-ordination and implementation of family reunification programmes.

Family reunification of children who have been involved as child soldiers or children who have been severely traumatised by war requires special assistance. Effective, community-based programmes will respect the cultural context, provide healthcare, psycho-social support, skills-training and liaison with the community to help with the transition back to normal life.

While humanitarian agencies know what needs to be done, political leaders are turning a blind eye to the situation of children, especially in some parts of Africa. Strong public support for the right of children to family life would help create the political will to allocate resources for family reunification. As an investment in future security, it would provide a higher return than much greater amounts invested in sophisticated weapons technology.

The right to protection from violence (Articles 5 and 37)

Child D has seen enough inhumanity to crush the spirits of an adult. After the provincial capital where he lived fell to UNITA rebels, he survived on scraps of food or none at all. A family friend suggested getting out of the area and walking to the government-held area of Dondo. D went with his 14–year-old brother, his sister and her one-year old baby. On the third day they were surrounded by UNITA soldiers. D watched while his brother was shot dead and his sister bayoneted. The baby was clubbed to death with a rifle butt. D ran through the bush in absolute terror. For hours he lay concealed listening to victims of the soldiers screaming. His escape was successful when he finally arrived in Dondo. Although he was now in a secure environment, he cried much of the night for the first weeks and experienced dreams of the killings for a long time. He returned to his family in Luanda, but the memories of his war experiences are likely to affect him for many years.

—World Vision International

"No child shall be subjected to torture or other cruel, inhumane, or degrading treatment or punishment" (Article 37). States also specifically commit to "take all appropriate measures to promote physical and psychological recovery and social reintegration of a child victim of such treatment" (Article 39).

In situations of armed conflict, children are subjected to various forms of violence and degradation or are eyewitnesses to these atrocities. Sometimes, in order to guarantee their own survival or safety, they may be required to carry out acts of violence against members of their own family or other adults or children.

Child soldiers are trained and forced to kill and torture. Once trained, they can prove to be highly effective and fearless soldiers, often sent to the front lines. According to a Khmer Rouge commander, "It usually takes a little time, but eventually the younger ones become the most effective soldiers of them all.[9]

It takes more than a little time to take the war out of the child when the war is over. Specialists in trauma counselling are often surprised at the resilience of children who survive brutal circumstances, but it can take years for former child soldiers to re-establish a normal life and be accepted in the community.

Gender-based violence

One can only be outraged by the abuse of children, sexually or otherwise, but when it is committed collectively by soldiers within the conditions of war it is doubly abhorrent.

—Michael Harbottle,
The Centre for International Peace Building[10]

Young girls in the context of armed conflict are vulnerable to sexual violence as a crime of opportunity. In Uganda and Sudan girls as young as 12 are given to soldiers as "wives" and subjected to sexual and physical abuse. Sexual violence is also used as a weapon of war. In Kosovo young girl refugees waiting at border crossings were systematically raped by Serbian soldiers as part of a programme of "ethnic cleansing." Refugee children in countries of asylum also experience an increase in sexual violence. In Albania, for example, refugee girls were at risk of attack or abduction by certain groups within the host country population. In other situations, such as Cambodia, research has shown that an increase in child prostitution accompanied the presence of peace-keepers in the country.

Children can also be required to witness sexual violence against family members or be forced to take part.

I was only 15 when I was abducted by rebels. . . . I lived in captivity for almost three years. Three days after my abduction I was given to a man to be his fourth wife. He was quite old and was a bad man who was harsh and rude. Twice he beat me and I almost died. In December 1995 I had a baby girl. Despite this I was given a gun and sent to the war front to fight with my baby strapped to my back.

—Former child soldier, Uganda, 1998

Young girls face physical and psychological trauma. They are vulnerable to infection by HIV/AIDs or other sexually transmitted diseases. Girls who are raped may be ostracised by their families and communities, and there are few reproductive healthcare services to meet their needs. As noted in a UN secretary general's report on the abduction of children, approximately 85 per cent of the girls who arrived at the Gulu Trauma Centre in northern Uganda had contracted sexual diseases during their captivity.[11] Sometimes, as a result of rape and rejection, children turn to prostitution for survival.

Since the Machel study, Article 7 of the Rome Statute of the International Criminal Court has classified rape, persecution, torture, sexual slavery, enforced prostitution, forced pregnancy, enforced sterilisation and any other forms of sexual violence of comparable gravity as crimes against humanity. Article 8 deals specifically with gender-based crimes as war crimes.[12] While this is a positive step, more has to be done to prevent sexual violence in times of both war and peace

Right to education (Articles 28 and 29)

Education is vital during armed conflicts, offering a sense of continuity and stability for children and for the whole community. Education gives shape and structure to children's lives.

Graça Machel, *The Machel Review 1996–2000*

Schools are often targets in conflict situations, and fear and disruption can make learning difficult. In spite of the difficulties, experience shows that maintaining or restoring education, even if only in informal activities, is an important form of security for children. When young people from conflict situations are asked about their priorities, education is always near the top of the list. Educational programmes can include safety and survival skills as well as assisting in the integration of injured youth, abuse survivors and former child soldiers. Educating children and communities about the rights of children can help to prevent recruitment, abduction and gender-based violence, and therefore serves as an important protection tool.

Education should be restarted as soon as possible in situations of conflict. Many donor countries consider education as long-term development and do not fund it as part of an emergency response. In situations where the conflict endures for many years, with children forced to remain in displaced persons' camps for years, the interruption in their education puts them at a disadvantage even after the conflict is over. In southern Sudan, for example, education has been disrupted for many years. While schools cannot be built in temporary settings, there are mobile, flexible, less formal ways to provide basic education.

Right to be heard, non-discrimination and identity

Article 12 of the CRC requires that "the views of the child be given due weight in accordance with the age and maturity of the child." Non-discrimination is a basic principle of the CRC, and other provisions protect freedom of expression, religious freedoms and the right to preserve one's cultural identity.

In modern conflict children are often targeted in campaigns to exterminate particular groups of people. In some cases local media and school curricula are used to foster prejudice. Earlier intervention to prevent discrimination could help to prevent attacks on children as part of ethnic or politically motivated conflicts. Local media and school curricula can be used positively to foster respect for other people.

Children are not only objects who suffer because of what others do; they are also active agents within their context. They must be allowed to participate in efforts to prevent conflict and in programmes designed to address their needs during and after armed conflict. Experience in WV programmes in Latin America and the Philippines shows that young people can be effective peace-builders and active participants in the process of reconciliation after conflict.

Youth participation in programme planning and implementation is an area for further learning from experience and research. More training for staff of development organisations would be helpful.

STRATEGIES FOR PREVENTION, PROTECTION AND REINTEGRATION

Circumstances in each country are different and must be reflected in country-specific strategies. A recommendation at the Oslo Conference called for UNICEF to facilitate country-specific strategies, including NGOs and civil society organisations in both their development and implementation.

Some common components of effective strategies are outlined below for consideration in the development of specific plans for specific situations. Other components are universal and must be implemented through the United Nations. The recommendations provide a summary of actions that would make a substantial improvement for children.

PREVENTION

Stop the use of child soldiers

Military necessity cannot provide a justification for conscription or the use of children in combat.

—Guy Goodwin-Gill[13]

One of the most alarming trends in contemporary armed conflicts is the reliance on children as combatants. A child soldier is defined as any person under 18 who is part of any kind of regular or irregular armed force or armed group in any capacity, including but not limited to cooks, porters, messengers, fighters and also girls recruited for sexual purposes.[14]

A profile of child soldiers today

- More than 300,000 children under the age of 18 can be categorised as child soldiers.
- The participation of child soldiers has been reported in 33 current or recent armed conflicts in almost every region of the world. In 26 of the reported countries the children are under 15 years of age. Some of the children are as young as 8 years of age.
- The increase in light automatic weapons and easy access to arms makes child soldiers an increasingly popular choice for armed forces.
- Shortage of military personnel, especially as a conflict drags on, often leads to forcing children into battle.
- Some commanders have noted the desirability of children as they are "more obedient, do not question orders and are easier to manipulate than adult soldiers."
- Particularly vulnerable to recruitment are children at risk under normal circumstances, such as children separated from families, street children, children in displaced persons camps, children in minority groups, poor children. These are the same groups vulnerable to exploitative child labour practices in peacetime.
- Forced recruitment may be through conscription, press-ganging, or kidnapping. Young people may also be "voluntarily" recruited; in some circumstances, however, it is questionable how voluntary such recruitment is. A lack of realistic alternatives for getting food, helping the family, social status, and so forth, may incline young people to choose military means to survive.
- In case studies in El Salvador, Ethiopia and Uganda, almost one-third of all child soldiers were reported to be girls. Girl soldiers are often raped or given to military commanders for sexual purposes.

The abuses

Using child soldiers is a form of exploitative labour. Child soldiers are physically and sexually abused; they have high incidences of sexually transmitted disease, HIV/AIDs, and pregnancy and abortion for the girls. They are often forced to commit atrocities; in some situations alcohol and drugs are used to induce them to commit violence, which leads to their subsequent addiction to these substances.

Physical wounds reveal little of the deeper emotional scars that these children endure as a result of being surrounded by violence. Psycho-social support programmes, including WV's programmes in Uganda and Rwanda, have shown that former child soldiers exhibit profound psychological trauma at levels exceeding that of adult soldiers. Even in situations where voluntary rather than forced recruitment is the norm, children carry the scars that such experiences bring.

Optional protocol to stop the use of child soldiers

The argument that the age of recruitment is merely a technical matter to be decided by individual governments fails to take into account the fact that effective protection of children from the impact of armed conflict requires an unqualified legal and moral commitment which acknowledges that children have no part in armed conflict.

Graça Machel, "Impact of Armed Conflict on Children"

In 1995 the UN Commission on Human Rights established an open-ended working group to draft an optional protocol to the CRC on the involvement of children in armed conflict. The objective was to raise the minimum age for recruitment and participation in military activities from 15 to 18 for any armed force, whether government, opposition, rebel or guerrilla.

The negotiations concluded with the adoption of an optional protocol which raises the age for participation to 18 and the age for voluntary recruitment to 16. The protocol includes specific provisions for non-state actors and requires states to provide assistance in the demobilisation and reintegration of existing child soldiers. This agreement is a step forward; it reflects the fundamental principle that young people under the age of 18 should not be involved in armed conflict. At the same time, failure to adopt a consistent age for all categories and limiting state responsibility for enforcement to "feasible measures" results in a protocol that is fairly weak.

Attention must now be focussed on ratification by as many states as possible and effective implementation in order to achieve universal acceptance of the basic value that children and war do not mix.

Progress is occurring on other fronts. In October 1998 the United Nations secretary general announced a new policy regarding age limits for UN peace-keepers, military observers and civilian police. The UN asks that "the troop-contributing countries do not send civilian police and military observers younger than 25 years to serve in peacekeeping operations. Furthermore, national contingent soldiers should preferably be at least 21 years old, and definitely not below the age of 18, when deployed in a United Nations peace-keeping operation."

In a statement to the UN Security Council on 12 February 1999 UNICEF Executive Director Carol Bellamy applauded the UN position as a model for country forces and emphasised the importance of a universal standard: "We would be derelict if we did not reiterate, in the strongest possible terms, that until the minimum age of recruitment is universally set at 18, the ruthless exploitation of children as soldiers will continue."

Recent ratification of the African Charter on the Rights and Welfare of the Child provides an additional tool for use in Africa. It is the first regional treaty which obliges states parties to the charter to take all necessary measures to ensure that no one under the age of 18 takes part in hostilities and that states refrain from recruiting anyone under 18 into their armed forces (Article 22).

Why age 18?

The arguments for adopting a consistent position of 18 as the minimum for recruitment and deployment include the following:

- All other provisions of the CRC use age 18. It is the most commonly accepted age for recognition as an adult around the world. It is inconsistent to lower the age for just one article.
- Voting age in most countries is 18. The age for participation in military activity should be consistent with the voting age.
- A higher standard will help to prevent illegal use of younger children. It is difficult to determine the exact age of children in

their teen years. A military commander, for example, can easily pass a 13 year old off as a 15 year old; but a 13 year old is unlikely to be mistaken for an 18 year old. Raising the age limit is, in particular, aimed at protecting the youngest and most vulnerable children and is especially effective in countries where children do not possess legal documents to prove their age.

- Only children who are non-combatants are entitled to benefit from the protection of civilians established in the Geneva Conventions and their additional protocols. If they do participate, even by being recruits or in support functions, they lose their inviolability as non-combatants and become legitimate military targets.
- Of the 191 states that have ratified the CRC, fewer than 50 currently have laws permitting the recruitment of those under 18 years of age.
- Experience in internal conflicts shows that children who start in support functions can be assigned easily to direct participation. The line between direct and indirect participation is blurred, and the absence of a clear definition prevents effective enforcement. A "straight 18" position would eliminate any ambiguity and allow for more effective enforcement.

In her report Graça Machel advocated immediate adoption of the optional protocol and a "straight 18" position. The report makes a direct correlation between standard setting in the international human rights framework and the use of child soldiers. Machel saw raising the age of recruitment and participation as a crucial intervention in the overall strategy to stop the use of child soldiers.

Control the small-arms trade – legal and illegal

Arming children, directly or indirectly, should not be tolerated and those countries which are exporters of arms should ensure that they are not sent to countries which arm children in violation of international law.

—Mary Robinson,
UN High Commissioner for Human Rights[15]

A recent report on small arms estimated that there are about 500 million small arms in the world; they have been used in 43 of the last 47 conflicts.[16] Small arms can be bought cheaply; they are simple to use; and they make it easier to arm children on the front lines. Approximately 90 per cent of civilian casualties are caused by small arms.[17]

In some countries it is not uncommon to meet young children who can assemble these weapons in a matter of minutes but who are unable to read properly. In some parts of the world guns can be bought for the price of a goat or a bag of corn and are less expensive than books. The increased participation of children in armed conflict has been linked to a proliferation in the availability of small arms.

The UN Security Council, in Resolutions 1261 and 1314 on Children and Armed Conflict, calls on member states, particularly those involved in the manufacture and marketing of weapons, to restrict arms transfer which could aggravate existing tensions and collaborate in combating illegal arms flows.

Welcome efforts are being made by governments to stop the illicit arms trade. Greater effort is required to control the legal sale of small arms. The European Union Code of Conduct on Small Arms provides a policy framework, but sustained work is required to tighten loop holes, call brokers to account, and increase the transparency and accountability of those who have signed it. A UN conference on small arms held in July 2001 provided an opportunity for all nations to show leadership and adopt international mechanisms to control trade in small arms.

Controlling access to small arms is a supply-side solution; attempts are also being made to reduce the demand for small arms. In a recent WV study, *Silent Revolution,* Tibebe Eshete and Siobhan O'Reilly-Calthrop demonstrate the potential of community development programmes to reduce the demand for small arms. Based on their research they recommend that disarmament programmes should include a more holistic approach, changing social attitudes as well as the behaviour of individual gun users.

Reduce the root causes of conflict

The best way to prevent the destructive impact of armed conflict on children is to invest in the reduction of the root causes of armed conflict, which include poverty, inequality, violations of human rights, poor governance and the need for alternative mechanisms to resolve disputes.

Investment in children and young people is a good investment in human security, especially in those countries which have a large and growing population of young people. The basic development needs of youth should be given higher priority in the development of country-specific development strategies used by the International Monetary Fund, the World Bank, donor countries and development organisations.

Resolving the root causes of conflict is feasible. A recent WV report, *10 Urgent Issues for the Children of the New Millennium*, documents that it is feasible to remove some of the major causes of conflict by the time a child born in 2000 reaches adulthood. The biggest problem is a lack of political will to take the necessary steps.

Make the IMF accountable

Members of the Jubilee 2000 network have drawn attention to the implications of the debt burden on the ability of countries to invest in their own children. The International Monetary Fund and finance ministers of developed countries must consider the impact for children at risk of fiscal policies forced on indebted countries. It is unfair to hold countries accountable for compliance with the CRC when their resource allocation is directed and controlled by the International Monetary Fund; the International Monetary Fund must accept its share of accountability for the consequences of its actions. In many cases structural adjustment policies have left children more vulnerable to the devastating impacts of armed conflicts. If developed countries take their statements about the importance of children seriously, then they will also do a child-impact assessment of the macro-economic policies they support.

Most developed countries are spending far more on promotion of trade and foreign investment than on investment in development assistance, and only a small portion of that goes to children. It would be a good investment for developed countries to shift some of the resources spent on trade promotion to investment in child-focussed community-development and community-security initiatives.

Give adolescents a higher priority

Effective prevention strategies in conflict-prone countries will pay particular attention to adolescents. In many developing countries young people constitute a growing percentage of the population, but they are ignored in national and international decision-making processes related to those countries. Adolescents are particularly vulnerable to military recruitment and sexual abuse. Adolescents in poor countries may face difficulties moving from a basic education to a sustainable economic livelihood and a meaningful role within their social structures. In other cases they may be forced to take on adult roles prematurely, such as in child-headed households, and miss educational opportunities. At the same time they are increasingly conscious of the gap between the images of the "good life" portrayed by advertisers and their own reality.

What takes place during adolescence shapes basic values and future attitudes. Unfortunately, adolescents often are overlooked in community development programmes, once they are finished with basic education.

On a positive note, there are examples of communities which work with young people to provide constructive activities, with a special focus on those who are likely to be drawn into armed activities. Effective strategies, based on an understanding of the role of adolescence in a particular culture, develop ways to channel youthful energy into peaceful and constructive activities. The use of microcredit with older teens is being explored as one tool toward economic livelihood. Other tools are sports and community leadership-training programmes. Helping adolescents obtain documentation regarding age and identity can be part of awareness-raising; evidence shows that youth who are aware of their rights are less vulnerable to forced recruitment. While respect for existing social structures is important, it may also be necessary to allow room for developing new structures, particularly where adolescents are a large percentage of the population.

Particular attention is required for adolescent girls with regards to reproductive health and the risk of sexual exploitation.

Support child protection networks

As part of community development programmes, greater attention needs to be paid to the development and support of child protection networks. The Africa Network for the Prevention and Protection of the Children Against Abuse is a good example. Effective strategies build on local leadership to support advocacy for children at regional and national levels. Such networks in vulnerable circumstances require active support by the international development community. They are an effective way to emphasise respect for children and implement systems for self-protection.

Local media and youth themselves can help to increase awareness of the dangers of involvement in conflict and promote alternative ways to resolve conflicts.

Increase the investment in peace-building

Investment in peace-building initiatives can be effective as a preventive measure. Young people, along with their communities, have a role to play in building a culture of peace, in using alternative methods for conflict resolution, and in reconciliation initiatives after conflict has occurred. Youth reconciliation programmes, such as those in Rwanda, can help the whole community.

Research shows that incorporating peace-building components into community development programmes can help to prevent conflict. Based on research in five different programmes on different continents, Siobhan O'Reilly Calthrop recommends specific steps that can be taken by NGOs.[18] Youth can be active advocates for peace, as shown in the Philippines and the Colombia youth peace movement. As well as learning conflict resolution skills, young people promote peace in their communities.

The Canadian International Development Agency and the Canadian Children and Armed Conflict NGO Network have developed an analytical framework for child-focussed dimensions of peace building activities. Community development programmes can incorporate a peace-building perspective to help prevent conflicts.

PROTECTION

For too long we have given ground to spurious claims that the involvement of children in armed conflict is regrettable but inevitable. It is not. Children are regularly caught up in conflict because of conscious and deliberate decisions made by adults.

—Graça Machel

Strategies of protection focus on helping those children already at risk of involvement in armed conflicts. The international tendency to turn a blind eye to violations of international norms has led to a culture of impunity in which abusers think no disciplinary action will result. Governments and NGOs must work together to remove the culture of impunity. Practical measures must reflect a basic principle that no amount of conflict justifies the abuse of children. Values, rules and standards matter even in times of war.

Protection of children during armed conflict must become a primary consideration for diplomatic initiatives and foreign policy, as well as in humanitarian and development policy. Effective implementation of the CRC requires more attention at the community level, in bilateral, diplomatic relations and through international channels.

National governments have the primary responsibility to protect children, and recognition of national sovereignty is an important part of the system of international law. At the same time, national sovereignty is not an absolute right. If the violations of the basic rights of children are large scale and serious enough to cause permanent damage and if a government does nothing to stop the violations, that government sacrifices its right to national sovereignty.

The United Nations also has a role to play. As stated by the secretary general, "The [Security] Council recognises that massive and systematic breaches of human rights law and international humanitarian law constitute threats to international peace and security, and therefore demand its attention and action."[19] The "Report to the Security Council on the Protection of Civilians during Armed Conflict" resulted in recommendations which: that the Security Council "consider deployment in certain cases of a preventive peacekeeping operation, or of another preventive monitoring presence"; that it investigate disputes at earlier stages; that it take concrete action in response to threats against peace; and that it make use of human rights information as "indicators for potential preventive action by the United Nations."

In keeping with this direction, the following suggestions provide additional mechanisms to improve compliance with the CRC and existing humanitarian laws which were developed to protect children.

Early warning systems

> *What does prevention entail? . . . It means having early warning systems in place so that signs of tension and potential conflict are spotted early enough to do something about them.*
>
> —Mary Robinson,
> UN High Commissioner for Human Rights

The United Nations and regional defence organisations are recognising the need to strengthen their early warning systems and develop strategies to prevent escalation of conflict before it threatens masses of the civilian population. Other players, such as international NGOs active in conflict-prone countries, can provide valuable assistance in development of appropriate, non-military strategies to diffuse developing conflicts.

More attention must be given to serious violations of the rights of children in the early warning system. Any attempts to recruit children for active deployment in armed conflict should be reported immediately and a strategy developed to deal with the problem. Organised campaigns of hatred against particular peoples, which often "justify" attacks on children, need to be countered in the early stages. If embassies, which focus the majority of their attention on trade-related matters, could be asked to give some attention to the situation of children and young people and make serious violations of the rights of children a matter for bilateral diplomatic relations, this would show that governments regard the development of children as seriously as they do economic and fiscal issues.

A child focussed early intervention team

Consideration should be given to the establishment of a highly skilled team of child rights monitors for deployment on an early intervention basis. Active and aggressive monitoring would provide documentation for prompt follow-up by appropriate UN officials. This team would operate under the direction of the UN Commissioner for Human Rights and report its findings to the Security Council in public sessions in order to enhance public accountability to take appropriate action by both country governments and the Security Council.

Some organisations are promoting the development of a civilian, global, nonviolent peace force. Dr. David Southall, honorary director of Child Advocacy International, went one step further and proposed the establishment of an apolitical international armed force designed specifically to protect children from war crimes. This proposal for an International Child Protection Force (ICPF) grew out of experience in Bosnia and Afghanistan and is based on an awareness that war crimes against children at the beginning of a conflict are often committed by a small number of dangerous and abusive people, spurred on by politicians. The ICPF would adopt an approach similar to a country police force in these situations. Since death and damage to children occurs early in a conflict, often in areas where humanitarian agencies have difficulty obtaining access, early intervention by the ICPF could also assist in protecting access for humanitarian workers in keeping with international law.

One advantage of a child-focussed protection team is that it would be hard for a political leader to argue against reasonable efforts designed to protect children. By focussing on children, regardless of their ethnic, religious, or social affiliation with any faction in the conflict, members of the international community are less likely to be accused of taking sides. Of greatest importance would be the speed and efficiency with which a small child-protection team could be mobilised, along with commitment to support its actions as necessary with strong diplomatic responses.

The primary objection to these proposals is the question of sovereignty. States will argue that it is their responsibility to protect their children. In situations of armed conflict, however, the evidence is clear that they are often unable to do this. Ideally, agreement for the use of a child-protection team would be sought from all factions in a conflict, but, if that were denied, it could be mandated by the Security Council in response to evidence that children were not being protected in accordance with international law.

While debate about the formation of a standing, international, protection team will take some time, it may be possible to deploy child rights monitors as a preventive measure under existing laws. This would be an important step in the direction of serious international action to protect the rights of children.

Another question is the feasibility of holding non-state actors accountable for violations of the rights of children. Globalisation means that even rebels and non-state actors depend on the good-will of the international community from whom they seek political legitimacy as well as their arms and funding. Examples of such groups responding to pressure include the Tamil Tigers, the SPLA and the Bouganvillian Revolutionary Army, which have openly denounced the recruitment and participation of those below 18 in armed conflict.

There are examples of non-state actors being held accountable for other human rights violations, such as the decision of the Inter-American Court in the case of Velazquez Rodriguez (Honduras), dealing with disappearances. Taking similar action under the CRC would require stronger enforcement mechanisms.

Reports by the UN secretary general have recognised that strat-egies such as targeted sanctions and public pressure could be used to cut off non-state groups from the international support and le-gitimacy most of them desire. The difficulty in getting a strong political consensus to implement such strategies consistently reflects the fact that protection of children is still a matter of words rather than serious action.

The UN secretary general has also proposed that the United Nations consider establishing a new mechanism to hold abusers financially accountable for the damage done to victims, including the capacity to seize assets such as equipment and bank accounts.

Compliance mechanism for the CRC

The CRC is highly regarded and has been ratified by every nation except the United States and Somalia. The Geneva Conventions are widely ratified, but the additional protocols specifically pro-tecting children have been ratified by fewer countries. The main problem, however, in both cases, is weak mechanisms for ensuring compliance.

Enforcement mechanisms of the CRC in particular are weaker than those provided for other human rights conventions. Countries are required to report on compliance once every five years. A com-mittee established by the United Nations reviews the country report and reports by other agencies, meets with the country delegation, and then issues a report with recommendations for improvement. Five years is a long time in the lives of children suffering serious impacts from armed conflict. Five years or even one year can do damage that will affect their lives forever.

Supporters of the CRC emphasise education and community work to achieve voluntary, progressive compliance with the spirit of the CRC as an integrated web, rather than pursuing violations of individual provisions. WV agrees that it is preferable to work through education to achieve implementation of the goals expressed in the CRC. But when large-scale and severe violations threaten the survival or do permanent damage to children through armed invasions or forced abductions, there must be an avenue for earlier and stronger action.

Under the present system, UNICEF provides protection programmes for children at risk in many countries and highlights abuses, but in some circumstances criticism of a government may put its programmes at risk. In difficult circumstances it is not realistic to expect the same agency which runs programmes in a country to pursue complaints which may result in risk to those programmes. The same difficulty faces humanitarian agencies which provide programmes in difficult circumstances. A separate mechanism for hearing petitions and conducting investigations would provide the independence to put the interests of the children first.

Consideration should be given to the establishment of a subcommittee of the Committee on the Rights of the Child with a mandate to hear and act immediately on complaints of violations of the rights of children, especially those which threaten their survival prospects in situations of armed conflict. If the committee, with the authority of the UN Commissioner of Human Rights, cannot achieve agreement to end serious violations, access should be granted to the Security Council to consider what other measures could be taken. Public pressure could also be used because both governments and rebel groups rely on international support for legitimacy.

As part of a child-protection strategy, consideration should also be given to pursuing violations of the rights of children under other international laws. This would reinforce the principle that children are as important as adults. The UN secretary general has emphasised the non-derogable rights in article 4 of the International Covenant on Civil and Political Rights, which prohibits torture and cruel and degrading treatment. The Convention Against Torture includes stronger enforcement provisions and the Convention on the Elimination of Discrimination Against Women could be used to pursue violations affecting girl children. The violations of children's rights occurring during contemporary conflicts certainly warrant the attention of other tribunals in addition to the Committee on the Rights of the Child.

Violations of the rights of refugee children can be pursued under the refugee conventions, and in some cases violations of the rights of displaced children could be pursued under national human rights legislation. The Convention Relating to the Status of Refugees (1951) clearly includes children, but the definition of "refugee" and the grounds for protection are limited. Under the African Charter, however, a broader definition of refugees would also apply to children who are internally displaced. The Committee on the Rights of the Child should also pay more attention to upholding the specific provisions of the CRC regarding the rights of children who are refugees.

Follow up the work of the special representative

The work of the Office of the Special Representative of the Secretary General for Children and Armed Conflict has resulted in a higher profile for the needs of children. Development of specific country strategies should follow up on visits made, including the identification of agencies responsible for action, regular monitoring and reporting of progress or lack of progress. NGOs active in the country would be asked to contribute to both the development and implementation of the strategy. In addition, the special representative for children and armed conflict should make earlier visits to conflict-prone countries with the aim of putting protection systems in place. In the case of East Timor, for example, there were warning signs; NGOs, as well as UN agencies, need to ask what could be done earlier in such situations to protect children.

Attacks on schools, hospitals and playgrounds

Facilities where children congregate or which have a significant presence for children, such as schools, hospitals and playgrounds, should be considered battle-free zones. Violations of the relevant provisions of the Geneva conventions need to be taken more seriously. This will, however, involve more than invoking the Geneva conventions and the CRC. It will take concerted international pressure at an official and public level to compel those who ignore conventional restraints to cease targeting children.

Protect children in displaced persons and refugee camps

In camps for internally displaced persons and refugees, children are the most vulnerable, succumbing to malnutrition, diseases, abuse and psychological trauma.

According to law, internally displaced children are eligible for the same protection as other children in the country. In reality, there is little effective protection. Nor are displaced persons camps temporary. In some cases children are spending many of their developmental years in camps, with minimal nutrition, poor healthcare and no education. When and if they return home, they are at a permanent disadvantage as compared to other children, which can be a cause of future conflict.

Words on paper, although important, do not protect children. Additional political will and resources are required to address the abysmal conditions faced by millions of children in the camps for displaced persons and refugee camps. The UN special representative for the secretary general on internally displaced persons, Dr. Francis Deng, is raising the profile of these issues but has no resources to take effective action.

International guidelines for displaced persons explicitly forbid recruitment. Principle 13 states: "In no circumstance shall displaced children be recruited nor be required or permitted to take part in hostilities." However, implementation of the guideline is a major challenge.

Training of peace-keepers in the protection of children

UN peace-keepers play a significant and positive role in missions throughout the world. But more deliberate training of peace-keepers in respect and protection for the rights of children is urgently needed. NGOs who have experience in working with children in difficult circumstances could assist in the training and development of civilian partnerships to best meet the needs of children. An important issue to be addressed in developing effective strategies is an early transition to civilian police forces and community-based organisations which can also protect children after the peace-keepers leave.

Similar training would help humanitarian workers and support staff who do not specialise in child care. Their actions often have a significant impact on children. With some training, they would also provide a large pool of people who could advocate for the rights of children.

REINTEGRATION

How well children are treated in the post-conflict situation affects the likelihood of future conflict. Focussing on children in the post-conflict situation is essential and a good investment in long-term stability. Yet it is often ignored. As the Machel report highlighted, many countries recovering from armed conflict fail to make adequate provision for children. The Machel report recommended that peace treaties and agreements should recognise the existence of child combatants and make suitable provision for their demobilisation.

Some progress is being made. In Sierra Leone, the Lome Peace Agreement included specific provisions for the children and young people involved in that conflict. Delays in implementation, according to both NGOs and government officials in the country, are leaving many young people with no alternatives to the use of force in order to survive. The challenge now is to implement the agreement in a way that will prevent future outbreaks of violence.

Taking children seriously in the post-conflict peace and reconstruction process would include the following steps:

- Give a high priority to children's issues early in the peace process, including civil society advocates for children in the process to help draft specific, practical provisions for inclusion in peace agreements.
- Implement child-specific components of demobilisation and reintegration without delay to provide a clear rupture with military life but with a long enough time frame to allow for

successful reintegration, with active participation of the young people and the communities.

- Avoid stigmatising child soldiers by providing help in the context of assistance for all the children affected by the war.
- Establish education as the fourth component of emergency assistance.
- Pay special attention to replacing the economic incentive of participation in conflict with other forms of economic livelihood for young people's survival.
- Use community-based approaches to deal with the psycho-social impacts of conflict, with respect for the cultural context of the children. Preparation for family reunification must be followed with family support and poverty reduction in order to ensure a successful reintegration. Long-term individual planning is required for children who cannot be reunited with their families.
- Recognise the spiritual dimension of child development, using culturally appropriate expressions. Research in Liberia showed that programmes which incorporated the spiritual side of Liberian culture, including the concepts of forgiveness and reconciliation, proved to be effective. Programmes which shied away from the spiritual inclinations of the children were strongly influenced by the children themselves to incorporate such elements. WV's programmes in Rwanda and Northern Uganda include a role for local church leaders and religious expressions of forgiveness, healing and reconciliation as one way children can deal with their past.
- Pay special attention to the needs of girls, including reproductive health services and work with communities to accept them, especially when rape results in shame and rejection by the community.

It is a mistake to treat children and their families as merely victims. Experience shows that active participation is the most effective approach. Children can be active agents for reconciliation and peace building in order to prevent future conflicts. Therein lies hope for the future.

It is also a mistake to think that the involvement of children in armed conflict is inevitable. Implementation of the prevention, protection and reintegration strategies presented in this report would go a long way to allow children to grow up free from the impacts of war.

SUMMARY OF RECOMMENDATIONS

Prevention

- Stop the use of child soldiers through ratification and effective implementation of the optional protocol to foster universal acceptance of age 18 as the minimum age for participation in any kind of military force.
- Implement the call of the Security Council to nations involved in the manufacture and sale of small arms to "restrict arms transfers which could aggravate existing tensions . . . and collaborate in combating illegal arms flows."
- Include detailed information about the trade in small arms in reports to the Security Council prepared by the UN secretary general. Specific information on transfers from individual countries should include the members of the Security Council themselves.
- Actively support the practical strategies being developed by the International Network on Small Arms. Member states of the United Nation should focus on implementation in their own countries and spheres of influence and then develop and adopt international mechanisms.
- Give the developmental needs of children, in the context of family and community, a greater priority in country assistance strategies developed by the World Bank, the International Monetary Fund, and donor countries. Child protection networks and education are essential.
- Give a higher priority to the needs of adolescents, especially in situations where they are a significant portion of the population and are at risk of becoming involved in armed conflict.
- Allocate more attention and resources to reduce the root causes of armed conflict, starting with the central issues outlined in *10 Urgent Issues for the Children of the New Millennium* (see summary in appendix).
- Increase support for long-term international development programmes to break the cycle of poverty and injustice that can lead to armed conflict. Developed governments are urged

to renew their commitment by meeting the UN goal of 0.7 per cent of gross national product to official development assistance.

- Ask the International Monetary Fund to present public child-impact assessments of their fiscal policy prescriptions for conflict-prone countries to demonstrate how they are helping to achieve the international commitments to children in the CRC.
- Invest more resources in preventive peace-building initiatives in the context of community development programmes and with the active participation of children.

Protection

- Strengthen early warning systems, monitor the situation of children at risk, and pay attention to violations of the rights of children through diplomatic initiatives. Promote and implement strategies, such as child-focussed humanitarian cease fires, to provide for the needs of children, based on the concept of children as zones of peace even in times of conflict.
- Establish a child-focussed early intervention team to monitor aggressively and to report appropriately systemic violations of the rights of children.
- Establish a subcommittee of the Committee on the Rights of the Child to investigate promptly complaints of violations which threaten the survival or do permanent damage to children during armed conflict and pursue appropriate action through other UN channels, such as the Security Council.
- Prosecute serious violations of the rights of children under other existing conventions with stronger enforcement measures.
- Follow up the work of the special representative of the security general for children and armed conflict with the development of country-specific strategies and frequent monitoring. Consider preventive missions to conflict-prone countries and follow-up visits.
- Enforce Geneva Convention prohibitions against attacks on schools, hospitals and places where children congregate and more actively protect the right of access for children to humanitarian assistance.
- Allocate more resources to the needs of children in displaced persons camps. Particular attention should be paid to nutrition,

healthcare, family reunification, non-formal education and support for especially vulnerable children.

- Strengthen efforts to make young people aware of the risks and consequences of involvement in armed conflict, including the active participation of young people themselves in awareness programmes and use of local media.
- Add a special focus on child protection in current training programmes for peace-keepers through the United Nations and member countries and include mechanisms for disciplining soldiers who violate the rights of children themselves.

Reintegration

- Give a high priority to children's issues early in the peace process, including civil-society advocates for children in the process to help draft specific, practical provisions for inclusion in peace agreements.
- Implement child-specific components of demobilisation and reintegration without delay to provide a clear rupture with military life. Allow a sufficient time frame for successful reintegration, and promote active participation of the young people themselves and their communities.
- Avoid the stigmatisation of child soldiers by providing help in the context of assistance for all the children affected by war.
- Establish education as the fourth component of emergency assistance.
- Pay special attention to the needs of girls, including reproductive health services and work with communities to accept them, especially when sexual abuse by enemy forces results in shame and rejection by the child's home community.
- Pay special attention to replacing the economic incentive of participation in conflict with other forms of economic livelihood for survival for young people.
- Use community-based approaches to deal with the psycho-social impacts of conflict, with respect for the cultural context of the children.

NOTES

[1] UNICEF, *State of the World's Children 1996*, Oxford University Press, Oxford, 1996, 13.

[2] United Nations, Convention on the Rights of the Child, 1989, the most ratified UN international instrument. Ratified by 191 states with only the United States and Somalia not having ratified.

[3] Graça Machel, "The Impact of Armed Conflict on Children," (United Nations/UNICEF, August, 1996).

[4] Carolyn Hamilton and Tabatha Abu el-Haj, "Armed Conflict: The Protection of Children Under International Law," *The International Journal of Children's Rights* 5 (1997).

[5] Thomas Hammarberg, Keynote speech entitled "Children as a Zone of Peace – What Needs to Be Done?" in *Conference on the Rights of Children in Armed Conflict*, ed. Aldrich and van Baarda (1994), quoted in Hamilton and El-Haj, "Armed Conflict."

[6] UNICEF, *State of the World's Children 1996* (Oxford: Oxford University Press, 1996), 13.

[7] "Landmines – The Year of Missed Opportunities," WV briefing (1996).

[8] WV Proposal Report (1999).

[9] International Save the Children Alliance, *Promoting Psychosocial Well-being Among Children Affected by Armed Conflict and Displacement: Principles and Approaches*, 3 n.2.

[10] Michael Harbottle, "Proper Soldiering – The Ethical Approach," written contribution to the Report on the Round-table "Armed Conflicts and Sexual Abuses of Children" by the NGO Group for the Convention on the Rights of the Child, Focal Point on Sexual Exploitation of Children (1997).

[11] United Nations Economic and Social Council, "Report from the Secretary-General," Document 27 (January 1999).

[12] Darryl Robinson, "Defining 'Crimes Against Humanity' at the Rome Conference," *American Journal of International Law* 93/1 (1999).

[13] In Ilene Cohn and Guy Goodwin-Gill, *Child Soldiers, The Role of Children in Armed Conflict* (Oxford: Clarendon Press, 1994).

[14] Machel, "The Impact of Armed Conflict on Children."

[15] Mary Robinson, *Report* (Geneva, March 1999).

[16] Thomas Rowell, "Small Arms – Trends and Statistics," a report for WV, Work Place Co-operative Project GEOG 3530 (April 1999).

[17] Salpy Eskidjian, ed., *Small Arms, Big Impact: A Challenge to the Churches* (Geneva: World Council of Churches, 1998).

[18] Siobhan O'Reilly Calthrop, "The Contribution of Community Development to Peacebuilding," World Vision UK special report (April 1999).

[19] Kofi Annan, "Protection of Civilians in Armed Conflict" (New York: United Nations, 1999), para 30.

APPENDIX

Executive Summary
Ten Urgent Issues for the Children of the New Millennium

World Vision proposes the following "To Do List" for the new millennium:

1. A liveable income. More than half of the world's nearly 6 billion people live on less than US$2 a day. Reaching a US$3 a day minimum with better income distribution would provide a liveable level while improving education, health care and economic growth. World Vision believes that appropriate economic policies and an extra US$22 billion in aid annually could eliminate absolute poverty by the time the first generation of the new millennium become adults.

2. Food for everyone. The world is capable of feeding itself. Increased production of food crops, investment in rural infrastructure, better distribution systems, agricultural programmes and land reform are among the measures that can end hunger. The Food and Agriculture Organisation (FAO) estimates that as little as US$8 billion a year, mostly for rural infrastructure and research, could greatly increase the global quantity of food.

3. Education for all. Education is essential if children are to realise their potential as healthy, informed and active citizens. Yet 125 million children, two thirds of them girls, do not attend primary school and 150 million children drop out of education before grade four. UNICEF believes that US$6 billion annually could provide education for all, less than the U.S. spends on cosmetics.

4. Clean water. Contaminated water, the biggest cause of preventable disease and death in the developing world, claims the lives of 5 million children a year. Some 1.3 billion people lack safe water and 2.5 billion are without adequate sanitation. Much could be done to provide clean water infrastructure for US$9 billion according to UNDP.

This appendix is taken from the "Executive Summary" of *Urgent Issues for the Children of the New Millennium* (Monrovia, Calif.: World Vision International, 2000), 5–7.

5. Debt relief for poor nations. Payments on international debt exceed spending on education in 30 African nations. Onerous debt deprives poor nations of revenue for schools, hospitals, roads, and economic development. Rich nations need the political will to forgo payments on existing loans. Theoretical costs of US$206 billion for debt write-offs really constitute a recognition that past debt agreements can never be paid.

6. Investing in peacebuilding. As the 20th century closes, some 15 million people are refugees; even more are displaced within their own countries. Families are driven from their homes by conflict and violence. Permanent peace-building measures, based on development and mutual self-interest, could contribute to safe and secure homes.

7. Girls Growing as Equals. Establishing equal rights and opportunities for girls is one of the best guarantees for development. A community that ensures equality for women is wiser, richer, and more fulfilled than one which does not. National governments across the world must find renewed commitment to making equality real.

8. A sustainable future. Poverty exacerbates environmental destruction by forcing the poor to clear forests, utilise marginal lands and accept man-made pollution. Good stewardship of the earth's resources guarantees a sustainable future for all. Rich nations must take seriously commitments already made on climate change, while helping poorer states to develop sustainably.

9. An end to child exploitation. Some 250 million children now work so their families can eat. Many are forced into prostitution, drug trafficking and debilitating jobs that adults refuse to do. Some 300,000 are soldiers. Investing in the future of children by prioritising an end to poverty will bring a liveable family income that releases children from exploitative labour.

10. Freedom to believe. The right of all women and men to hold to personal beliefs and to participate in society – politically, economically, socially, and spiritually – is fundamental to their ability to construct a safe and sustainable future.

9.

Development and the Deadly Pandemic

Small Arms and Light Weapons

DON BRANDT

> *Virtually every part of the United Nations system is dealing in one way or another with the consequences of armed conflicts, insecurity, violence, crime, social disruption, displaced peoples, and human suffering that are directly or indirectly associated with the wide availability and use of these weapons (small arms and light weapons).*
>
> —"Small Arms" (19 August 1999)

The plethora of small arms and light weapons (SALW) is a concern of every humanitarian organisation. The earth is now home to about 1 billion lethal arms that are relatively cheap, portable and easy to use. This means that the ratio of weapons to people is an astounding 1 to 6. Indications are that the number of guns will continue to grow, probably outpacing the increase in population.

To reduce significantly the use of weapons, more attention must be placed on the demand side of the arms equation. Even organisations and agencies trying to restrict the supply of SALW recognise that the reduction of arms ultimately depends on cutting demand. Yet, curtailing demand is much harder than reducing supply. An analogy with the drug trade is appropriate. The United States spent billions of dollars in the past decade to reduce the sup-

---

Material in this chapter was previously published in Don Brandt, *A Deadly Pandemic: Small Arms and Light Weapons,* working paper no. 4 (Monrovia, Calif.: World Vision International, 2001).

ply of illicit drugs originating from other countries. This vast expenditure of resources was largely wasted, as the overall demand for drugs in the United States has not fallen. The tale of guns is similar. Codes, conventions and protocols to limit arms are needed. These supply-side actions are significant but not the primary factor in reducing the amount of legal and illicit SALW. Cutting demand is paramount.

Reducing demand is very difficult because it requires the creation of a "culture of peace." Where inequities and injustice now prevail, societies must be transformed into inclusive democracies. This is a Herculean task. Still, in their own small, incremental way community development programmes of many operational NGOs appear to be doing just that. For example, findings from two World Vision (WV) studies in India and Ethiopia indicate that community development reduced the level of violence and the use of lethal weapons.[1] NGOs need to take the next steps and intentionally introduce programmes of reconciliation and peace to the places where they work.

Reconciliation efforts and other recommendations conclude discussions of various topics bearing on SALW. One issue is the glut of weapons and the high price paid by children, whether as civilians or child soldiers. Next, definitions and examples of SALW try to more accurately illustrate the variety and profusion of arms. Supply-side matters are then reviewed, followed by demand-side concerns and the arms trade. Regional and national codes of conduct and UN conventions are cited as examples of attempts to better regulate the legal trade of arms and to restrict the illicit arms trade.

BACKGROUND

SALW are likened as a scourge or plague of worldwide proportions. SALW are responsible for 90 per cent of war fatalities, 90 per cent of whom are civilians. That added up to about 4.8 million civilian deaths between 1990 and 1998. Due to increasingly open borders, no country is unaffected by the spread of arms. For many states, wide and indiscriminate access to small arms has been a disaster rivalling that of famine and disease. Examples that readily come to mind are Colombia, El Salvador, Haiti, Afghanistan, Sri Lanka, Angola and DR Congo. The earth is now saturated with

SALW. Unless checked, the worse is yet to come. William Benson, a researcher on Saferworld's Arms Trade Programme, writes: "It has been estimated that there are eight times as many arms awaiting disposal as have been transferred in the entire post cold-war period."[2]

WV and other operational NGOs are especially affected by the glut of SALW. Staff, project people and programmes are increasingly at risk. Consider –

- Most post–Cold War conflicts are intrastate. Combatants have little knowledge or respect for the Geneva Conventions or the protocols.
- Most refugees and internally displaced persons are victims of civil strife and war.
- Criminal, random and non-political violence using rapid-firing weapons is escalating.
- Although most SALW are relatively low-tech machines, more sophisticated and deadly arms, such as rocket-propelled grenades and shoulder-fired missiles, are now being used by rebel groups.
- Light in weight, easy to use and maintain, small arms makes it possible for children to be exploited as combatants.
- The disastrous toll on children due to wars fought by SALW is truly staggering. Children comprised over half the 24 million refugees and 27 million internally displaced persons in the mid 1990s.[3]

While pro-gun lobbyists argue that "guns don't kill people, people kill people," SALW certainly makes killing easier. "Modern weapons have made the ability to kill, more than ever before, a utilitarian act, unrestrained neither by age nor gender."[4] Studies indicate that automatic weapons allow slighted ethnic groups to resort rapidly to violence, reducing the time for nonviolent actions, including reconciliation efforts.[5] Taking a cue from other regions, insurgent groups in Asia are co-operating to enhance the movement of guerrillas, drugs and arms.[6]

As insurgents, criminals have more firepower than ever before. Their arsenals are often more lethal than those of the police. Gangs that form coalitions with rebel groups make it difficult to tell the two apart. Rocard calls these partnerships "alliances of death" in the South. In the North they are a "complicity of silence" among those who stand to profit by SAWL sales.[7]

The losers of SAWL-related violence are non-criminal civilians. They lose in two ways. One is directly through violent crime such as armed robbery, kidnapping and murder. For example, 20,000 people have been killed since the 1992 "peace" in El Salvador, most of whom were not criminals.[8] Second, people lose indirectly because crime, like war, frightens away overseas and domestic investment.

CHILDREN

The greatest losers of all are children. The effect on children was especially negative between 1990 and 1998, resulting in 2 million dead children, 4-5 million crippled children, 12 million homeless children, and 10 million psychologically traumatised children. This is bad enough. Yet most children affected by war die of disease and hunger, as dysentery, cholera, typhoid and malaria take their tolls on malnourished bodies.

A subset, child soldiers, has riveted the attention of many NGOs and child-centred agencies such as UNICEF and WV. This is not surprising given that:

- 300,000 children under 18 are fighting in one of the world's 36 armed conflicts. About 120,000 of these children are African.[9]
- Children as a percentage of total combatants have increased. Today, 30-45 per cent of all soldiers are children less than 15 years old.
- Radda Barnen (Swedish Save the Children) reports that child soldiers under the age of 15 fought in 26 countries in 1995 or 1996, either on the rebel or government side. Included in this list are 19 countries in which WV works.
- Although most combatants are boys, the composition of many rebel bands contains between 10 and 30 per cent women and girl soldiers.
- Most girls serve as domestic servants. Many girls are used as sex providers and are euphemistically termed the "wives" of older soldiers.

- Besides injury, death and psychological trauma, children are highly susceptible to sexually transmitted diseases, including HIV/AIDS.

Why are children recruited in rebel and government armies?[10] This question is easily answered – children are cheap and obedient. But given the barbaric life of the child soldier, why are so many children serving in wars? Some children join to avenge the death of their parents or other relatives. Others hope for excitement, glamour, and adventure. More enlist to escape hunger and poverty. Poverty also encourages desperate parents to send off their sons and daughters as recruits. Most children probably do not volunteer but are forced to become soldiers. Rogue armies, rebel groups and right-wing militias all see children as a valuable military asset.

DEFINITIONS

What are SALW and why are they so lethal? Definitions of SALW vary. For consistency, most researchers now use the definition formulated by the United Nations in 1997. Small arms are weapons that can be handled and maintained by one person. They include revolvers and self-loading pistols, rifles and carbines, sub-machine guns, assault rifles, and light machine guns. Light weapons usually require a vehicle or pack animal for transport and often two people to operate and support them. Examples include heavy machine guns, hand-held under-barrel and mounted grenade launchers, portable anti-aircraft missile systems, and mortars of calibres less than 100 mm. Ammunition and explosives are also included as SALW.[11]

The Organization of American States' (OAS) definition is both more generic and more precise: "Firearms are defined as any barrelled weapon which will or is designed to or may be readily converted to expel a bullet or projectile by the action of an explosive (except antiques) [or] any other weapon or destructive device such as any explosive, incendiary or gas bomb, grenade, rocket, rocket launcher, missile, missile system, or mine."[12] Information on the more popular SALW models is found in Table 9-1.

Table 9-1 dramatises the dominance of the Kalashnikov (AK-47 family). The table also shows the large number of countries that

Table 9-1. Popular SALW Models

Name	Type	Maker	# Countries Using	# Countries Manufacturing	# Weapons Made (in millions)
FN MAG	Machine gun	Fabrique Nationale* (Belgium)	74	—	—
HK21	Machine gun	Heckler & Koch** (Germany)	14	—	—
Uzi	Submachine gun	Israeli Military Industries	47	—	10
HK MP5	Submachine gun	Heckler & Koch**	42	—	—
AK-47, AK-74	Assault rifle	Soviet State Arsenals (Russia)	78	14+	35-70
M-16	Assault rifle	Colt (US)	67	7	8
FN-FAL family	Assault rifle	Fabrique Nationale*	94	15	5-7
G-3 family	Assault rifle	Heckler & Koch**	64+	18	7
Galil	Assault rifle	Israeli Military Industries	14	—	—
AUG	Assault rifle	Steyr-Daimler-Puch	11	—	—
FN35	Pistol	Fabrique Nationale*	35	—	—
M92/M34	Pistol	Beretta (Italy)	15	—	—

*Now part of Giat (France) **Now part of Royal Ordinance of Britain (UK) Steyr-Daimler-Puch
Sources: Michael T. Klare, "The Kalashnikov Age," *The Bulletin of the Atomic Scientists* (January/February 1999), 25; "Small Arms," Dept. of Disarmament Affairs (1999), 15.

use and/or manufacture arms under franchise arrangements. Over 300 companies in at least 52 countries make SALW. In 1994, 22 Southern nations produced SALW; 16 of those countries exported small arms.[13]

The arms listed in Table 9-1 are characteristic of SAWL in general. They tend to be low in cost; widely available; lethal, especially at short ranges; simple to operate and maintain; durable, with long life expectancies; and portable. Many have civilian as well as military uses. Brute strength and/or skill are no longer operating requirements. Children as young as 10 can use and maintain an AK-47. These traits make SAWL ideal weapons for rebels and terrorists.

SUPPLY SIDE

Table 9-1 illustrates a world that is awash in arms. Not including landmines, the estimated number of SALW range between 500 million and 1 billion. The latter figure is probably the more accurate.[14] This is one reason that an AK-47 in working condition may be found for as little as US$6 in some parts of Africa. Guns, ammunition and explosives get into the market in one of six ways: (1) over 50, and perhaps as many as 70 or more, countries make weapons; (2) sales brokered through legitimate private arms dealers; (3) official gifts or sales by governments of surplus military SALW; (4) unofficial government supplies of arms sent to other governments or insurgents (grey market); (5) theft of government stocks; and (6) illicit, non-government-sanctioned sale of arms (black market).

Governments have finally awakened to the threat of SAWL to national security. Unfortunately, the new codes of conduct and the proposed UN convention and protocol only address part of the problem. Glaringly missing is the recognition that legal and illicit sales are functionally related and closely interwoven in today's global market.

Many SALW are recycled from past wars. Examples include AK-47s from Mozambique that are now freely circulating in southern and eastern Africa; Stinger missiles transported from Afghanistan, some of which are probably in the hands of terrorists;[15] and a huge supply of M-16s and other US arms left in Vietnam only to fuel wars in other places. States are also trying to unload large stockpiles of weapons left over from the Cold War. Desperate to earn foreign exchange, Eastern European nations and countries that made up the former USSR are the main culprits. Yet Western countries are also guilty. Annually the United States dumps SALW on friendly nations. Between 1995 and 1999, the US military gave away over 300,000 rifles, pistols, machine guns and grenade launchers. After unification, Germany disposed of 304,000 Kalashnikovs by giving them to Turkey.[16] Exacerbating the problem is the expansion of NATO. States admitted to NATO are required to upgrade their arsenals. This has pressured countries to unload old Soviet-era conventional weapons at bargain prices on the world market.

Part of the global market is supposed to be forbidden by UN sanctions. Yet sales to National Union for the Total Independence of Angola (UNITA) have been brisk. Eastern European and other countries made scuttling the Lusaka Peace Accords by UNITA possible. Several African countries ignored the arms embargo on Burundi and either supplied or transhipped weapons to that nation. Somalia is another example. Other states in the Horn and Libya bought weapons for various factions in direct violation to the UN embargo mandate. Nothing has been done to prevent or even stem the flow of these and similar infractions of international law. As stated by Laurence:

> Several UN peacekeeping and postconflict peace-building operations have resulted in the incomplete disarmament of former combatants for two reasons: peace agreements or mandates did not cover small arms and light weapons disarmament, or inadequate operational guidance or resources led to shortfalls in the implementation of mandates. Weapons left in circulation thus became available for criminal activities, recirculation, and illicit trafficking.[17]

To help correct the oversupply problem, governments must be held more accountable for their production and transfer of SALW. This task will be difficult to do because "at the global level, the primary supply-side factor is the basic principle governing the conduct of relations among member states of the United Nations, that states have a right to export and import small arms and light weapons."[18]

Unwilling to restrain legitimate SAWL sales, gun-producing countries have leapt on the bandwagon to cut the illicit movement of arms. States can do much more, if nothing else than to help break the dearth of information on small arms. Michael Renner's comments on a global lack of information on ammunition apply equally well to all SALW in general. Specifically, more information is required on the location and number of production facilities; direction and volume of trade; stocks held for legitimate use; surplus and obsolete stocks; and data on explosives, including incidents, production, and use.[19]

DEMAND SIDE

Development may actually promote disarmament.[20]

The abundant supply of cheap weapons, especially assault rifles, encourages lethal violence and retribution. However, SALW experts agree that civil unrest and wars will diminish only if the demand-side for arms is reduced.[21] Much less work and thought have gone into how demand for small arms may be decreased. The majority of the advocacy initiatives and lobbying recommendations on tackling the small-arms problem have dealt primarily with the control of the supply of SALW, such as export controls, illicit trade and embargoes.

Several compelling reasons for putting greater emphasis on reducing demand may be cited. First, a vast quantity of arms is already in circulation throughout the world, in part left over from the Cold War; these weapons are recycled from one conflict region to another. Policies that address restricting supply of new weapons, therefore, cannot be sufficient on their own. Second, those states that are signing codes of conduct or agreements do not include some of the worst offenders such as countries located in Eastern Europe and East Asia. Such codes leave the field clear for states desperate for hard currency but with a glut of AK-47s and other small arms. Third, the rise in primitive types of warfare as witnessed in Rwanda, Sierra Leone and Northern Uganda demonstrates that removing sophisticated weaponry does not preclude violent, large-scale intra-state conflict.

Attention must be paid to address motives for taking up arms, whatever their mechanics. WV works with communities that frequently become vulnerable to using such weapons. This places the organisation in a unique position to speak about methods that might alter motives or attitudes towards the "gun culture." In contrast, the types of NGOs active in lobbying on small-arms issues are almost all non-operational. This helps explain why the general NGO approach has been largely "supply" focussed. It also demonstrates the gaping need for insight, knowledge and ideas from those working directly with the impact of SALW. Then, too, focussing on reducing demand also helps overcome some of the obstacles that the supply-side approach poses for an organisation with a diversity of opinion on calling for restraint on the manufacture and traffic of SALW. Alternatively, focussing merely on curbing illicit trade gives states the chance to use this as a "safe" option as opposed to the more integral path of seeking restrictions on legal and illegal trade, both of which are interlinked.

Examples of demand-side activities likely to reduce the flow of small arms include:

- Support for building an inclusive democratic, civil society that will not tolerate violence. Many countries have a democracy in form. Still, without a population that understands the concept of democracy and the people's role in it, it can only be a puppet democracy.

- Employment programmes that give young men a stake in peace and disincentive for participating in violent groups. "With no employment opportunities, lack of food and physical security there are few incentives to give up arms."[22]

- Informing donors and key decision-makers on the impact of small arms, their origin and perpetrators of abuse and misuse, including mercenaries contravening embargoes.

- Advocate for passage and compliance of the Optional Protocol that limits the age of soldiers to 18. The use of children in modern conflict is an important motivator for continuing trade in light weapons.

- Promote community-development programmes that build a culture of peace by encouraging interdependence and dialogue among people groups so that they lose the incentive to fight with one another. In Antsokia, Ethiopia, for example, the Oromo and Amhara have lost the motivation to use their weapons against one another as a result of the community development activities.

Recent research within World Vision suggested that integrated community development programmes can have a strong role in promoting cultures of solidarity and reversing cultures of violence. One particular example of this was found during an evaluation of an Area Development Programme (ADP)[23] in a remote district in Amhara region, Ethiopia. In addition to considerable socio-economic and environmental improvements achieved within the community, it was observed that gun-related violence had dramatically declined, in particular between two rival tribes. This was not an area that could be identified as a "war zone," but it suffered from an entrenched culture of revenge and violence, and small arms have been widely available for much of this century.[24]

Reduction of the demand for arms may result in disarmament and the disposal of weapons. Successful destruction of SALW stocks was carried out in several countries, including Albania, Liberia, Mali, Mozambique and South Africa. The demolition of 3,000 rifles in Mali in 1996 set the stage for the October 1998 agreement of seven Economic Community of West African States
(ECOWAS) to ban exports and imports of SALW for three years. Mozambique has earned worldwide recognition for its arms-disposal programme. Beginning in 1995, 4,400 firearms and 75,000 weapons and accessories were destroyed. Many of the decommissioned weapons were turned into sculpture created by former combatants.[25] Unfortunately, this innovative programme run by the Christian Council of Mozambique is handicapped by a lack of resources.

The Christian Council programme is successful not only in the number of arms destroyed but also in how the weapon buy-back scheme works. Experience shows that cash for arms should be avoided because a seller may use the money to buy another gun. Incentives, though, must be sufficient to entice former combatants and others to turn in their weapons. A recent NGO study suggests that desirable items include food, clothing, education scholarships, computers, agricultural tools, bicycles, sewing machines and housing construction materials.[26]

Building more inclusive democracies with enhanced economic opportunities for all groups will help reduce demand for SAWL.

Unfortunately, this classical "liberal" position is not sufficient. As a recent World Bank study indicates, "greed" soon overtakes "grievance" as the prime motivating force that prolongs civil disturbances and war. Economically or politically disenfranchised ethnic groups that take up arms to "right the wrongs" tend to turn into gangs of thugs and bandits.[27] Examples abound and include UNITA in Angola, the Revolutionary United Front in Sierra Leone, Abu Sayyif in the Philippines, the Free Aceh Movement in Indonesia and the LRA in Sudan. In the words of Peter Lock, "Fighting parties turn into complex economic conglomerates, often commanded by wealthy traders turned warlords."[28]

Indeed, it is becoming increasingly difficult to separate legitimate grievances from criminal activities. Many revolutionary and para-military groups finance their causes, including the purchase of SALW, through criminal activities such as kidnapping (Abu Sayyif) the drug trade (Taliban, Latin American guerrilla groups), and the sale of illegal diamonds (RUF, UNITA). Investigations show that the world's annual US$500 billion in illegal drug sales[29] moves along the same routes as illicit arms. To a large extent, the demand for drugs in the North pays for the flow of illegal SALW to rebel and criminal groups in the South. Unfortunately, this probably indicates that a meaningful reduction in illicit exports of arms to the South must wait for the demand for heroin and cocaine to sharply drop in the North. If this is the case, then both the UN protocol and proposed UN convention to stop the illicit trade of SALW will largely be ineffectual.

THE ARMS TRADE

The illicit or black-market trade in SALW has received the most attention from governments. Somehow the demand for weapons, legal or illicit, is misplaced or forgotten. Often neglected, too, is the recognition that 60-70 per cent of SALW exports are legal – or at least done with government sanctions. Modes of legal trade in SALW include government-to-government sales and arms give-away programmes; government sanctioned private sales by arms brokers (probably the largest source of SAWL exports in the Europe and the United States); and clandestine or grey-market exports from governments to insurgent groups. In other words, states already have a great deal of power to curb the flow of small arms if they choose to do so.

Most arms exporters have chosen to intervene minimally in the legitimate SALW trade. Some of the reasons have to do with supporting friendly governments. Other factors may be more ideological. An example is the fear expressed by the National Rifle Association that curbing foreign exports of small arms may ultimately lead to restricting domestic SALW sales in the United States.[30] Probably the main reason that states shun from seriously regulating exports of SALW is economic. SALW are big business.

For years the dollar worth of SALW was overlooked as states and NGOs concerned with arms concentrated on planes, tanks and the like. Today, SAWL sales amount to US$7 to $10 billion a year. That is a significant amount, even though it is dwarfed by the US$34 billion a year in total international arms sales.[31] Still, the weaponry responsible for most civilian casualties is SALW, not attack helicopters, Katyusha artillery rockets, Leopard tanks and other large conventional weapon systems.

Leading the pack of conventional arms traders, including SALW, is the United States. With US$18.4 billion dollars worth of weapon sales in 1999, the United States counted for 54 per cent of all arms deliveries. Other major arms exporters are the UK, France, China and Russia. Russia is rapidly trying to re-establish its place as a premier arms supplier; its increase in sales of SALW between 1998 and 1999 was an astonishing 77 per cent, partly due to the brisk trade in Kalashnikovs.[32] All told, the above five nations account for about 85 per cent of the arms trade.

Despite new and proposed codes on the sale and export of weapons, indicators point to an increase in the arms trade. The reasons include:

- Weapons are a prime source of export revenue for countries of the former Soviet Union and Warsaw Pact, especially Bulgaria, the Czech Republic, Slovakia, Russia and Ukraine.
- Russia sees the export of arms as a way to reassert its significance as a world power.
- Eastern European countries wishing to join NATO must upgrade their arsenals to make them compatible with NATO standards. Most of these states have elected to buy Western arms,

including light weapons, and sell the older Soviet era stock to developing countries.

- An agreement to facilitate the co-production and export of arms was signed by six European nations in July 2000. The agreement indicates Europe's desire to sell more weapons by competing more aggressively with the United States.[33]
- More countries in the South are becoming significant SALW manufacturers and merchants to other developing nations. The primary examples are Brazil, Chile, Egypt, India, Indonesia, Iran, North and South Korea, Pakistan, Singapore, South Africa and Turkey.[34]

While countries continue to expand their arms exports abroad, governments are becoming more concerned with the illicit or black-market trade. Wearing nationalistic blinders, states such as the United States refuse to acknowledge the direct association between the easy access to domestic weapons and illicit exports. For example, 99 per cent of arms seized during drug raids in Brazil were made in the United States. Most of these weapons were illicit imports. A similar case may be made about drugs and illicit US-manufactured guns in Mexico.[35] Similarly, the arms-exporting countries conveniently overlook evidence that much of the black-market weaponry started as government-sanctioned sales or transfers. Arms became illegal due to theft from government arsenals or elsewhere; grey-market sales to insurgents who later sell the arms to other rebel groups, often in bordering countries; illicit arms transfers from militaries to para-military groups; and sales to countries that re-sell weapons without requiring adequate background checks and documentation of arms purchasers.[36]

This is not to deny the case against illicit export of SALW. Accounting for 30 per cent or more of the small-arms trade, illegal weapon sales are big business because of high demand for guns. Like drugs, reducing demand is key to curbing illicit SALW sales in the long term. Shrinking the supply of SALW, both legal and illicit, will help by making it more difficult to acquire arms. If this is done, non-criminal civilians may be the net beneficiaries.[37]

In order to curb the illicit arms trade, much more about the black market in weapons must be known. As Lock says, "No institution collects continuously data on the illicit proliferation of small arms."[38] James McShane states that the largest problem is to identify clearly illegal shipments. Among other suggestions he recommends in-transit licensing and marking firearms for identification.[39] Arms transfers often are unchecked. Louise maintains that it is difficult to manage the "free-flowing, transient supply and demand markets."[40] Klare concurs. Regarding SALW exports, he says that government-to-government transfers present few control problems. Large exports of illegal arms are more difficult to control, but it can be done. The real difficulty is the huge number of small-scale illicit exports. If Western governments seriously clamp down on individuals, then civil liberties issues may arise.[41]

CODES, CONVENTIONS AND PROTOCOLS

Generally, there are two intertwined topics to consider regarding the small arms trade. One is the legal transfer of weapons, usually from industrial to less developed countries. Although legal, government condoned trade in SALW has tended to operate in an ethical vacuum lacking accountability. In the words of Krause, "Currently, few states compile or exchange information concerning actual transfers, indigenous production, or stockpiles of light weapons and small arms."[42]

To help correct the defects in the legitimate arms trade, including SALW, a group of Nobel Laureates wrote an International Code of Conduct in 1997. Subsequently, European Union (EU) foreign ministers passed a code in May 1998. The US code passed the House of Representatives in 1997 but languishes in the Senate. Both the EU and US codes use the Wassenaar Arrangement developed by the Organisation for Economic Co-operation and Development (OECD) in 1996 as their point of reference.

The second topic of concern is the illicit trade of light weapons. Borders are indeed porous when transporting small arms. Probably over one-third of arms transfers are illegal. Exporting countries have done little to stop this illicit trade. Some experts believe that many of the illegal exports from the United States are actually undertaken by legitimate or registered arms dealers. On the receiving end, innumerable means are available for arms dealers to get high-value products safely to customers. Regional and international actions against illicit trade of arms were developed or proposed by the OAS and Economic and Social Council (ECOSOC), respectively.

LEGAL TRADE

The OECD recognised the devastating effect of conventional weapons on sustainable development in the South. This concern led in July 1996 to the Wassenaar Arrangement on arms and dual-use goods (high-tech items such as computing systems that may have both civilian and military uses). Basically, the Wassenaar Arrangement tries to harmonise the actions of signature states. For example, all 33 participating countries agreed to adopt trade controls and notify one another on transfers of dual goods, including technologies. Another stipulation in the arrangement is that signatory nations shall inform each other about "undercutting." Undercutting takes place if country A, an arms buyer, purchases weapons from country B after first being denied arms from country C.

NGOs evaluating the Wassenaar Arrangement state that the agreement addresses mostly major weapon systems.[43] Further, controls on arms transfers may be exempted for national reasons. While notification of undercutting is required, undercutting activities are permitted. NGOs feel that no undercutting should be permitted without in-depth and wide-ranging consultations.[44]

The Wassenaar Arrangement as well as the International, US, and EU codes of conduct deal with conventional transfers of all arms, not only SALW. Under the leadership of Oscar Arias, an International Code of Arms was released in May 1997. According to this code, arms transfers would be barred from countries that could not show:

- Promotion of democracy;
- Protection of human rights, including vigorous attempts to bring perpetrators to justice;
- Transparency in military spending;
- Non-aggressive actions against other nations or people;
- Non-violation of the Geneva Convention of 1949 and the protocols of 1977;
- Non-involvement in armed conflict in the region (unless self-defence);
- Final destination of the arms, including end-user certifications; and
- Health and education budgets that exceed military outlays (justify if not).

The International Code is rigorous and is hailed as a model for other codes to follow. Unfortunately, the comprehensive nature of the International Code will probably doom it to failure. Although the Arias Foundation is still pushing for passage of the International Code, modification of the Code is probably needed before widespread ratification will occur. Both the US and EU codes are watered-down versions of the International Code. However, NGOs are expending considerable effort in trying to strengthen these codes.

The proposed US Code of Conduct can be effective when used in conjunction with other legislation. The code stipulates that arms cannot be sent from the United States unless the president certifies that the importing country promotes democracy (such as free and fair elections and the rule of law); respects human rights; is not engaged in certain acts of armed aggression; fully participates in the UN Register of Conventional Arms (unfortunately, most SALW are not on the register); and adheres to the Wassenaar Arrangement.

Current federal laws and regulations working in tandem with the proposed US Code should go a long way towards effectively controlling the legal trade in arms. The Arms Export Control Act requires that the purpose for the arms to be exported is given and that foreign governments involved must get approval before transferring weapons of US-origin to a third party. The Arms Export Control Act also requires the registering and licensing of brokers wishing to sell arms abroad. Subsequent legislation requires all brokers who are US citizens or have permanent residency status, no matter where they reside, to obey all US laws and regulations on the export of arms. The Export Administration Act covers the shipment of dual-use goods. The Foreign Assistance Act governs military aid to foreign governments. Theoretically, states that show a "gross and consistent" pattern of human rights abuse are barred from receiving US military aid.[45]

Regulations enacted since 1996 greatly increased the transparency of arms sales and military aid. The Pentagon must submit annual reports of weapons delivered under the Foreign Military Sales provisions of the Foreign Assistance Act, commonly called the 655 Report. The 655 Report also lists arms given away by the US military (Excess Defense Articles). More important, the 655 Report tracks the enormous quantity of commercial arms sales on an annual basis. From this report, for example, one learns that the

State Department approved of US$590 million worth of SALW export sales in 1996.[46]

The main weakness with the US Code is that the president can make exceptions without congressional approval. Currently, about 85 per cent of the countries that receive US arms are in violation of the proposed code. Compliance would force the United States to forego arms sales to Saudi Arabia and Israel, among others.

Another serious deficiency with the US Code is that end-use certification is not required. Not being able to establish final destinations has been a major problem in the small-arms trade. Governments (or corrupt officials) often re-sell arms to other states or factions engaged in conflict or repressive activities. Finally, the US Code ignores the ineffectual registration laws for arms dealers. Forfeiture of licenses or other penalties are not built into the code.

Although the EU Code of Conduct is more comprehensive than the US Code, NGOs hoped that a stronger code would be passed. On the positive side, several countries including Norway, Canada, Poland, Slovakia and the Czech Republic have altered their arms-trade laws in order to conform to the EU Code. The present code is in two parts. Guidelines for arms exports are found in part one. These include the prohibition of arms exports if an importing country does not respect human rights, including export of arms for internal suppression; engages in prolonged armed conflicts; uses weapons other than for self-defence; employs arms against other states; does not assure that arms will not be re-exported; and does not assure that arms sales are congruent with the "technical and economic capacity" of a country (that is, that a country can pay its international debt and social and educational programs).

Part two deals with operations: procedures on notification and consultations between states before granting export licenses. Here, states agree to notify other EU countries with names of arms dealers and reasons why they are refused licenses. Licenses are automatically forfeited if dealers do not honour UN and EU embargoes or inter-treaty obligations.

NGOs point out some correctives to the deficiencies in the EU Code:[47]

- As in the Wassenaar Arrangement, the "no undercutting without serious and in depth consultations" clause should be added;
- Member states should agree on a list of sensitive destinations;

- More vigorous human rights requirements should be included;
- The code should require parliamentary and public oversight and accountability;
- The code should require a comprehensive list of items (arms) exported from each member state;
- The code needs end-user contracts, safeguards and monitoring;
- The code should demand a clamp down on arms brokers who violate the code;
- The code should require enactment of arms-broker laws similar to those of the United States. Brokers who are citizens or permanent residents of the United States must obey the relevant arms-transfer laws and regulations whether they live in the United States or abroad.
- Agree that contracts are voided if the clause "non-adherence (to the code) should not preclude countries receiving arms" is used by arms dealers.

ILLICIT TRADE

More operational NGOs, such as WV, should be involved in promoting viable codes of conduct. These NGOs also have a high stake in pressing for action to halt the flow of illicit arms. Under the auspices of the Consultative Committee of the OAS, the Convention against the Illicit Manufacturing and Transfer of Firearms, Ammunition, Explosives, and Other Related Materials was signed by 27 member countries in November 1997. Among its articles, the OAS Convention requires:

- Arms, including light weapons, to be marked (identified) by the manufacturer;
- Markings on arms at point of import;
- Co-operation and exchange of information and training among member states;
- Standard arms importing and exporting systems; and
- Standard border controls.

Missing in this commendable document is the requirement to destroy illicit arms. The current wording specifies "auction, sale or other disposal." As arms experts repeatedly report, the re-transfer of light weapons is a major problem. For example, South African AK-47s sold to Renamo and UNITA are now being used by gangs in South Africa itself. The United States left 1.8 million small arms in Vietnam; many of those weapons are now widely spread over the globe, including within militia groups within the United States.

The UN's concern with illegal trafficking of firearms is handled primarily through the Centre for International Crime Prevention and the Commission on Crime Prevention and Criminal Justice, both branches of ECOSOC within the Department of Economic and Social Development (DESA). In April 1998 the Centre for International Crime Prevention released a resolution, endorsed by representatives of 56 countries entitled "Measures to Regulate Firearms for the Purpose of Combating Illicit Trafficking in Firearms." The key recommendations are three. First, countries should develop an "international instrument" to combat the illicit manufacture and trade of small arms (including ammunition). In doing so, states are to seek the views of NGOs, and to use the OAS "Convention Against the Illicit Manufacturing and Transfer of Firearms." Second, the instrument or resolution should include methods to identify and trace firearms, including import, export, and in-transit licenses for the international transfer of light weapons and ammunition. Third, the International Criminal Police Agency (Interpol) should be asked to provide "views and proposals" towards a system of technical co-operation designed to increase the ability of security forces to combat the illegal trade of small arms.

The Centre for International Crime Prevention's call to fight the illicit arms trade evolved into the Protocol against the Illicit Manufacturing of and Traffic in Firearms, Ammunition and Other Related Materials of the UN Convention Against Transnational Organised Crime. The Group of 7 Industrial Countries and Russia (G8) strongly favoured passage of the protocol, which was shaped after the OAS Convention – some would say too closely modelled for an international treaty. The protocol contains the current weaknesses of the OAS Convention and a couple of omissions. It doesn't include explosives and the provisions to mark weapons. Nor does the protocol recognise the ties between legal and illicit arms sales. For example, there is no specification to regulate arms brokers and no provisions are made to guard against the inadequate transfer and storage of weapons.[48]

Concurrent with the development of the protocol, a UN Conference on the Illicit Trade in Small Arms and Light Weapons in All Its Aspects was held in July 2001. Promoting the conference was the Mechanism for Co-ordinating Action on Small Arms within the Department of Disarmament Affairs. NGOs hoped that the "in all its aspects" phrase would open the door to include conditions of legal trade that affect illicit sales. Unfortunately, indications from three preparatory-commission sessions proved to be true. The conference was narrowly limited to illegal arms sales and a voluntary policy statement, not a treaty, was the final product.[49]

Better news is that other groups besides the G8, OAS and OSCE want brakes applied to the illicit arms trade. Most of the ECOWAS countries agreed to an arms import and export moratorium between 1998 and 2001. Unfortunately, there are no mechanisms in place to enforce the moratorium that Liberia and Burkina Faso violate with impunity. Other regional initiatives to control illegal sale of SALW are associated with Southern Cone Common Market, Declaration of Rio (between Latin American countries and the EU, Euro-Atlantic Partnership Council, Organisation of African Unity and Southern African Development Community). Indications are that policies, albeit voluntary and weak, to halt the illicit flow of guns may soon be produced by blocks of Asian countries.

RECOMMENDATIONS

Suggestions for improving the code of conduct in regards to legal arms transfers and the UN convention and protocol regarding the illicit trade in SALW were discussed in the previous section. Some of those recommendations are repeated because they may be enacted separately from codes or protocols. These and other measures to reduce SALW are found in "General" below. "Operational NGOs" recommendations are specifically applicable to operational NGOs, such as WV.

General

- The UN and/or regional organisations should attempt to stabilise the legal transfer of SAWL. To do so effectively will require governments to divulge data on production and stockpiling. Arms and ammunition should also be marked before either are exported or imported.[50]

- Restricting the export of ammunition primers to belligerents may retard the use of SALW.[51]
- Knowledge gained through the greater transparency in the sale of ammunition may also serve as an early warning indicator.
- Like alcohol and tobacco, a tax should be placed on ammunition to reduce its use.[52]
- States should be encouraged to pass laws that better regulate the activities of arms brokers. The United States requires brokers with US passports, no matter where they reside, to obey all US laws and regulations on the export of arms.
- In the United States and similar states, guns should not be manufactured that do not meet the standards set for imported arms. Restricting the supply of these "Saturday Night" specials should both reduce domestic violence and the transfer of these handguns to other countries.
- Restricting the advertisements of small arms might be a way to reduce demand.[53]
- Regional collection and destruction of weapons should be encouraged. Financing should be primarily from the industrial countries that are responsible for most of the export of arms.
- Related, and more radical, Lock calls for an arms' recycling deposit, as occurs in other environmentally unfriendly products that can be reused for other things.[54]
- With enough political will, other remedies to reduce arms are possible. An example is to require substantial export deposits to cut down on the tremendous amount of fraudulent documentation. The deposits would be refunded upon receipt of the arms to the legitimate buyer.
- A more controversial recommendation is to hold the original owner responsible (liable) for weapons that are subsequently sold or traded.[55]

Operational NGOs

Some NGOs have begun to educate parliamentarians and government officials on the benefits of reducing the trafficking in SALW. These NGOs must do more. WV and other operational NGOs' right to speak is based on firsthand knowledge about the effect of

SALW on staff and on the way they work. Effectiveness in petitioning for stiffer codes and laws will be more effective if more operational NGOs:

- Join the International Action Network on Small Arms, "an attempt to generate co-ordinated NGO advocacy on curbing the proliferation and misuse of small arms. The aim is to create a network of likeminded organisations to build capacity, support and momentum for agreed common purposes."[56]
- Join NGOs advocacy groups in their attempts to reduce the number of SALW. For example, WV United States recently became part of the Small Arms Working Group and WV Brazil intends to work closer with Viva Rio and its nation-wide disarmament campaign.
- Participate in the collection and destruction of SALW.[57]
- Consider expanding demobilisation and reintegration programmes with child soldiers to include adults.
- Intentionally build upon their organisations' "comparative advantage" of reducing demand for arms through their community-development programmes. Peace-building initiatives could be introduced to enhance development efforts.
- For faith-based NGOs, involve the church whenever possible. Churches are deeply rooted in most communities where WV works and will be instrumental to any successful local peace-building efforts.[58]

CLOSING

Most reasonable people probably believe that one billion SALW exceed the globe's carrying capacity for these weapons. Data on fatalities caused by combatants and criminals using SALW would lead one to think so. Yet despite codes, conventions and protocols, the number of weapons will continue to grow. This is because the synergy between supply and demand has not been dampened.

On the supply side, states tend to ignore the damage done by legal arms transfers. Conveniently discarded or overlooked are issues of second-party transfers, shoddy inventories of arms in insecure armouries, evasion of UN embargoes, and grey markets. Instead, governments led by the G8 are pushing for the passage of a protocol aimed at the illicit arms trade. Accounting for about one-third of SALW transfers, the black market is important. Yet, states continue to be blinded by the deadly effect of the loosely regulated, legal weapons' trade. Nor do governments want to recognise the functional interdependence of the legal and illicit sales of arms.

Most analysts recognise that reducing supply for SALW ultimately depends on lowering demand. Cutting demand, unfortunately, is a long-term and precarious solution in situations of deep injustice and/or where internecine rivalries are fraught with retribution and revenge. The cheap and abundant availability of weapons aggravates the problem by reducing the time when negotiation might be possible. Despite the difficulties, it is possible to cut the demand for weapons. WV has shown this to be so in its community-development work, where violence noticeably declined. Now the organisation must learn how to strengthen more intentionally the forces of reconciliation and peace-building. Local churches are natural allies to do so.

NOTES

[1] Tibebe Eshete and Siobhan O'Reilly-Calthrop, "Silent Revolution: The Role of Community Development in Reducing the Demand for Small Arms," World Vision working paper 3 (September 2000); Siobhan O'Reilly, "Building on Our Comparative Advantage: The Case for a 'Demand' Focused Approach to the Small Arms Problem," World Vision internal report (December 1998).

[2] International Alert, "Light Weapons Conrol and Security Assistance: A Review of Current Practice," available on the Web.

[3] Judith L. Evans, "Children as Zones of Peace: Working with Young Children Affected by Armed Violence" (New York: Consultative Group on Early Childhood Care and Development, 1996), 4.

[4] Christopher Louise, "The Social Impacts of Light Weapons Availability and Proliferation," *Journal of Humanitarian Assistance* (September 1995), 7.

[5] Edward J. Laurence, "Light Weapons and Intrastate Conflicts: Early Warning Factors and Preventative Action" (Washington, D.C.: Carnegie Commission, 1998), 14.

[6] Tara Kartha, "Controlling the Black and Gray Markets in Small Arms in South Asia," in *Light Weapons and Civil Conflict*, ed. Jeffrey Boutwell and Michael T. Klare (Landham, Md.: Rowman and Littlefield, 1999), 50. Rebels are the beneficiaries of a large "grey" arms market in Asia, in

which governments provide insurgents with weapons. The most visible example is Pakistan's support for the Taliban in Afghanistan and rebel groups in Indian Kashmir.

[7] "Statement by H. E. Mr. Michel Rocard Before the International Press Conference," UN Conference on the Illicit Trade and Light Weapons in All Its Aspects, preparatory committee meeting at UN Headquarters, New York, New York (29 February 2000), 1.

[8] Criminal and gang violence is a notorious problem in most countries of Central America. Other states, including the United States, aren't immune from "cultures of violence." In an 11 September 2000 IRIN News Brief, South Africa's Safety and Security Minister Steve Tshwete warned that tough action must be taken to control urban terror to avoid a situation similar to "violence-wracked" Algeria. *Can Anyone Hear Us? Voices from 47 Countries*, makes it clear that a paramount anxiety of the poor is criminal violence (Deepa Narayan et al., Poverty Group [Washington, D.C.: World Bank, December 1999]).

[9] *UN Wire* (14 June 2000). Countries with especially large numbers of child soldiers include Sierra Leone, Burundi, Guinea-Bissau, Somalia, Angola and Sudan. Afghanistan and Myanmar are leaders in Asia, Colombia in Latin America. The numbers of child soldiers in these countries are at least 100,000, 50,000, and 19,000, respectively (Jeffrey Boutwell and Michael J. Klare, "A Scourge of Small Arms," *Scientific American* [June 2000], 4).

[10] Children are primarily used by guerrilla bands, although government armies in Colombia, Myanmar, Liberia, Sudan and Sierra Leone are all guilty of recruiting child soldiers. Government recruiters target the poor and dispossessed. Recruitment is often forced. Unless children can prove they are under age, they are inducted into the state security forces (Rachel Brett and Margaret McCalin, *Children: The Invisible Soldiers* [Vaxjo, Sweden: Radda Barnen, 1996]).

[11] Landmines are an explosive and technically a sub-type of SALW. However, since anti-personnel mines received so much attention over the past few years, they tend to be treated as a distinct weapon system.

[12] Inter-American Convention Against the Illicit Manufacturing of and Trafficking in Firearms, Ammunition, Explosives, and Other Related Materials (13 November 1997), 2.

[13] Michael Renner, "Arm Control Options," *The Bulletin of the Atomic Scientists* (January/February 1999), 26.

[14] There were 40 million military-style SAWL in the South 10 years ago (Michael T. Klare and Robert Rotberg, "The Scourge of Small Arms" [Cambridge, Mass.: World Peace Foundation, 1999], 8). Not surprising, the country with the largest number of SAWL is the United States.

[15] Klare and Rotberg say that Afghanistan is the world's leading country of unaccountable weapons, with at least 10 million SAWL in circulation. About 60 per cent of the arms from Afghanistan are illegally exported ("Small Arms," 35).

[16] Lora Lumpe, "The Leader of the Pact," *The Bulletin of the Atomic Scientists* (January/February 1999), 28; Michael T. Klare, "The International Trade in Light Weapons: What Have We Learned?" in Boutwell and Klare, *Light Weapons and Civil Conflicts*, 17.

[17] Laurence, "Light Weapons and Intrastate Conflicts," 39.

[18] Ibid.

[19] Michael Renner, "Small Arms Found in All Nations," in *Vital Signs*, ed. Linda Starke (Washington: Worldwatch Institute, 1999).

[20] Quoted in Natalie J. Goldring, "Coordinating Action on Small Arms," in Natalie J. Goldring, "Overcoming Domestic Obstacles to Light Weapons Control" (British American Security Information Council [BASIC], April 1997).

[21] Much of the information from this section is borrowed from O'Reilly, "Building on Our Comparative Advantage."

[22] Susan Willett, "How Could the Emerging Donor Agenda for Security Sector Reform Help the OSCE [Organisation for Security and Co-operation in Europe] Curb Small Arms Proliferation?" in *Small Arms and Light Weapons: An Issue for the OSCE?*, workshop organised by the governments of Canada, Norway, the Netherlands, and Switzerland in association with BASIC (November 1998), 92.

[23] WV's ADPs are large community-development projects. Expansion of size permits economies of scale.

[24] Eshete and O'Reilly-Calthrop, "Silent Revolution," executive summary.

[25] "The Tools for Arms Project in Mozambique," *IANSA Newsletter* (May 2000).

[26] Bonn International Center for Conversion and Monterey Institute of International Studies, "Tackling Small Arms and Light Weapons: A Practical Guide for Collection and Destruction" (February 2000), 7-8.

[27] Paul Collier and Anke Hoeffler, "Greed and Grievance in Civil War," World Bank website (new version October 2001). According to this report, funds to fuel rebellions are often derived from ethnic populations living in diaspora. These expatriates believe that they are funding a just cause. Moves towards peace and reconciliation may depend on reducing the resources sent by expatriates.

[28] Peter Lock, "Comprehensive Measures to Reduce Illicit Small Arms Availability," Forty-ninth Pugwash Conference on Science and World Affairs (September 1999), 2.

[29] Louise, "The Social Impacts of Light Weapons Availability and Proliferation," 6, 9. Before the oil price increases last year, the sale of illegal drugs probably exceeded petroleum revenues. The expanding arms-for-drugs (marijuana) trade in Papua New Guinea fuels both criminal activities and tribal feuds. In addition, the trade threatens to further destabilise the situation in neighbouring Papua, one of Indonesia's restive provinces ("Arms Smuggling Menace in Papua New Guinea," Stratfort Global Intelligence Update [13 September 2000]).

[30] In testimonies at UN and OAS hearings, one gets the impression that the National Rifle Association would rather not have the US enter treaties that curb the illicit trade of SALW.

[31] Boutwell and Klare, "A Scourge of Small Arms," 2-3. Possibly US$2-$3 billion are illicit sales.

[32] Pamina Firchow and Tamar Gobelnick, "The US Is No. 1 in Global Arms Sales," *San Diego Union Tribune* (30 August 2000). In "US Arms Sales Rise," *Arms Trade News* (September 2000), a distiction is made between arms deliveries and sales and deliveries. In 1999 the United States's share of sales and deliveries was 38 per cent or US$11.8 billion. Kalashnikovs are about six times cheaper than the US-made M-16-A1 ("Russia: Arms Sales," *Oxford Analytica* [5 January 2000], 1). However, better-financed criminal groups seem to prefer the M-16 because the quality of ammunition is higher and bullets are easier to get.

[33] "Framework Agreement Concerning Measures to Facilitate the Restructuring and Operation of the European Defence Industry," in "Europe Signs Defense Industry Cooperation Pact," *Arms Trade News* (September 2000), 2; Kathleen Miller and Theresa Hitchens, "European Accord Threatens to Lower Export Controls," BASIC papers no. 33 (August 2000). The United States fears that the agreement will eventually force US armsmakers out of "Fortress Europe."

[34] Renner, "Small Arms Found in All Nations," 155.

[35] Sussanah Dyer and Geraldine O'Callaghan, "Combating Illicit Light Weapons Trafficking: Developments and Opportunities," BASIC (January 1998), 12.

[36] Laurence, "Light Weapons and Intrastate Conflicts, 17-18; Lock, "Comprehensive Measures to Reduce Illicit Small Arms Availability," 6-8.

[37] A World Bank report emphasised that lack of security due to rising armed criminal activities is one of the paramount fears of the poor (Narayan et al., *Can Anyone Hear Us?*).

[38] Lock, "Comprehensive Measures to Reduce Illicit Small Arms Availability," 5.

[39] James P. McShane, "Light Weapons and International Law Enforcement," in Boutwell and Klare, *Light Weapons and Civil Conflict*, 178.

[40] Louise, "The Social Impacts of Light Weapons Availability and Proliferation," 4.

[41] Klare, "The Kalashnikov Age," 18.

[42] Keith Krause, "Prospects for Agreeing Common Controls on Legal Transfers of Light Weapons within the OSCE," in *Small Arms and Light Weapons: An Issue for the OSCE?*, 87.

[43] To a large degree, the Wassenaar Arrangement is patterned after the principles set forth in the OSCE's 1993 "Criteria on Conventional Arms Transfers" code of conduct (Krause, "Prospects for Agreeing Common Controls on Legal Transfers of Light Weapons within the OSCE," 86).

[44] For a short discussion of SALW and the Wassenaar Arrangement, see Luigi Lauriola, "Prospects for Agreeing Common Controls on Light Weapons Within the Wassenaar Arrangement," in *Small Arms and Light Weapons: An Issue for the OSCE?*, p. 84. Lauriola is head of the secretariat of the Wassenaar Arrangement.

[45] Lora Lumpe, "U.S. Policy and the Export of Light Weapons," in Boutwell and Klare, *Light Weapons and Civil Conflict*, 66-67.

[46] Ibid., 70-73. Goldring makes the point that passage of the Violent Crime Control and Law Enforcement Act in 1994 may have indirectly cut the amount of illicit arms exported by reducing the number of weapons dealers from 250,000 to 100,000 (Natalie J. Goldring, "Domestic Laws and International Controls," in Jeffrey and Klare, *Light Weapons and Civil Conflict*, 105; Lumpe, "U.S. Policy and the Export of Light Weapons," 70-73.

[47] More European than US NGOs are watching proposed code of conduct legislation. The result is far more critiques on the EU Code than on the US Code.

[48] For these and other omissions, see Susannah Dyer and Geraldine O'Callaghan, "One Size Fits All: Prospects for a Global Convention on Illicit Trafficking by 2000," BASIC research report 99.2 (April 1999).

[49] NGO input was invited during the first preparatory commission in February-March 2000. NGOs were not invited to the intersessional session in July 2000, in which no substantial decisions were made. NGOs sat as observers in the March 2001 preparatory commission. The report following the conference is available on the UN website.

[50] From Rocard, "Statement by H. E. Mr. Michel Rocard Before the International Press Conference," 2. Renner suggests that states follow a head stamping method for ammunition that is universally applicable ("Small Arms Found in All Nations," 12).

[51] Primers are the most difficult part of ammunition to manufacture. Restricting the sale of primers is not a panacea to stem the illicit use of SALW. Yet it might be an effective choke point to reduce the effectiveness of arms in specific instances (Rachel Stohl, "Deadly Rounds: Ammunition and

Armed Conflict," BASIC research report 98.4 (May 1998); Goldring, "Overcoming Domestic Obstacles to List Weapons Controls."

[52] Lock, "Comprehensive Measures to Reduce Illicit Small Arms Availability," 8.

[53] In the United States, for example, weapons may be legally advertised in magazines, although arms can't be legally bought through the mail.

[54] Lock, "Comprehensive Measures to Reduce Illicit Small Arms Availability," 11.

[55] Assessing responsibility will spur a corollary business in third-party insurance that should also serve as a brake to the free flowing arms trade (ibid., 6).

[56] O'Reilly, "Building on Our Comparative Advantage," 2. Currently, World Vision UK and World Vision International are members of the International Action Network on Small Arms.

[57] This potential role for WV was mentioned or affirmed by personnel from five policy-based NGOs located in Washington, D.C. (interviews by the author, 25-26 September 2000).

[58] "Ecumenical Consultation on Small Arms in Latin America," Project Ploughshares (28 July 2000), 4.

10.

Thinking Politically

NGOs, Religious Nationalism and the Language of the People

ALAN WHAITES

Average NGO workers now face a daunting set of expectations in terms of their skills and abilities: media savvy, political sensitivity, academic credibility, organisational competence and development awareness. Aside from these pressures on individual aid workers, the issues facing agencies as a whole are on occasions even more daunting. This is never more true than when agencies are trying to tread an intelligent political path in a complex environment. NGO workers may not personally combine in superhuman form the skills of political scientists, social anthropologists and efficient managers, but collectively their agencies must do so. NGOs need to look at their skill sets in each of these areas, that is, if they are to work for poverty reduction without doing long-term political and social harm in the process.

An often ignored but neatly illustrative issue in relation to contextual sensitivity is religious nationalism. In "Let's Get Civil Society Straight: NGOs and Political Theory," I argued that if a particular concept of political theory (civil society) were not taken seriously at a conceptual level, then NGOs could unwittingly reinforce homogeneous, primordially based groups in their confrontational competition for resources.[1] This chapter goes on to suggest, using religious nationalism as an example, that all NGO programmes (operational or not) need to be aware of the inherently political nature of even the simplest development process.

The neutrality of any action is, after all, not defined so much by the perceptions of the actor as by those of the observer. NGOs pursue humanitarian principles within a social context, and it is by the principles and norms of that context that their actions are judged. Nobody's intentions can be so obvious as never to be misconstrued. When an NGO begins a project, signs an MOU, or recruits staff, it is acting politically. When those dynamics involve highly charged issues of religion and politics, it is easy for an NGO to move rapidly into unintended situations of conflict. Seeing actions in the light of the social sphere in some ways comes more easily at the micro-level (with a wealth of Participatory Learning and Action tools, partner organisations and social anthropology to help). Greater problems can exist when NGOs, particularly Northern NGOs, consider broader strategic goals within their operational contexts.

The politicisation of religion points to the necessity of considering long-standing social and political dynamics. For Western NGOs, religious dynamics are frequently marginalised, even within local communities, as part of the spiritual (corollary assumption: non-developmental) sphere of life. Figures from the local mosque or watt may be put forward by a community as part of its chosen leadership but are not necessarily one of the first ports of call for staff of a visiting NGO.

Yet outside of the village, the power of religious institutions is not felt simply through local, institutional representatives. Politicised religion has become a feature of many developing societies at the macro level. National politics can bear out the effect of religion whether through the influence of radical Catholic priests, the revolutionary zeal of fundamentalist Islam, or the electoral draw of the BJP (a right-of-centre Hindu revivalist party). The rise of politicised-religion means that, rightly or wrongly, NGOs are evaluated or interpreted in the light of a prevailing religious worldview. Depending on the context, observers evaluate NGOs as Western, pro-market, the vanguard of immorality, liberal, secular, feminist and so forth.

Can NGOs operate effectively in such a complex and sometimes emotional political world? A few experiences, such as the clash between NGOs and the Taliban over women workers, may suggest not. It would be wrong, however, to be too pessimistic; in many instances NGOs do manage to anticipate and side-step emerging problems. The key to such action is effective analysis. Agencies must be committed to the process of trying to understand the roots and dynamics of local political power structures. Inevitably this means a willingness to undertake Political Impact Assessments (PIAs). The idea of such assessments at the local level has gained momentum through work on conflict prevention, particularly Mary Anderson's Local Capacities for Peace *(Do No Harm)* ideas. PIAs are, however, usually unfamiliar territory for NGOs at the macro-level and yet have much to offer in enhancing programme effectiveness and avoiding problems.

PIAs will in most cases show that the linking of religion, ethnicity and nationalism is not inherently a cause for NGO alarm, despite the simplistic trap set by Huntington and others which sets up religio-nationalism as inevitably liable to confrontation.[2] Nor is religious militancy, a growing factor in the NGO world, necessarily something that will be identified as needing dedicated strategies and policies.[3] Rather, PIAs will help NGOs to identify which factors do need constructive planning on their part and which can safely be left alone. This chapter, therefore, simply offers a basic plea to the international development NGO to get to grips conceptually with the political history of its contexts as a guide to the current obstacles facing the aspirations of the poor.

RELIGION: THE LANGUAGE OF THE PEOPLE

The rising role of religion within the power politics of many states is intimately linked to popular religion's role amongst nationalist elites as a means to articulate and convey political messages.[4] Religion is often the conceptual language of the people, rather than merely a primordial identity.[5] Religion is not static. All popular religions embody a set of ideas and explanations for social norms which is interpretative. Religion becomes a means to express our fears and hopes, allowing us to make sense of our environment. Religion offers an elevated language through which we can rationalise our world and keep our defining national myths alive.[6] Elie Kedourie provides an example of religion's power to embody and codify mass popular behaviour when she says of Hinduism that "the new national spirit has found apt vehicles for expressing itself in the current religious rights and formulas of the people."[7]

This connection between religion as core to people's identities and its ability to provide an interpretive framework for our world – including ideas of community – lies at the heart of its role in politics in any country. Religions may point towards particular political directions as a natural corollary of their founder's vision and teaching. But in reality, agreement on which road to take is rarely achieved; Christianity, for example, is frequently politicised in a right-wing way in North America, whereas its European counterpart is more likely to identify with the left. The variable is not the religion's teachings but the experiences and interpretations of its adherents. Hence in Europe, Christian Socialism grew from the experience of industrialisation and nineteenth century movements for social reform.[8]

This interpretative dynamic, through which religious elites critique society, also provides opportunity for political elites to weave ideology and events into religious themes. Religion can be a malleable tool in either group's hands. Those who see religion's role as limited to providing what Bendix has called the "shared understandings" which "determine the character of the political community"[9] forget that religious understandings evolve and mutate. Changes within religions can have radical effects on the wider polity.

This is particularly the case in those instances in which, instead of supplying reference points, religious groups seek not only to influence, but also to control the state itself. In these situations religion becomes a direct player in the game for power. Political ideologies, after all, rely on stories and images to capture the imaginations of potential supporters. Throughout the twentieth century those images more often than not drew on the well of primordial memory and identity.

The interaction of political rhetoric with a people's sense of nationhood or ethnicity becomes a self-reinforcing process, in which national symbols become a powerful force in public life. This does not mean that diverse states are immune to nationalist manipulation, or that a sense of common community cannot be built. In some states, such as the United States, the very heterogeneity of the population pushes the political elite towards the use of unifying myths (the American Way, the land of the free, etc.) which become tools of political rhetoric and manipulation.

For the nationalist elite, however, appealing to a sense of common purpose can be greatly facilitated where religious and/or ethnic rallying points of identity exist. In situations of religious homogeneity, use of religious rhetoric and symbols as a means to reach the masses can become a temptation beyond forbearance for the often urban and middle-class nationalist leadership. Tom Nairn and Eric Hobsbawm were instrumental in framing a discussion exploring the role of elites in manipulating identities as part of the nationalist cause.[10] The need on the part of elites for points of connection with a mass audience is so acute that where a religious vehicle for symbolism does not exist an alternative has to be created through the use of secular religion, of which Communism was particularly effective in the last century.

Nationalism has long tended to combine with political or religious philosophies in its articulation of national ideals. Sometimes these political idioms are either religious (Hinduism and Islam) or secular (Vietnam), although on occasions they have included an interesting mixture of both (such as the Integrationist and then Pancasila philosophies of Indonesia). Elsewhere this concept has been termed "political religion,"[11] and this notion is discussed briefly below, but for the purposes of clarity this chapter will focus on the idea of political idioms.

While defining *nation* and *nationalism* continues to inspire academic debate,[12] much of this discussion can seem to be arguing the obvious for an NGO practitioner immersed in the charged environments of Bosnia, Palestine, East Timor, or India. This chapter therefore focusses on the universal goal of nationalists to mobilise a sense of common political purposes around a cause defined in terms of the community itself.

RELIGION, ETHNICITY AND NATIONALISM

The reputation of nationalism has risen and fallen with the decades. In the 1960s nationalism was synonymous with struggles for independence in many parts of the developing world. In the 1990s nationalism acquired connotations of ethnic cleansing and genocide. Neither inference is new. Nationalism was both integral to the movement for Indian independence and a mainstay of the

Nazi cause. The call to achieve a common goal based on a sense of political community brings no guarantees that the ultimate goals will be good (or evil), although such a call does create a tendency to crudely characterise nationalism as a product of ethnicity. Nationalism is therefore inherently neither good nor bad and modern multi-ethnic states can exhibit just as much nationalistic and patriotic sentiment as more homogeneous neighbours.

Recognising that nationalism does not depend on ethnicity does not alter the reality that in many parts of the world the sense of community does frequently include a strong ethnic dimension. Although religion, ethnicity and nationalism can be a powerful combination, they can also be the roots of division in those heterogeneous contexts in which unifying national myths are weak. Ethnic identity may therefore subvert the concept of nation itself (as has happened all too painfully in Rwanda, Sri Lanka, Bosnia, etc). Equally, religion has constrained national unity for Kashmiris, Punjabis and others.

Nationalism is therefore never uniform, neither is it the simple result of a social equation that can be applied globally. Nationalism's components and foundations alter from political community to political community, dictating that any fuller definition must absorb numerous other possible points of common identity. This wider sense of community, which we term *nationhood* and *nationalism,* embraces issues of geography and history that can push ethnicity as such into a minor role. Whatever the nature of nationalism's specific components in any given context, the myriad of factors that together create a sense of nationhood merge to form a distinct set of shared political understandings. Indeed, John Dunn believes nationalism has become the "common idiom of contemporary political feeling."[13]

Both religion and nationalism are capable of carrying forth the "common idiom" of Dunn or the "shared understandings" of Bendix. In fact, if, as Dunn says, nationalism plays this role now, then religion was its immediate predecessor. In terms of Western political understanding, Andersen claims, it was only with the Enlightenment that it became necessary to find "a secular transformation of fatality into continuity, contingency into meaning."[14] Not only do religion and nationalism share this ability to provide a conceptual framework for political life, but they also are invariably important to each other in doing so.

THE INTERESTS OF ELITES:
SYMBOL MANIPULATION AND POLITICAL IMAGERY

The advantages to religious elites of identifying with ethnic/national sentiments include coming to terms with and becoming consolidated within "existing cultural and economic divisions".[15] In other words, there are distinct advantages for any religious hierarchy in becoming associated with national identity. These advantages vary from overt protection by the state itself to growth of a peer pressure barrier to apostasy (for example, the sense that to be Thai is to be Buddhist). In some cases the link is itself a vehicle to intellectually re-invigorate a religious system in decline.[16]

Any idiom used by nationalists (religious or secular) can enjoy considerable longevity. But, politicisation of religion brings peculiar and frequently uncontrollable long-term forces into play. The major religions tend to include a distinct and organised religious elite who are distinct (apart from some notable exceptions) from the political elite – a crucial factor in the long term. Politicisation of religion for nationalist purposes creates a potential for unfulfilled expectations and, in some cases, open rivalry.

In effect, the relationship between religion and nationalism does not necessarily bridge the gap between religious and nationalist elites. The separate ambitions of these elites may coalesce during a nationalist phase or struggle, but more permanent association would imply not only sharing power but, for the nationalists, acceptance of an irrefutable and uncontrollable "divine" political actor. Examples such as Pakistan offer stark lessons regarding use of religion during the independence struggle – followed by post-independence cold shouldering of the religious elite. Interestingly, the sole Asian country to institute a formal relationship between state and clergy during transformation to modern nation-statehood, Thailand, also had a religious elite dominated by members of the ruling royal family and the absence of a concept of an interventionist deity.

Case Study One:
South Asia – Religion as the Idiom of National Struggle

Perhaps of all those places where religion has been a significant factor in the nationalist struggle, its role has been most thoroughly studied in relation to South Asia, a context in which NGOs now face strong religious-political force in all states. Religion in South Asia was not only an important focus of nationalist myth and ethnic pride, but it also provided one of the few constant channels of communication between elites and masses as Western education and economic methods replaced traditional forms. The link between the Hindu worldview and nationalism was forged as early as 1828 by Raja Rammohan Roy, who believed that before political freedom could be attained, Hinduism would have to be reformed.[17]

By the end of the nineteenth century both Hinduism and Islam were undergoing revival within India as theological debate flourished. New liberal thinkers and movements such as the Brahmo Samaj in Hinduism and Sir Syeed Ahmed Khan in Islam had their traditionalist alter-egos (such as the Dharma Sabha in Hinduism[18] and the Deoband school of Islam[19]). Religious reformers and traditionalists tried to come to terms with Western rationalism (for the former) or to reject it in favour of cultural introspection (for the latter). Chandra describes the process as "a cultural-ideological struggle against the backward elements of traditional culture, on the one hand, and the fast hegemonising colonial culture and ideology on the other."[20] The fruit of this struggle was re-invigoration of religion as a social and, potentially, political force.

In 1883 Surendranath Banerjea became the first Indian journalist imprisoned on a nationalist issue. His sentence for contempt of court was the result of an article decrying a judicial decision on the question of ownership of a family idol, a judgement viewed by many as insulting to Hinduism.[21] This incident, only two years before the founding of the Indian National Congress, was a precursor to realisation by nationalists that Hindu symbolism was a powerful populist force in the struggle against the British. B. G. Tilak, the first truly charismatic figure of the nationalist movement, used not only Hindu symbols but also Hindu chauvinism to popularise nationalist ideas.[22] Although more Westernised (and constitutionalist) elements of Congress were to reclaim leadership of the nationalist movement in the period after the First World War, the importance of religion as a motivational force was not lost.

The power of religion to embody those aspects of national identity which united Hindu Indians was crucial to Congress in bridging the chasm between its Western educated leadership and the rural poor of the Indian hinterland. The figure of Mahatma Gandhi, both an educated lawyer and a dhoti-wearing holy man, provided the nationalist elite with an effective bridge to the rural peasant.[23] Fred Riggs has asserted that nationalism in poly communal societies uses the symbols of the dominant elite;[24] in fact, the elite in India recognised the importance of speaking the symbolic language of the masses.

Gandhi and Congress may today be frequently associated with a non-sectarian or even secular nationalist creed, but in reality this more complex message was only imperfectly transmitted to India's populace. Judith Brown has said "part of Gandhi's public image was that of a Hindu holy man, and in places this almost shaded into veneration of him as semi-divine. There were reports of Gandhi puja worship. But this charismatic appeal was not the foundation for a stable and disciplined political following."[25] The result of this strategy was that the pre-independence Congress was identified closely with Hindu interests not only by Muslims but also by its own members, as Brown has recounted.[26]

Politicised Religion after Independence

With independence, Congress's secular leadership had neither the desire nor mandate to respond to the role of Hinduism in the nationalist movement by bestowing upon it the position of a state religion. Instead the new government sought to displace the religion it had helped to politicise from a central role in setting the political agenda by instituting a new "political religion" – Nehruvian Socialism.

Political religion, a term coined by David Apter, consists of the ideology of the state used to bind ruler and ruled together. Apter asks, "What bridges the gap between ruler and ruled, individual and society? . . . An ideological position is put forward by government that identifies the individual with society. Modern political leaders come to recognise quickly, however, that no ordinary ideology can prevail for long in the face of obvious discrepancies between theory and practice. A more powerful symbolic force, less rational, although it may include rational ends, seems necessary to them."[27] This powerful symbolic force is political religion, and in India, the strength of Nehruvian Socialism was such that it enabled Indira Gandhi not only to ditch and then reform Congress, but also to transform politics into a more populist form.

An almost identical situation quickly emerged in Pakistan, where the Pakistan movement used local Pirs (sufi holy men) and clerics extensively to persuade the Muslim majority provinces to vote for partition. Ian Talbot has described the work of local clergy in achieving the dramatic successes by the movement as it reversed previous electoral defeats.[28] The movement's aim, a homeland for the subcontinent's Muslims, seemed to suggest the advent of a religious state. But Pakistan proved, in its first decades, to be established on the secular Western principles of Mohammad Ali Jinnah and Liaquat Ali Khan. I have previously argued that the ideological idea of Pakistan itself can be said to have become the state's new basis of shared understandings.[29]

However, for political religion to succeed in displacing the pre-independence role of traditional religion, it must establish its own legitimacy by living up to the expectations created. In India the 1980s brought crisis to the political religion of Nehruvian Socialism as economic stagnation and political instability weakened popular belief. Mayall believes that economic development is used to detach people from primordial loyalties, but in India, as elsewhere, development failed to materialise as rapidly as had been promised.[30]

The undermining of political religion by failure to live up to economic expectations provided renewed opportunity for the re-emergence of Hinduism as a serious political force. Right-of-centre Hindu revivalist parties, particularly the BJP (successor to the Jan Sangh), articulated a Hindu platform of "shared understandings" which seemed to fit more comfortably with the process of political and economic reform than Nehruvian Socialism ever could. For the BJP, the goal was no less than redefinition of Indianness.[31] Although anti-Muslim rhetoric and condemnation of increasing provisions for minorities were important to the BJP in creating popular support, the main target of its attack has been the secular Nehruvian elite. A sympathetic commentator stated, "One of the first tasks in the awakening of the Hindu society is to scrutinise and expose the Nehruvian establishment in the political and in, more fundamentally, its intellectual dimensions."[32]

In Pakistan, religious leaders found post-independence politics equally frustrating. Political descendants of Pirs who had campaigned for partition (embodied in the Jamaat-i-Pakistan party) and even the clerics who opposed the creation of Pakistan (whose successors form the Jamaat-i-Islami) claim the promised state has failed to materialise due to the insistence on secularism. Muslim political parties have become increasingly vocal, demanding creation of a more fully Islamic Muslim state. In effect, the religious elites deny the "completeness" of the nation-forming process without a greater theocratic dimension.

Politicisation of religion in the nationalist struggle has proven, in India and Pakistan, to have awakened long-standing political ambitions amongst the religious elite, which the new political religion failed to contain. Writers such as Geertz and Migdal[33] suggest that the creation of the nation-state introduces a new prize over which to contend. For the BJP and other religious parties, the prize is claimed as rightfully theirs, an unfulfilled promise of the national struggle. "How could you fashion a strong Indian state which did have a Hindu identity?"[34]

Case Study Two:
Vietnam – Communism as a Secular Idiom

It is possible to argue that adoption of a firmly secular approach by nationalists has had the effect of defusing the role of religion in the political sphere. In effect, nationalists avoided the later need to depoliticise religion through political religion by instituting an equally or more effective alternative source of unity during the national struggle.

An interesting case study of the secularisation of politics by a nationalist elite is provided by Vietnam, a country in which the diversity of belief systems made religion a poor unifying idiom – leading to the search for a broader, more generic idiom of mobilisation. The history of overlap between religion and nationalism in Vietnam was not in itself unimpressive – indeed, secular nationalists faced a strategic need to overcome rival religious idioms. But, ultimately, history suggests that an entirely different approach to mobilisation – such as the secular idiom of Communism – was always a more promising route in Vietnam than often ill-defined and poorly articulated religious principles.

Although Buddhism was the majority religion of the masses in Vietnam, Confucianism predominated amongst the traditional elite. During the subjugation of Vietnam by the French in the latter half of the nineteenth century, a resistance movement continued under the leadership of gentlemen scholars educated in the Confucian tradition. For the Vietnamese gentry, a classical education included several years under the tutelage of a local Confucian teacher, learning the Confucian classics in Chinese script. This inculcated into the gentry Confucian principles of conservatism and loyalty to the monarchy. The central political principle offered by Confucianism was the need for harmony within the state. Harmony was said to be best secured by loyalty to the emperor, family and the nation.[35] For the mass of the Vietnamese population, religious belief took the form of Mahayana Buddhism, less organised and hierarchical than Theravada Buddhism. Buddhism was tolerated by the Confucian elite, as were growing numbers of Catholic converts – a tolerance which rested on an implicit understanding that the status quo was not to be questioned.[36]

With the coming of French rule and establishment of a puppet Confucian court in Hue, the role of Confucianism in Vietnamese society was increasingly questioned. Confucianism, with no concept of the absolute but only of harmony, seemed to offer little response to Western rationalism other than reversion to traditionalism. Ralph Smith states, "As a political orthodoxy Confucianism all but deified the Emperor. But it did not compel him to defend and develop his power against rival source of authority: nor did it lead him along the path of the modern dictator to seek control over his subjects' every thought and deed. Being itself absolute, universal harmony had no need of absolutism."[37]

The Vietnamese elite, led at first by classically trained scholars such as Phan Boi Chau, increasingly felt that Confucianism itself was retrogressive.[38] The only positive element of Confucian thought which could now form a focus for identity was the concept of nation. This now provided "a focus for their borrowings from the West."[39] Nationalists embraced the new Romanised alphabet and launched a Free School Movement which was closed down by the French in 1907 due to its overt nationalist stance.[40] New Vietnamese elites were therefore no longer taught the Chinese script or Confucian classics, nor did they learn Confucian principles of loyalty to the Crown, seen by some as a collaborationist institution.[41]

The nationalist movement within Vietnam engaged in what Dunn has termed the "brutal natural selection of belief systems"[42] and looked towards Western ideologies which might be used to unify the elite and masses. Phan Boi Chau followed the trend amongst his Chinese counterparts and adopted a quasi-socialist stance, but his successors, particularly Ho Chi Minh, embraced a more clearly defined Marxist-Leninist philosophy of national liberation. The adoption of Communism by large parts of the nationalist elite in the 1920s and 1930s did not take place against the backdrop of a society with strong organised religion. Instead, this process filled the vacuum left by the disappearance of one religious form and the lack of organisation in another (Buddhism). As Ralph Smith states: "On a philosophical level Marxism has provided its adepts with a set of beliefs and ideas which answer many of the questions most puzzling to twentieth century Vietnamese."[43]

During the pre–World War II period, other belief systems were not entirely dormant. A Buddhist revival led by more disciplined Japanese schools, such as the Lotus school, made considerable headway in the 1930s and encouraged a more militant approach to politics on the part of monastic orders.[44] However, the new religious and secular groups were competitors with Marxism for the minds of the nation and proved unequal to the discipline, organisation and leadership of the Communists. Communist-inspired rebellions in the 1930s and the role of the party as a rallying point for resistance during Japanese occupation meant that, as Duiker states, "the American presence, like that of the French before Geneva, obscured the fact that the Communists had already won the civil war in Vietnam at the end of World War II and that foreign power alone had prevented them from consolidating their victory."[45]

The Vietnamese experience and that of states such as China suggest that where religion has little potential as a unifying force for the nationalist cause, political religion is unlikely to develop. Although religion became a political issue during the Vietnamese war and has been a peripheral issue since (with Catholics still viewed primarily as a threat to the regime),[46] it has periodically been continued economic stagnation which has eroded support for the Hanoi government rather than the appeal of a religious alternative.

Vietnam underlines the key role of nationalist elite in providing or not providing a political role for their religious counterparts. For religion to be adopted as a tool of the nationalist struggle, its ideology must provide an effective, unifying idiom for the nationalist ideal – qualities religion seemed unable to offer in Vietnam. But if Vietnam highlights the weakness of religion when beliefs are too diverse and tied to social class, the examples of India and Pakistan highlight the impact of politicisation using the religious elite. Indeed, the stirring of political ambitions amongst religious elites has been strengthened by belief that nationalist goals can only be realised through theocratic or quasi-theocratic forms of government.

Development of a religious agenda amongst the religious elite and of a politicised view of religion amongst the masses does not inevitably suggest a path towards theocracy. As we have seen, nationalist elites have attempted to displace religious power through a secular political idiom or political religion rather than surrender any power to their religious counterparts. In India and Pakistan this has been undermined by disillusionment with Nehruvian socialism on one hand and reversion to Islam (as a unifying force in the light of ethnic tension) on the other. It is perhaps ironic that in the state founded explicitly on religious-nationalist principles – as in a homeland for the subcontinent's Muslims – religious parties have found it most difficult to secure power.

WHAT DOES THIS MEAN FOR NGOS?

Religion as a political idiom clearly has the potential to play a valuable role in the struggle for justice, independence, or reform. The ability of religious leaders to articulate the aspirations of the poor has allowed such leaders to become a rallying point for those seeking justice. The Desmond Tutus of the world have used faith as a nonviolent weapon against oppression. Recent work on Africa has underlined this potential in relation to a number of states, linking religion in particular to various pro-democracy causes.[47] The political role of religion, however, also clearly brings the potential for a union with nationalism in its more confrontational sense. Religious nationalists, like their secular counterparts, often require a focus for animosity to provide the momentum for popular support, whether it be the BJP's view of religious minorities and Pakistan, Iran's anti-Americanism, or the bizarre demonisation of the UN system by some US Christian fundamentalist groups.

The result is that for NGOs the emotive power of politicised and nationalistic religion creates a hazard-strewn working environment. The tendency to identify a focus for animosity leads to even greater scrutiny of NGO actions according to criteria of the prevailing religious worldview. NGOs find that every decision is a potentially sensitive issue, and temptation increases to avoid points of known contention, whether projects focussed on gender or alignment with partners who are themselves seen as suspect. Often NGOs will decide that continued operationality will mean avoiding some engagement that might otherwise be seen as strategically important. But, in determining a path through the mine-field of religious nationalism, NGOs should also be conscious of the cause of the phenomenon itself.

The rise of religious nationalism is directly linked to opportunities presented by religion to politicians as a vehicle through which to articulate their message. For many, religion embodies the language of the people; its images and concepts are the easiest way to relate to and interpret even a *globalised* world. This gift to politicians presents an important lesson for the secularised, philosophically Western NGO. Even in contexts where religion has become an inherently charged political issue, there is cause to listen to and speak the language of religious discourse. Through it, important messages will be relayed.

Amongst NGOs, the tendency has been to offer a language of our own. Even participatory tools tend to focus on need and wealth over worldview. This, in its worst expression, becomes no more than simply allying with the process of building a secular idiom. Aligning with the secularisation of the language of popular discourse often does much to reinforce the prejudice of those religious nationalists who see NGOs as the harbingers of destructive, Westernising change. In some contexts it can also provide unintended service to those who seek to offer their own political religion, their own secular idiom, to reinforce and consolidate a differing political agenda.

Religion as a language of political articulation is not necessarily something for NGOs to fear. Politicised religion can bring focus to altruistic and egalitarian values of faith to empower and liberate, without seeking to dominate and control. In the hands of a Tutu, Boff or Bonhoeffer religion becomes the language of the poor seeking neither to dominate nor to marginalise others. When silenced, an avenue for participatory change is lost. NGOs should also recognise that driving religion out of politics does not always replace religious nationalists with a nicer, more preferable sort. The process of de-spiritualising politics may not only deny the poor their voice but may also come at a high human cost.

In Asia, for example, secular political religion has been less effective in displacing the role of religion in national life, leading to direct repression of religious institutions. In states such as Burma and Lao PDR religion retains considerable importance as a focus for national identity. Religious elites are, however, carefully controlled by the respective ruling elites, who ensure that political aspirations are kept firmly in check. A further example of the ability of elites or government to remove religion from the political sphere has been provided by David Laitin's studies of the Yoruba in Nigeria, where colonial policy promoted other primordial loyalties which became a key focus of identity.[48]

For the nationalist elite, post-independence government has shown considerable faith in the ability of the state to mould political and social attitudes. Experiments in political religion have underscored the potential of the state to change primordial sentiments, demonstrated by the case of the Yoruba. But in those cases where the nationalist elite had previously manipulated the call of religion, the attempt to displace it has been a high-risk strategy. In replacing the role of religion after first contributing to its political renewal, elites have weakened their own grasp of the shared understandings which underpin social attitudes to political life. Alexis de Tocqueville misunderstood the nature of faith when, having stated the benefits of religion in providing common, altruistic, reference points, he went on to suggest that religion should confine itself to its proper sphere if it was not to run the risk of being disbelieved.[49] Most of the world's great religions reject the separation of faith and society, instead seeing the two as inherently joined. The call of faith usually entails a vision of a national community organised around the religion's principles and ideas.

For religions to deny themselves any role in politics would be to deny their own most basic beliefs. The issue, therefore, is to recognise the positive and negative roles the language of the people can play – providing vehicles for social doctrine and aspirations for freedom and justice, or tools of elite manipulation, a focus for confrontation and even hate. Where politicised religion has become the means to convey a message of harsh nationalist animosity, the future nature of the politicised religious elite should come as no surprise. Nationalist struggles have provided religion not only with the opportunity to lay claim to new spheres of common dignity, personal freedom, and altruism but also to add an aura of belief to the state itself.

NOTES

[1] Alan Whaites, "Let's Get Civil Society Straight: NGOs and Political Theory," *Development in Practice* 6/3 (1996).

[2] Samuel P. Huntington, "The Clash of Civilisations?" *Foreign Affairs* (1993), 22–49.

[3] See David Little, "Religious Militancy," in *Managing Global Chaos*, ed. Chester A. Crocker and Fen Osler Hampson (Washington D.C.: US Institute for Peace Press, 1996); see also, Ankie Hoogvelt, *Globalisation and the Postcolonial World* (London: Macmillan, 1997), chap. 9.

[4] See Hoogvelt, *Globalisation and the Postcolonial World*.

[5] Clifford Geertz lists religion as one of a small group of such identities, which also includes ethnicity, nationality, language group and religion (Clifford Geertz, "The Integrative Revolution," in *Old Societies and New States*, ed. Clifford Geertz et al. (New York: The Free Press, New York, 1963), 111–13.

[6] Anthony D. Smith, "The Origins of Nations," in *Nationalism*, ed. John Hutchinson and Anthony Smith (Oxford: Oxford University Press, 1995), 151.

[7] Elie Kedourie, "Dark Gods and Their Rites," in Hutchinson and Smith, *Nationalism*, 206.

[8] Alan Wilkinson, *Christian Socialism: Scott Holland to Tony Blair* (London: SCM Press, 1998).

[9] R. Bendix, *Nation Building and Citizenship* (Berkely and Los Angeles: University of California Press, 1969), 23.

[10] See E. J. Hobsbawm, *Nations and Nationalism Since 1780* (Cambridge: Cambridge University Press, 1990); T. Nairn, *The Break up of Britain* (London: New Left Books, 1977).

[11] David E. Apter, "Political Religion in the New Nations," in Geertz, *Old Societies and New States*.

[12] See Hutchinson and Smith, *Nationalism*, 4.

[13] J. Dunn, *Western Political Theory in the Face of the Future* (Cambridge: Cambridge University Press, 1979), 56.

[14] B. Anderson, *Imagined Communities* (London: Verso, 1991), 11.

[15] Anthony D. Smith, *The Ethnic Origins of Nations* (Oxford: Basil Blackwell, 1986), 34–45.

[16] Anthony D. Smith, "The Crisis of Dual Legitimation," in Hutchinson and Smith, *Nationalism*, 117.

[17] B. Chandra, *India's Struggle for Independence* (New Delhi: Penguin Books, 1989), 82.

[18] J. M. Brown, *Modern India: The Origins of an Asian Democracy* (Oxford: Oxford University Press, 1991), 156.

[19] Ibid., 157.

[20] Chandra, *India's Struggle for Independence*, 87.

[21] Ibid., 106.

[22] Brown, *Modern India*, 167, 173–91.

[23] A. Copley, "Indian Secularism Reconsidered: From Gandhi to Ayodhya," *Contemporary South Asia* 2/1 (1993), 49–50.

[24] F. Riggs, *Administration in Developing Countries* (Boston: Houghton Mifflin, 1964), 160.

[25] J. M. Brown, *Gandhi: Prisoner of Hope* (New Haven, Conn.: Yale University Press, 1989), 164.

[26] Brown, *Modern India*, 302.

[27] Apter, "Political Religion in New Nations," 61.

[28] I. Talbot, *Provincial Politics and the Pakistan Movement* (Karachi: Oxford University Press, 1988), 17–18, 40–49.

[29] A. Whaites, "Political Cohesion in Pakistan: Jinnah and the Ideological State," *Contemporary South Asia* 7/2 (1998), 181–92.

[30] J. Mayall, *Nationalism and International Society* (Cambridge: Cambridge University Press, 1990), 117; see also Pranab Bardhan, *The Political Economy of Development in India* (Oxford: Basil Blackwell, 1990).

[31] S. Khilnani, *The Idea of India* (New York: Farrar Straus Giroux, 1997), 190.

[32] K. Elst, *Ayodhya and After* (New Delhi: Voice of India, 1991), vii.

[33] Geertz, "The Integrative Revolution," 24; J. Migdal, *Strong Societies and Weak States* (Princeton, N.J.: Princeton University Press, 1988), 39–41.

[34] Copley, "Indian Secularism Reconsidered," 53.

[35] R. Smith, *Vietnam and the West* (London: Heineman, 1968), 14.

[36] Ibid., 18–21.

[37] Ibid., 17.

[38] William J. Duiker, *Vietnam Since the Fall of Saigon*, Southeast Asian Studies Series no. 56 (Athens, Ohio: Ohio University Press, 1989), 58–59.

[39] Smith, *Vietnam and the West*, 34–35.

[40] Duiker, *Vietnam Since the Fall of Saigon*, 159.

[41] Ibid., 58–59.

[42] Dunn, *Western Political Theory in the Face of the Future*, 59.

[43] Smith, *Vietnam and the West*, 140.

[44] Ibid., 81.

[45] Duiker, 13.

[46] Duiker, *Vietnam Since the Fall of Saigon*, 80.

[47] See J. A. Wiseman et al., *Democracy and Political Change in sub-Saharan Africa* (London: Routledge, 1995), particularly the sections on Malaw and Zambia. Also, for the role of religion in fostering civil society, see Naomi Chazan, "Engaging the State: Associational Life in Sub-Saharan Africa," in *State Power and Social Forces*, ed. J. Migdal, A. Kohli and V. Shue (Cambridge: Cambridge University Press, 1994).

[48] D. Laitin, "Hegemony and Religious Conflict: British Imperial Control and Political Cleavages in Yorubaland," in *Bringing the State Back In,* ed. P. B. Evans et al. (Cambridge: Cambridge University Press, 1985), chap. 9.

[49] Alexis de Tocqueville, *Democracy in America* (London: Collins, 1977), 2:570.

Conclusion

ALAN WHAITES

This book has, to an extent, deliberately opted to divorce the challenges that face development activists/workers employed in civil society organisations from those that preoccupy the staff of bilateral or multi-lateral agencies. The fascination with the changing world of that part of civil society we term NGOs has not been intended as unhealthy self-absorption. The historical role of the NGO community as a driver for conceptual and methodical change provides a legitimate basis for questioning how these diverse groups will respond to a range of complex issues.

When our authors have brought attention to bear on the potential of governments and multi-laterals to affect development beneficially (or negatively), it has often been related to the work of NGOs. The focus of the contributors is perhaps not surprising at a time when private assistance to developing countries through charities often exceeds national budgets for aid. It is perhaps also a reflection of the fact that in terms of staff size, budgets and available expertise, some NGOs are now difficult to ignore in the development field.

In reviewing the dilemmas facing all those who make development their goal, this volume began with questions of legitimacy and accountability. The chapters that followed have reminded us that simplistic assumptions have often been the stumbling blocks ready to trip those who seek to work alongside the poor – assumptions that occasionally betray the willingness of development workers to buy too easily into rhetoric that is difficult to translate into substance. Nyamugasira has laid bare the tendency among all kinds of development organisations to use glibly terms such as *partnership* without necessarily tackling the complex issues of organisational culture that lie beneath the concept. His chapter reiterated the need to remember that NGOs are not the poor and can never assume their role. NGOs are organisations, and like all organisations they are inevitably flawed.

The problem of organisational roles can be seen as the constant need to balance ideological NGO objectives with the deeper obligation objectively to serve the cause of the poor. It is this balancing act that lies at the root of many of the dilemmas we have discussed. NGO failures to provide an effective analysis of macro-economic analysis and their inability to consider adequately the spiritual dimension of development or the consequences of nationalism are simply facets of a determination to remain within a comfort zone of existing development thinking.

The NGO comfort zone, founded in a basic needs worldview of village and slum, has through the imperative towards advocacy gradually embraced some issues of human rights and macro-economics (for example, trade and debt). But it has not enabled the development community as a whole to create a systematic model of development that can be set against the empirically questionable neo-liberal models favoured by governments and institutions in the West.

The NGO comfort zone has also made it difficult to apply advances in other areas of thinking (such as human rights) to many aspects of their own operations. David Chandler has sought to break through some of this log jam by bringing non-NGO organisational theory to bear. He has provided a framework for seeking to view the work of NGOs in contexts with repressive regimes in a more strategic and planned way. His call to look at local operations and methodologies in the context of the big picture of economic and political change should be a basic requirement for all those who engage in the process of development.

The need to consider the ultimate ramifications of the way we work is central to the dilemmas development practitioners face. Moving from doing no harm to trying to do some good is increasingly a question of analysis. We live in a world in which our participatory methodologies for identifying local needs and aspirations must be complemented by our ability to read the tea leaves of political and economic change.

Brandt's overview of the complex and challenging context that will continue to face most NGOs is a starter for some of the issues that need to be discussed. But the need to think long term and broad goes beyond global trends. It is implicit within the overview of issues that face development workers each and every day, such as the problem of small arms or the impact of conflict on children. It is also brought home by the potential impact of NGO awareness-raising, education and advocacy among donors and policymakers and the increasing tendency of NGOs to dialogue with other bodies such as transnational corporations.

The greatest dilemma facing those who struggle with the challenge of development is to analyse the world in which we work with a willingness to step away from our past. For NGOs, the problem with our external analysis is often the problem of coming to term with ourselves. This is a challenge for organisations to accept their inherent flaws and to recognise the rhetoric-reality gap. NGOs and aid workers need to recognise that theirs is an industry laden with values, ideology, bias and disparate agendas. As Bruce Bradshaw has reminded us, nobody can claim to do development value free.

The ideologies that NGOs bring to development, whether faith, politics or socially based, are not to be shunned or repressed. Provided those ideologies are openly admitted, they add to the diverse debate that has always enriched development. Honest admittance is especially important to the poor, who have the right to a dignity free from the underhand pushing of other people's agendas and yet who are also not as naïve and gullible as some in development often imply.

Coming to terms with the role and future of NGOs is not just a matter of accepting our value-based origins. It also means recognising and hopefully rejecting our desire to view the world through a lens that constantly gives priority to civil society's own role. We must learn to admit that sometimes big development actually does work, and that sometimes small development does not need our help. Equally, we must strive to ensure that we never confuse the interests of the poor with those of the NGOs that exist to work alongside them.

Coming to terms with the reality of the role of NGOs lays the basis for re-energising the very real potential for civil society to find its greatest legitimacy through the expertise brought by its own grass-roots work. More important, it will enable civil society to voice more strongly the need for others to engage directly with the poor. It is a constant call on policy-makers and institutions to engage continually and directly with the poor that should become the new mantra for NGOs. NGOs should not be excluded from the table, for there is much that we can bring of value, but the onus lies on us to make clear that without the poor the table is not complete.

sharing knowledge

working papers

$4.95 X-007 104pp 2000

No. 2–The Right to Peace: Children and Armed Conflict
Melanie Gow, Kathy Vandergrift and Randini Wanduragala

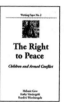

Children today are increasingly deliberate targets, as well as unintended victims, in armed conflicts around the world. Children are killed, seriously injured/permanently disabled, left homeless, orphaned or separated from their parents, traumatised or used in armed conflict. World Vision believes that the protection of all children from armed conflict is essential and presents avenues for action.

$4.95 X-003 98pp 2000

No. 3–The Role of Comm. Dev. in Reducing the Demand for Small Arms
Tibebe Eshete, Siobhan O'Reilly-Calthrop

It is widely agreed that the global proliferation of small arms is responsible for greater prolonged conflict, instability, crime and deeper poverty. World Vision is concerned with the impact this is having on children and presents valuable lessons learned from peace-building programs and the implications for humanitarian NGOs and governments with similar programs.

$6.95 X-012 72pp 2002

No. 5–Working the Soil: Land Reform and Poverty Reduction
Don Brandt

Culture, environment, economics and equity are all relevant perspectives in the issue of land reform, however, the ideal

to order

call:
1.626.301.7720
1.800.777.7752US

fax:
1.626.301.7789

email:
wvpp@wvi.org

that land reform could be utilised to fractionally alleviate poverty is tenable. Because the conditions of poverty are harshest in rural areas, World Vision views land reform as a multifaceted partial solution. By reviewing past efforts and making clear recommendations on future programmes and implementation, Don Brandt shares World Vision's dedication to the likelihood that land reform can become an essential element in a holistic approach to reducing rural poverty.

sharing
knowledge

World Vision
Publications

current issues

$6.95 X-009 45pages 2001

The Approaching Storm: HIV/AIDS in Asia
Don Brandt

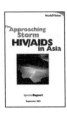

"Asia now accounts for about half the number of new HIV infections each year... Asia's overall fortunate position as a 'nascent' region may have lulled many countries into complacency. Now is the time to confine the disease through preventative programmes that target high-risk populations. Depending on the country, these tend to be injecting drug users, mobile groups and commercial sex workers." *excerpt*

$4.95 X-002 31pages 2001

HIV/AIDS and Human Development in Africa
Moses Dombo, Joe Muwonge and Don Brandt

By the end of 1999 more than 80 per cent of the people infected with or killed by HIV/AIDS were Africans. Most of Africa's increased vulnerability to HIV/AIDS may be attributed to conflict, poverty and cultural and behavioural practices. World Vision believes that HIV/AIDS in Africa now must be a global concern today because of the terrible human costs tomorrow.

$6.95 X-010 52pages 2001

A Safe World for Children
Melanie Gow, editor

"This World Vision report documents the appalling scale of violence against, abuse and exploitation of children. The report contains original research compiled from... some of the 90 countries in which World Vision works. Sadly, much of this documented violence occurs in the home. This report compels us to take action. It offers specific recommendations on influencing our respective governments so that public awareness is heightened, community resources are mobilised and children are protected."
— *Dean Hirsch, president of World Vision International*

to order

call:
1.626.301.7720
1.800.777.7752US

fax:
1.626.301.7789

email:
wvpp@wvi.org

sharing knowledge

books

$6.95   X-004   79pages   2001

Precarious States: Debt and Government Service Provision to the Poor
Alan Whaites, editor

In many poor countries, debt payments alone exceed the funding of health and education programs combined. World Vision attempts to elevate the debate on debt, conditionality and state capacity to a globally applicable level with these case studies from Ecuador. Whaites examines the chain effect of the way that debt repayments force governments to cut the level of service provisions (resources to government, health and education) they provide to the poor.

$24.95   Y-007   288pages   2000

Complex Humanitarian Emergencies: Lessons from Practitioners
Mark Janz & Joann Slead, editors

In this volume, experienced practitioners address the question of how we can respond appropriately to CHEs by linking conceptual and theoretical thinking to practical application at the grassroots level.

to order

call:
1.626.301.7720
1.800.777.7752US

fax:
1.626.301.7789

email:
wvpp@wvi.org

$14.95   S-022   148pages   2000

World Vision Security Manual
Charles Rogers & Brian Sytsma, editors

Global trends and recent events signal the growing vulnerability of international aid workers. By sharing our own personnel security rules, this pocket-sized book fills the void for safety manuals and is designed to help create a complete personnel safety policy.

sharing knowledge

World Vision
Publications

economics   **$2.95**   X-001   28pages   2000

PRSPs: Good News for the Poor?
Alan Whaites

Poverty Reduction Strategy Papers (PRSPs) are an important innovation in the evolving area of social conditionality. World Vision's assessment of the reasons for hope and concern are presented here. This is an honest inventory of World Vision's issues juxtapositioned with realistic perceptions of the World Bank, IMF and "business as usual."

$29.95   Y-022   288pages   2002

Development Dilemmas: NGO Challenges and Ambiguities
Alan Whaites, editor

"The range of issues covered in this volume reflects the breadth of dilemmas that face development workers. Aid professionals have become acutely conscious that even the most local of problems is shaped by its wider context and is likely to have hidden political connotations... The authors map out only a fraction of the micro- and macro-problems that face NGOs, yet the honesty of the perspectives offered suggests that development practitioners do bring something unique to the shifting sands of the development debate."
—*from the introduction, Alan Whaites*

coming soon

to order
call:
1.626.301.7720
1.800.777.7752US

fax:
1.626.301.7789

email:
wvpp@wvi.org

March 2002
Masters of Their Own Development? PRSPs and the Prospects for the Poor